# Rethinking Educational Leadership

Published in Association with the British Educational Leadership, Management and Administration Society

This series of books published for BELMAS aims to be directly relevant to the concerns and professional development needs of emergent leaders and experienced leaders in schools. The series editors are Professor Harry Tomlinson, Leeds Metropolitian University and Dr Hugh Busher, School of Education, University of Leicester.

Titles include:

# Rethinking Educational Leadership

## Challenging the Conventions

*Edited by*

# Nigel Bennett and Lesley Anderson

SAGE Publications
London • Thousand Oaks • New Delhi

First published 2003

SAGE Publications Ltd
6 Bonhill Street
London EC2A 4PU

SAGE Publications Inc
2455 Teller Road
Thousand Oaks, California 91320

SAGE Publications India Pvt Ltd
B-42, Panchsheel Enclave
Post Box 4109
New Delhi - 100 017

**Library of Congress Control Number: 2003101545**

A catalogue record for this book is available
from the British Library

ISBN 0 7619 4924 0
ISBN 0 7619 4925 9 (pbk)

Typeset by C&M Digitals (P) Ltd., Chennai, India
Printed by Athenaeum Press, Gateshead

# Contents

# Acknowledgements

We wish to express our sincere thanks to Tina McCay for her work on this manuscript and to Marianne Lagrange and Saleha Nessa of Sage Publications for their support and assistance throughout the preparation of the book. We also gratefully acknowledge the financial support provided by BELMAS for the preparation of the index.

# Series Editor's Preface

Nigel Bennett and Lesley Anderson were instrumental in organizing the highly successful BELMAS (British Educational Leadership Management and Administration Society) International Research Conference in 2000. The conference papers have been revized and restructured to provide two complementary edited books, the first on evidence-informed practice, and this book *Rethinking Educational Leadership: Challenging the Conventions*. The two editors have asked the authors to rewrite their conference papers to more fully address the themes of this book. Four of the chapters were specially commissioned for this book. Educational leadership has been given even higher political and educational priority by the establishment of a National College for School Leadership and plans for the provision of similar support for further education leaders and leadership. In this centralizing context it is particularly important that conventional thinking on leadership is challenged.

The authors who have contributed to this book are all leading thinkers internationally. The introduction explores the current context and debate about leaders and leadership. The first section presents four alternatives to the current conventional theorizing about educational leadership. The second section explores the significance of these four models by asking six leading researchers to consider their empirical research evidence and its relationship to them. In section 3 the two chapters examine the implications of alternative views of leadership for professional preparation. The final chapter offers a critique of all the theoretical perspectives and attempts to structure their relationships through a mapping process. There is a right, and indeed a necessity, to challenge the approved in a political context where the rhetoric is of empowerment but the practice is greater authoritarianism. Given the central significance of leadership, and a tendency to devalue theory and research, Nigel Bennett and Lesley Anderson are to be congratulated on providing a collection which has such a clear, simple and effective structure, and on editing and focusing so successfully a book which should be read by all those who might otherwise accept the current orthodoxy. That means those who exercise educational leadership.

*Professor Harry Tomlinson*

# Biographical Notes

*Lesley Anderson* is a Lecturer in the Centre for Educational Policy and Management at the Open University.

*Nigel Bennett* is a Senior Lecturer in the Centre for Educational Policy and Management at the Open University.

*Megan Crawford* is a Senior Lecturer in School and Teacher Development at the University of Warwick.

*Christopher Day* is Professor of Education and Co-director of the Centre for Research on Teacher and School Development at the School of Education, University of Nottingham.

*Peter Gronn* is currently Associate Dean (Development) in the Faculty of Education, Monash University, Melbourne.

*J. Tim Goddard* is an associate professor in the Graduate Division of Educational Research, Faculty of Education, University of Calgary.

*Helen Gunter* is Reader in Educational Leadership and Management in the School of Education at the University of Birmingham.

*Lynne M. Hannay* is Professor in the Department of Theory and Policy Studies in Education and Head of the Midwestern Field Centre at the Ontario Institute for Studies of Education of the University of Toronto.

*Alma Harris* is Professor of School Leadership and Director of the Leadership, Policy and Improvement Unit at the Institute of Education, University of Warwick.

*Dian-Marie Hosking* is Professor of Development and Change in the Department of Organizational Studies, the University of Tilburg, Netherlands.

*Jane McGregor* was a secondary school teacher for many years before being awarded the TES Research Fellowship in Educational Policy at Lucy Cavendish College Cambridge. She is now completing a PhD at the Open University.

*Ian E. Morley* is a Senior Lecturer in Psychology at the University of Warwick.

*John O'Neill* is a Senior Lecturer in the Department of Social and Policy Studies in Education at Massey University, New Zealand.

*Rodney T. Ogawa* is Professor of Education at the University of California, Santa Cruz.

*Peter Ribbins* is Emeritus Professor in Educational Management at the University of Birmingham and visiting Professor at the University of Leicester.

*Christine Wise* is a Lecturer in the Centre for Educational Policy and Management at the Open University.

# Introduction: Rethinking Educational Leadership – Challenging the Conventions

NIGEL BENNETT AND LESLEY ANDERSON

'Leadership' has become a key concept in the organization, management and administration of educational organizations and systems, and this development is reflected in both academic and educational policy statements throughout the English-speaking world. In England, for example, all school inspections must report on the quality of *leadership* found, heads of subject departments are referred to as 'middle *leaders*', and the government has created the National College for School *Leadership* for the training of head-teachers and others in activities not directly related to curriculum and teaching. At the time of writing (late 2002) proposals are being considered for a *leadership* college for the post-compulsory sector. Many similar developments exist elsewhere.

Much traditional writing on this topic focuses on the leader as a person. Sometimes this person acts in a formal role, exercising leadership on the basis of that role and position, and sometimes exercising it through some kind of informal acknowledgement of his or her authority. In this analysis, leaders 'do' leadership 'to' their followers. Although there is some reciprocity in the relationship, the leader is the dominant member and the relationship is frequently portrayed as a one-way process: one person leads, and the others follow. This view is particularly dominant in current English writing on leadership in education, and reflects a long tradition of headteacher leadership that stretches back through nineteenth-century private education to Dr Arnold at Rugby School, immortalized in *Tom Brown's Schooldays*. It is the underlying assumption of charismatic leadership theory (Conger, 1989). It is also the foundation of transformational leadership, which Earley *et al.* (2002, pp. 80–1) call one of the two pre-eminent prescriptive models of school leadership in England (the other is instructional leadership, which they describe as focusing on ways in which classroom practice can embody more fully the aims articulated in the school's mission statement). As they construct

1

it, transformational leadership emphasizes a number of strongly person-centred dimensions, including building vision, establishing commitment to shared goals, providing intellectual stimulation, offering individualized support, and explicating high expectations of staff (*ibid.*, p. 80). The transformational leader is therefore concerned with transforming staff expectations, creating individual learning by emphasizing intellectual stimulation and individual support, and generating organizational learning by drawing on that individual stimulation to formulate and gain consent to the goals through which the vision is to be realized.

The transformational leader, then, is charismatic and works, not by force, but through the articulation of a vision that others are prevailed upon to subscribe to. This concept fits comfortably into Schein's (1993) analysis of the relationship between organizations, their cultures, and their leaders. Schein writes of the importance of the 'founder' who sets up the organization and creates its culture (Ch. 11). Whilst a headteacher might not be the founder of a school, in England they have the capacity, over time, to re-create its membership. Campbell, Gold and Lunt (forthcoming) point out that the ability to recruit staff is a key dimension of successful transformational leadership, and quote one school principal as stating, 'I've been lucky now. I've selected about eight per cent of the staff. At selection, I make it clear what is the vision and the ethos. They must want to work at [this school]' (*ibid.*, p. 8).

From this point of view, leadership is concentrated in the hands of one or, perhaps, a small number of individuals. Leaders set direction and create the culture – the norms that constrain and prescribe action – that others conform to and follow. They stand on the boundary between the organization and its environment, scanning the horizon for future developments, filtering them and reinterpreting them so that their organization's members know how to respond to them (Goldring, 1997). They are the source of change and transformation, and the follower is essentially a passive participant in the process. Even when an individual member of the organization generates ideas for change, their implementation is dependent on the approval of the leader. Depending on the degree of direct control that the leader seeks to exercise, she or he may be seen as the apex of a hierarchy or as the centre of a web.

More recently, there has been an upsurge in the idea of leaders being found in other parts of the organization. Writing about schools, Sammons, Thomas and Mortimore (1997) and Harris, Busher and Wise (2001) have emphasized the leadership potential of heads of subject departments, who in England have been renamed 'subject leaders' (TTA, 1998). Those in formal positions as heads of department are now receiving attention as 'middle leaders' and England's National College for School Leadership began in 2002 a national programme of training for such people, entitled 'Leading from the Middle'. However, we should emphasize that middle leaders exercise that leadership within the clear constraints of policy and culture created by those senior to them, and still carry out the tasks required as individuals with formal responsibilities in a system.

Conventional leadership theory is to be found in the emphasis on collaboration and collegiality (Earley *et al.*, 2002). However, as Hargreaves (1992) points out, we can distinguish between 'true' and 'contrived' collegiality. The former is an organic development that develops spontaneously between those colleagues who wish to work and take decisions on a collective basis; the latter is a created form of action that has the appearance of collegial decision-making but within carefully defined limits. Hargreaves suggests that contrived collegiality is often about creating an illusion of support for pre-determined decisions: at best an advisory service, and often a control device.

However, within this conventional view of leaders acting within systems and, in particular, in the developing concept of 'middle leaders', there is a recognition of an important extension of leadership as an individually located function. Leaders, even charismatic leaders, cannot lead alone. Leaders may exercise their role as leaders in other parts of the organization. From this recognition it is but a short step to depersonalize leadership from individuals and relocate it as a function of, and within, organizations. This move opens up some questions that it could be argued receive insufficient attention within the conventional theories just summarized. Could leadership be about more than delivering the vision as articulated from 'on high'? Might organizations be less monolithic than charismatic or hierarchically located person-centred leadership models assume – structurally loose (Weick, 1976) or culturally diffuse (Martin, 1992)? Could leadership be exercised in contradiction of the articulated 'organizational vision', perhaps in order to resist change or to restate a form of organizational culture that is under challenge? If leadership is not simply about delivering the articulated vision through the exercise of formally designated authority, what is the basis upon which it is exercised? This view suggests that leadership might be exercised by many different people at different times, and in relation to different issues, depending on the circumstances and the demands of each occasion. It is the basis of the concept of 'distributed leadership' which has become the focus of extensive discussion in the last 18 months (see especially Gronn, 2000; Chapter 4 this volume).

A further question that arises from a view of leadership as a function is what is involved in its exercise. Leadership in pursuit of change and leadership in opposition to change both rest on a range of perceptions and understandings. Change and resistance involve engaging with both explicit knowledge – publicly articulated knowledge, such as a teacher's subject knowledge – and tacit knowledge – what underpins our actions and our practice, but which it is difficult, and often impossible, to articulate (Lam, 2000). This combination drives both individual and collective practice. Achieving change involves both forms of knowledge, not just explicit knowledge, for without engaging with tacit knowledge, the innovator-leader will only influence colleagues' espoused theories and will not affect their theories in use (Argyris, 1992). From this point of view, change involves learning, both by individuals and by the collectivity within which they work. Learning has to be seen as a reciprocal activity: to see the relationship as largely one way, as we suggest the current emphasis on charismatic visionary leadership does, is to see the task of instruction or teaching as coterminous with learning rather than as a catalyst of it.

Analyses which incorporate this more sophisticated and dynamic view of the relationships which exist between 'leaders' and 'followers' can go beyond the orthodox distinction between transactional and transformational leadership and explore the implications for leadership studies of non-unitary conceptualizations of organizations. They can create alternative locations and understandings of leadership functions.

Such alternative ways of looking at leadership provide a basis for analysing critically what we have called the conventional or orthodox view of it, and it is important that such critical analysis should be made available to policymakers, those in senior positions in educational systems, and those involved in their training and development. There is already evidence of this taking place, some of it being written by contributors to this volume. However, as any field of study and research develops, many separate but related ideas are advocated, with their authors often paying little attention to other writing as they jostle with one another for intellectual and political domination. Furthermore, at least in the early phases of this development, relatively little attempt is made to compare them dispassionately or to test them, either through significant new research or by revisiting and reanalysing existing research. This book is an attempt to begin that process.

In this volume, we explore the utility and explanatory power of three particular perspectives on leadership, drawing on institutional theory, activity theory as developed in theories of distributed leadership, and the implications of the concept of communities of practice. We also examine further the value of a view of leadership that rests on contingency theory. These alternative views raise questions about

- the nature of leadership as a function within organizations and communities;
- how it is constructed by individuals and the communities in which they operate; and
- what is seen as legitimate action by those charged with such responsibilities.

These appear to be largely taken for granted in the more 'conventional' literature.

In order to explore these questions and the utility of these alternative perspectives in addressing them, this book examines their theoretical bases, re-examines a number of empirical studies to test the utility of these alternative perspectives, and explores their implications for the professional development of educators. Its origins lie in a number of presentations to the sixth international research conference of the British Educational Management and Administration Society (BEMAS),[1] held in Cambridge in March 2000. Eight chapters in the book are reanalyses of research data presented at that conference, which have been carried out in order to assess the utility of one or more of the alternative perspectives on leadership presented in Section 1. Two other chapters are reworkings of papers to other BEMAS conferences. The other chapters have been prepared especially for this book.

The book is divided into four sections. Four chapters in Section 1 outline perspectives on leadership that stand as alternatives to what has been suggested here is the current conventional theorization of leadership in education. In Chapter 1, Tim Goddard extends contingency theory into a wide range of leadership styles and approaches. Using the analogy of an Inuit dog-team, he suggests that the art of successful school leadership lies in relating together the demands of the environment, the students, the community and the staff, so creating an understanding of each situation. The successful leader then draws on knowledge of a wide repertoire of possible strategies in order to respond successfully and keep the school and its environment in balance. Goddard emphasizes the uncertainty of the school's situation in terms of its destination and the problems that might be met along the way, the knowledge both tacit and explicit the individual has to draw on in order to analyse and respond to each situation as it arises, and the capability to utilize that knowledge in order to make the response that is necessary.

In Chapter 2, Rodney Ogawa develops the concepts of uncertainty, knowledgeability and capability through the lens of institutional theory. He argues that both the purpose and technology of education are deeply contested, and that organizations exist as a means of attempting to create a sense of order out of the disorder that such contestation breeds. However, effective leadership must create a balance between order and disorder, enabling teachers to deploy the knowledgeability and capability that they need in order to do their work whilst encouraging learning and the development of both that can only arise when they are sufficiently uncertain about their work to question their practice.

Chapter 3 further extends these analyses. Ian Morley and Dian-Marie Hosking propose that the relationship between people and their context is one of mutual creation, and that both contexts and persons are created, maintained and changed through conversation, most of which can be described as negotiation. This social constructivist position argues for the dynamic interaction of people and their contexts, and the importance of forms of negotiation to create, sustain and change this dynamic relationship. In this, they link their analysis to concepts of organizational culture and, more specifically, communities of practice. Once again, leadership is concerned with enabling this communication and negotiation to take place, and ensuring that it is sufficiently located in the existing context to be creative and constructive. They outline key dimensions of leadership activity that may help to achieve this.

The last chapter of this section is by Peter Gronn, who examines the concept of distributed leadership within schools. Starting by questioning the leader–follower duality, he argues for de-centring analysis from 'the' leader and exploring two possible alternatives – 'stretching' leadership across two or more individuals so that potentially the entire workforce can exercise it, or 'conjoint agency', which involves plural member work units. He explores three kinds of conjoint agency that might be identified, and then examines their utility – perhaps even necessity – as a response to the work-intensification being experienced by those with formal accountability responsibilities, such as principals and headteachers. He concludes by arguing against models of 'designer leadership' as intruding into the demands faced by those with formal leadership roles.

In Section 2, six authors review their research into school leadership in the light of one or more of these perspectives. In Chapter 5, Megan Crawford begins the test of Gronn's arguments for distributed leadership by re-examining her study of leadership in a primary school which 'failed' its national Office for Standards in Education (OFSTED) inspection. Her original study of the leadership provided by the headteachers who brought the school out of 'special measures' was originally based on charismatic theory, but she concludes that a distributed leadership analysis was able to identify additional influences and challenge some of her original arguments.

Alma Harris and Christopher Day draw on two of the perspectives outlined in Section 1. They acknowledge the merits of Goddard's typology, but feel that it does not address sufficiently the more structural issues they encountered in their study of 12 successful headteachers. Strongly critical of the cult of the individual leader that we have identified as current orthodoxy, they argue for a view of leadership that supports the principles of distributed leadership and stresses the social and contextual dimensions emphasized by Morley and Hosking.

A similar melding of perspectives is offered in the next chapter by Lynne Hannay, who brings together elements of three chapters in Section 1: those of Ogawa, Gronn and, to a lesser extent, Morley and Hosking. She examines ways in which one Canadian school responded to a district requirement that all its schools should restructure, and that the status quo was unacceptable. Hannay tracks the ways in which staff opinion and commitment changed from hostility to the innovation into total commitment to it, so much so that when the school district was amalgamated with another and the school was forced to return to its previous structure there was great anger among the staff.

Three of our authors in Section 2 have focused on the concept of communities of practice. In Chapter 8 Jane McGregor explores its utility in relation to her study of teacher collaboration in three secondary schools. She draws on the analyses of leadership presented by Gronn and Morley and Hosking to argue that communities of practice provide a powerful analytical tool for examining forms of collaboration and their implications for shared values and the generation of new knowledge. Then, in Chapter 9, Christine Wise discusses the secondary school subject department as a community of practice, drawing strongly on Wenger's (2000) analysis. She relates it to the issue of teacher monitoring, a responsibility of all heads of department, and considers how working to re-create the formal organizational unit of the subject department as a community of practice might help to overcome the resistance to monitoring by offering it as a form of collective learning.

In contrast to these two chapters, John O'Neill launches a strong attack on the idea, directing his criticism in particular at Wenger (1998). He finds that his original analysis, which drew on a range of more established sociological analyses, was far more helpful in interpreting his data.

Section 3 examines the implications of alternative views of leadership for professional development in the fields of leadership development. In Chapter 11, Nigel Bennett re-examines data from a pilot study exploring how schools and teachers might assess the impact of their professional development experiences on individual and collective practice. Drawing on the institutional theory perspective put forward by Ogawa in Chapter 2, he suggests that the concepts of uncertainty, knowledgeability and capability provide a useful theoretical framework within which to assess both individual and organizational needs from professional development and what is achieved as a result.

Peter Ribbins then presents a critique of current models of headteacher preparation and offers an alternative view which emphasizes the significance of values and philosophy. He relates this to the perspectives put forward in Section 1, and suggests that they contribute to a powerful and practical alternative approach to the task that creates a stronger and less instrumental model of leadership.

A volume that presents a range of theoretical perspectives and attempts to apply them needs a discussion that looks across the whole range of ideas and provides a dispassionate critique. In Section 4, the final chapter of the book, Helen Gunter reflects on the book as a whole. Drawing on her own recent work on mapping the field of leaderhip studies, she suggests that the chapters in this book have contributed to that process by successfully challenging conventions and legitimizing the challenge. She argues that the contributors have raised significant issues relating to both theory and day-to-day practice of leadership in education. She concludes that the chapters in this book succeed in demonstrating how 'thinking' and 'doing' are not separate but integrated, and that both are alive and well in the field.

## NOTE

1. Now BELMAS – the British Educational Leadership, Management and Administration Society.

## REFERENCES

Argyris, C. (1990) *Overcoming Organizational Defenses: Facilitating Organizational Learning* . Boston, MA: Allyn and Bacon.

Campbell, C., Gold, A. and Lunt, I. (forthcoming) 'Articulating leadership values in action: conversations with school leaders', forthcoming in *International Journal of Leadership in Education.*

Conger, J.A. (1989). *The Charismatic Leader: Behind the Mystique of Exceptional Leadership.* San Francisco, CA: Jossey-Bass.

Earley, P., Evans, J., Collarbone, P., Gold, A. and Halpin, D. (2002) *Establishing the Current State of School Leadership in England.* London: DfES.

Goldring, E. (1997) Educational leadership: schools, environments and boundary spanning, in M. Preedy, R. Glatter and R. Levačić (eds), *Educational Management: Strategy, Quality and Resources* (pp. 290–9). Buckingham: Open University Press.

Gronn, P. (2000) Distributed properties: a new architecture for leadership, *Educational Management and Administration,* 28(3), 317–38.

Hargreaves, A. (1992) Contrived collegiality: the micropolitics of teacher collaboration, in N. Bennett, M. Crawford and C. Riches (eds), *Managing Change in Education: Individual and Organizational Perspectives* (pp. 80–94). London: Paul Chapman Publishing.

Harris, A., Busher, H. and Wise, C. (2001) Effective training for subject leaders, *Journal of In-service Education,* 27(1), 83–94.

Lam, A. (2000) Tacit knowledge, organizational learning and societal institutions: an integrated framework, *Organizational Studies,* 21(3), 487–513.

Martin, J. (1992) *Cultures in Organizations: Three Perspectives.* Oxford: Oxford University Press.

Sammons, P., Thomas, S. and Mortimore, P. (1997) *Forging Links: Effective Schools and Effective Departments.* London: Paul Chapman Publishing.

Schein, E.H. (1993) *Organizational Culture and Leadership.* San Francisco, CA: Jossey Bass, 2nd ed.

Teacher Training Agency (TTA) (1998) *National Standards for Subject Leaders.* London: TTA.

Weick, K. (1976) Educational organizations as loosely coupled systems, *Administrative Science Quarterly,* 21(1), 1–21.

Wenger, E. (1998) *Communities of Practice, Learning, Meaning and Identity.* Cambridge: Cambridge University Press.

Wenger, E. (2000) Communities of practice and social learning systems, *Organization,* 7(2), 225–46.

# SECTION 1

# LAYING OUT THE PERSPECTIVES

# 1

## Leadership in the (Post)Modern Era[1]

### J. TIM GODDARD

### OF DAFFODILS AND DOG TEAMS: LEADERSHIP IN THE (POST)MODERN ERA

When my grandmother saw the first daffodils bursting through the ground, she knew exactly what to expect. Stately yellow blooms nodding on big green stems, the same in her Yorkshire garden as Wordsworth had observed on the Lake District hills. Now, as I watch the young shoots fight their way through the mud of a Canadian spring, I have to consult my planting guide (Breck's, 2002). Is this a clump of the pure white blooms of the Mount Hood, or the clustered heads of the Avalanche, or the orange-red of the Fortissimo ...

As it is with daffodils, so it is with leadership. It seems there are as many definitions of leadership as there are those who write about the concept. In graduate courses and programmes around the world a new generation of aspiring administrators are taught about Theories X, Y and Z, about 9-9 managerial grids and System 4 organizations, about linking pins and loose coupling ... often failing, it seems, to take into account the warnings of Hughes (1994, p. 7) and others that we 'must be skeptical of simplistic models of leadership'. In this chapter I do not attempt to provide a single conceptualization of what leadership is, nor do I attempt to develop a scale by which leadership ability might be measured and analysed. To do so would be to suggest that leadership is a concept which can be pinned down like a butterfly on a board, or bottled like glacial water, and that a single person can, on their own, provide the consumers with such a product.

### INTRODUCTION

In this chapter the focus is on leadership as it relates to the role of the school-based administrator, headteacher or principal. In locating leadership within this role I ignore those elements that pertain to other decision-making functions within education, such as the superintendency (Berg, 1995; Patterson, 1993). Further, the role of the principal is presented within the context of a 'western' education system, specifically one that draws upon the Anglo-Canadian

11

experience. Thus those issues raised by Hallinger and Leithwood (1996) and Heck (1996) concerning leadership outside the western context are not part of this discussion. Similarly I do not attempt to explore the nuances of application that are related to issues of post-coloniality (Smith, 2001) or race and gender (McGee Banks, 2000). Finally, I take an individual, rather than institutional (Ogawa and Bossert, 1995), perspective and thus ignore those elements related to the sharing of leadership functions (Hajnal *et al.*, 1997) or the development of teacher leaders (Hart, 1994).

This is not to say that issues of race, gender, institution, geography, culture and class, among other ethnocultural variables (Goddard, 1997), ought to be ignored. Such factors form part of the weft and warp of the fabric of leadership. These issues not only constitute the context within which leadership is exercised but are also part of the concept itself. Similarly, the notion of shared leadership must be recognized and acknowledged. Indeed, the development of schools as learning organizations, or communities, is predicated on the understanding that leadership is spread throughout the organization (Beck, 1999; Leonard, 1999; Wallace, 2000). A sign on a door does not a leader make. However, for the purposes of the analysis presented here it is useful to restrict the description to within the confines of a single role. Although presented from a singular perspective, it should be understood that the leadership styles presented and discussed here have application outside the principal's office. The role of leadership is not *contained* within a single individual by virtue of their positional authority; however, the function of leadership is *exercised* by individuals acting within a certain organizational position.

From this dichotomy there emerges an important contradiction. Although Fiedler (1996, p. 241) regales us with stories of idiosyncratic leaders and cautions us to accept that 'leadership does make a difference', for many North American educators the notion of a 'great man' theory of leadership has been placed on the compost heap of history. Conversely, in England and Wales, the Fresh Start approach for 'failing' schools has championed the idea of a 'super head' who can single-handedly redress the situation. In this chapter the focus is not on the individual role incumbent but, rather, on the styles, or strategies, that might be part of the repertoire of an effective leader.

In reviewing the literature it is apparent that many different types of leadership have been identified. The administrative equivalents of Dutch botanists are working overtime to develop new varieties for the jaded palates of those who would analyse the role and function of practitioners who somehow seem to make a difference in the operation of schools. In this chapter I briefly summarize 14 different strains of leadership which have been identified; the shelves are so crammed that this is not an exhaustive list, but rather one that is representative of the literature. I then suggest that to adopt any one of these forms is, in itself, not a means to achieve success as a principal. Rather, it is necessary for the administrator to select from a variety of leadership styles as the situation permits. The metaphor of an Inuit dog-team is used to illustrate how this may be achieved.

## LEADERSHIP

To define leadership is a task which has caught the imagination of both practitioners and academics over the years. There are those who exhort practitioners not to confuse leadership with status, power, or official authority (Gardner, 2000). Others suggest that leadership can be examined as a function rather than as a role, for a role is essentially located in the person who occupies it, whereas a function can be conceived of and discharged in other ways (N. Bennett, personal communication, August 2001). I tend to view leadership in anthropological terms, drawing upon my experiences working with communities from the western Pacific to northern Canada. In such communities there are rarely formal roles or job descriptions, and yet leaders abound. In my experience, therefore, leading is surely the act of working with a group of individuals to achieve communal goals. As such there need be no official authority in place; people listen to those with the best ideas, not those with the biggest name tag. Any power or status achieved through leadership is fleeting and transient, good only for the current situation and then transferred to someone else who has better ideas about the next challenge. Leadership is functional in that it is only present when it is being exercised. To define leadership in any categorical way has proven both difficult and, perhaps, unnecessary.

The problem arises that once the concept is defined to our own personal satisfaction, we then attempt to teach the concept as though it were learnable (e.g., Smith and Piele, 1997). Herein lies the difficulty. Leadership is not learnable in the sense that one might learn how to boil an egg; once the basic idea of boiling water and leaving the egg in that water for three to five minutes is mastered, one might boil eggs all over the world with a certain degree of impunity. Unless, of course, one finds oneself high in the Himalayas, where altitudinal differences in air pressure mean that significantly more time is required. I have never been to the Himalayas, but I do know how to boil eggs at lower altitudes and am confident that I would be able to amend my practice, if required, based on knowledge learned from those who have travelled to Tibet, Nepal and Bhutan.

Leadership is not so simply learned. In schools, leadership is a concept both multidimensional and multifaceted, where the values, goals, beliefs and decision-making skills of the principal give purpose and meaning to the policies and procedures which she or he is duty-bound to implement. These policies and procedures, however, together with the norms of the school context within which they are implemented, are not set by the principal or the school but rather are established and affected by national, provincial, divisional and local pressure groups.

To respond to this pressurized and unstructured environment requires a multiplicity of skills. Such skills can be conceptualized as ways, or styles, of leading a community of others in an attempt to help achieve the collective goals. In this chapter I argue that the contextuality of leadership is such that the principal must have knowledge of, and be able to appropriately adopt, a variety of different leadership styles.

The adoption of such an approach, predicated as it is on the tenets of contingency theory, suggests that there is no 'correct' answer or response to any situation. While true, this does not mean that all responses are appropriate. Rather, it is incumbent upon the leader to select the response appropriate for that particular situation in that specific time and place, and which is also sensitive to the beliefs and values of all participants to the decision.

This requires the leader to make a 'flexible and appropriate adaptation to the immediate situation' (Davis, Sumara and Luce-Kapler, 2000, p. 130). Such an adaptation is not future focused but rather grounded in 'the present, as conditioned by past experience and biological predisposition' (*ibid.*, p. 130). Similarly Hales (1993), Kelley (2000), McGregor (Chapter 8 this volume) and others have stressed the importance of context in influencing the decision-making and learning processes that occur within an organization such as a school.

Here follows a description of 14 styles, identified from the literature. The list is neither exhaustive nor prescriptive, merely illustrative. One might argue that situational leadership is the only 'true' leadership style and that the others are simply examples of this in action. However, I would suggest that significant differences of focus, value and action found between the different styles require each to be considered separate and independent from the others. The styles are presented as potential strategies for leaders to implement in different contexts.

### Situational leadership

The work of Hersey and Blanchard (1977) has been expanded to embrace the tenets of contingency theory. Through boundary scanning and the judicious development of contingency plans, the effective leader utilizes the situation to gain power, control, and influence over the actions of subordinates (Fiedler, 1993). Such negotiation, compromising, coalition building and resource allocation are the hallmarks of the political actor (Bolman and Deal, 1991). Situational leadership requires administrators to fully immerse themselves in their school community and be intimately knowledgeable about the context within which they work.

### Managerial leadership

The managerial leader focuses on the maintenance of a system. She or he puts great effort into planning and organizing the day-to-day operations of the school. Budgets are carefully constructed and rigorously monitored, resources are located and allocated, subordinates are co-ordinated and controlled, strategic and tactical plans are designed, prioritized and implemented. The focus, as Bolman and Deal (1991) have observed, is on the rationality, efficiency, structure and policies of the structural frame. Drawing on the writings of business and public administration (e.g., Hales, 1993; Simon, 1960), such a techno-rational or 'scientific' approach has been embraced by educational administrators since the middle of the twentieth century.

Although this approach often results in a hierarchical and bureaucratic structure that is anathema in these postmodern times, there is still the need for such diligence. Teachers do not want to spend their lives making decisions about which company provides the best deal for buying photocopier paper or what colour the paper clips should be for the office. There is a need for managerial leadership in moderation, and moderation in management. To determine the overall budget parameters may be within the purview of the administrative team of the school; to involve teachers in the process of deciding how that budget is expended is good management practice.

### Instructional leadership

This style of leadership was very popular in the early 1980s. The focus of the principal was seen to be on the promotion of an effective instructional climate, on providing teachers with advice and support as they delivered the curriculum. On such understandings were predicated the efforts of the effective schools movement (e.g., Edmunds, 1979; Lezotte, 1989) as attempts were made to develop a menu of strategies from which a principal could draw.

It rapidly became apparent that headteachers were not able to be curriculum experts in all fields. Some teachers became disgruntled when principals were perceived to be overstepping their professional boundaries. 'What the heck does he know about teaching the sciences? It's facts, it's real learning, not touchy-feely like the humanities stuff' exclaimed one teacher. This was after a principal with a background in English language arts had critiqued a high school physics lesson as being 'rather boring' and 'quite teacher focused, not utilizing the more modern collaborative learning techniques' (John MacDonald, personal communication, 16 March 1999). Although instructional leadership has become less common as a declared priority, responsibilities for many instructional decisions have been divisionalized (Hales, 1993) to the department level.

### Servant leadership

Greenleaf (1977) argued that the legitimate power of the leader only develops if the leader sees him or herself as a servant of those being led. Leaders have to achieve balance between their operating and conceptual talents; the former carries the organization forward in its daily tasks and objectives, and the latter permits leaders to see the whole within the perspective of time, both past and present. The leader is not so much a charismatic visionary preacher as a cloistered monk or nun, one who views the role as a vocation where the desire to serve outweighs any need for peer recognition or professional advancement.

This approach has touched a chord with those (e.g., Thom, 2001) who see authenticity in simplicity. To have the leader as servant of the people calls to mind some of the great religious teachers of the past, for example Mohammed, Buddha or Christ. If the leader has no personal gain from her actions, it is argued, then the cause must be just and right for no ego or benefit is satisfied. This notion of stewardship resurfaces in contemporary discussions of community.

## White knight and black hat leadership

Sometimes, a leader is 'parachuted' in to a school in order to 'fix' real or perceived problems. Often dubbed a 'white knight', she or he brings rescue to those isolated in the dragon's cave. No matter how tense the situation or how hopeless the odds, such a 'super head' will be able to save the day. If wholesale staff transfers or redundancies are required, however, the metaphor changes from chivalry to the Wild West, and the new leader is said to 'wear a black hat' as she or he cleans up the lawless town. Incompetent teachers tremble as she or he comes stamping down the corridors, clipboard in hand, ready to assess and judge.

Such perspectives assume that schools are tightly coupled organizations within which the actions of one person, who embodies all the leadership qualities in that school, might have a significant and lasting impact. As Murphy, Hallinger and Mitman (1983) observe, this perspective also assumes that the principal can control her or his own work flow. For those caught in the maelstrom of public school life such an idea is ludicrous. I have often challenged administrators to sit down for a few moments before leaving for work and write a list of the 'ten things I would like to achieve today', then, at the end of the day, to check that list against what actually happened. There is seldom any correlation. From the moment of arrival in the school they are enmeshed in tasks, situations and circumstances over which they have very little control. They achieve many things over the course of a day's work, but these are seldom the things that were written on the list over an early morning coffee.

## Indirect leadership

We recognize that not all leadership is embodied within an individual. Strategies to facilitate the empowerment of all staff to provide leadership focus on the human and symbolic frames of the organization (Bolman and Deal, 1991). It is recognized that the 20-year veteran teacher may be a more powerful leader than the person with their nameplate on the office door.

The indirect leader often leads by example. Rather than making a big fuss over teachers not being present to welcome children to the school in the morning, for example, she or he may take to being proudly visible in the entry way and the corridors. To encourage support for social or sporting events, the indirect leader is present at many of the events and makes friendly contact with any colleagues encountered. Teachers are usually quick to pick up on such messages.

## Collaborative leadership

Lugg and Boyd (1993) suggest that the principal establish external and internal linkages for the school. Externally, these linkages require better communication, co-operation, collaboration and co-ordination with social and community agencies. Internally, trust and collegiality must be established between teachers, students and administrators. The principal must facilitate this collaborative process if leadership is to be effective.

The establishment of external linkages is intended to establish much closer relationships between the school and other societal institutions and organizations. It goes beyond the identification of a local business that might sponsor certain events in order to be proclaimed a 'partner' in the education process.

## Ethical leadership

There is a growing recognition that the work of leaders is predicated on the value and belief systems they hold. Notions of caring, justice and ethics are the foundations on which observed behaviour is constructed. The works of Greenfield (1993) and Hodgkinson (1996), for example, address these issues. The actions of the leader cannot be separated from the value positions held, for understandings of 'right', 'wrong', or even '(not) appropriate', depend upon recognition of individual world views and beliefs.

## Dialogical leadership

Freire (1970) suggested that those with whom the leader was interacting often had a more complete understanding of their situation than did the leader. Thus, it was incumbent upon the leader to establish a dialogue with those whom she or he wished to lead. Only through discussion could truth be determined and appropriate action developed and implemented – action appropriate not only to the leader but to the followers as well.

There is a need for leaders to immerse themselves in their community of learners, to understand how certain actions are perceived and understood. For those in marginalized communities, school leaders are predominantly outsiders (Goddard and Foster, 2001). These principals must recognize that there will be attempts to mislead and misguide, and that not all actions will ever be fully understood by those who do not share the cultural heritage from which the actions emerged.

## Transcultural leadership

The recognition that contemporary workforces are not culturally homogeneous has led to the development of the notion of transcultural leadership (Simons, Vazquez and Harris, 1993). There is a need for leaders to be sensitive to, recognize and accept different cultural values and beliefs. The leader must recognize both the *emic* (perspective of self) and *etic* (perspective of the observer) in every situation. Thus, when someone of an ethnocultural background different from that of the principal behaves in a certain way, the effective leader is able to not only determine her or his own perspective but to recognize the underlying values and meanings of that behaviour from the perspective of the person making the action.

The notion of transcultural leadership embraces issues of communication. It has been suggested that 55 per cent of communication is through non-verbal cues (Barbour, 1998). This can lead to confusing and contradictory situations. The Anglo-European, used to a more verbal culture, tends to accept the spoken and ignore the more subtle hints proclaimed by body language. The effective administrator must be aware of, and react appropriately to, non-verbal interactions with the staff, students and parents in her or his school.

## Influencing leadership

The purpose of this leadership style is to achieve organizational goals by enhancing the productivity and satisfaction of the workforce. Such a person must be sensitive to the issues of the day, know the source of those issues and be able to recognize what values are involved (Miklos, 1983). In maintaining a balance between contradictory forces, the leader can use these tensions to bring about change in practice.

Influencing leadership differs from indirect leadership in the intentionality that is involved. An indirect leader often leads by example, but her or his actions are grounded in a personal belief system that makes such action taken for granted in its nature. The influencing leader, however, is purposive in using that influence. The distributed nature of influence is such that this strategy, perhaps more than the others, is often demonstrated by those who have no formal leadership role.

## 'Marxiavellian' leadership

The principal cannot act alone in achieving the goals and objectives she or he has set for the school. The micro-political interactions that exist among any staff provide opportunities for an alert administrator. Recognizing that there are class distinctions within the staff, student and parental bodies, the principal uses persuasion and exchange to manipulate the allocation of resources (Goddard, 1993). The subclasses of gender, ethnicity, age, socio-economic status, and so forth, are played off against each other so the goals of the organization can be better achieved. Resources are allocated to the area where they might best serve the long-term needs of the organization.

It is sometimes necessary for the head to make strategic alliances with groups of teachers within the school. These groups have their own agendas in play, and it is up to the head as to whether she or he ought to accept the realpolitik of the situation or not. The timely distribution of scarce resources might assist here. For example, the percentage of a budget used for new mathematics textbooks might influence the vote received from the mathematics department on an issue related to student discipline. Such lessons may then be reinforced if a negative vote is followed by the withdrawal of previously enjoyed resources.

## Transformational leadership

The principal is not content with being the only leader in the school. Rather, she or he facilitates the development of leadership abilities within all staff. She or he does this by identifying and articulating a vision for the school, conveying expectations for high levels of performance, and providing both intellectual stimulation and individualized support (Burns, 1978; Leithwood, 1994). The staff are transformed from followers to leaders within the organization.

Such a transformation requires a heavy investment in the professional development of teachers, enabling and mobilizing them to act as change agents in their own professional development. However, as Hales (1993, p. 217) observed, 'the mobilisation of employees is only a powerful management force if the mobilisation is in a positive direction'. Such a direction might be found in the 'reculturing' (Hargreaves, 1997) of schools.

It must be recognized, of course, that a collaborative and professional school culture will not arise from the ashes of current practice without a major influx of resources. Of these, perhaps the most critical is time. It is through the allocation of time that a principal can facilitate the spaces necessary for teachers to talk to teach other, to observe each others' lessons, to provide support and encouragement as required.

In a truly transformational school, not just the 'regular' teachers are involved in the initiatives. All too often supply or substitute teachers are the 'untouchable' class, brought in on the whims of daily need. A school that wishes to become truly transformational ought to develop a small but appropriate pool of possible replacement teachers. Then, using the sports analogy of 'bench strength', the principal has a core group of regular and reserve teachers from whom to draw when allocating tasks, constructing committees, and so forth.

## Constructivist leadership

Lambert *et al.* (1995) suggest that leadership is not learned but, rather, is made by the leader and the followers, working together. They argue that traditional models are male-thinking and need to be carefully analysed, as women's ways of knowing may lead to different leadership methods. In constructing what leadership is, and, perhaps as importantly, agreeing on what it is not, all members of the staff participate in both its development and practice.

It is though the construction, deconstruction and reconstruction of meaning that a school might develop its own understandings of effective leadership. In this way it becomes possible for a school to determine a less hierarchical and more collaborative approach to 'the way things are done around here'. In this manner the lines of demarcation between 'leadership' and 'followership' are blurred and, in some cases, erased. The skills, abilities and knowledge of all individuals are accepted in the decision-making process. The role of the formal leader is to ensure that all constituents are involved, to the extent that they wish, in the construction and enactment of leadership within the school.

## LESSONS FROM THE INUIT

The preceding description of 14 leadership styles might be considered part of the 'science' of administration. These are skills that can be learned and practised. It is in the implementation, however, that the 'art' of leadership becomes apparent. To understand the science of school administration is one thing. To understand which style is appropriate under which circumstances, and to make an instantaneous decision in this regard, is quite another. It is in discussing the art of leadership that I turn to the metaphor of an Inuit dog-team.

In the high Arctic the winds scour the land. There is little precipitation. The low plains are covered with a thin veneer of snow, which then blows around for months, alternatively obscuring and revealing the natural features of the landscape. The ice cracks and heaves, sometimes forming high ridges and at other times parting to reveal the cold slate sea.

Across this land travels the Inuk, his primary means of transportation the *komatiq*, a sled drawn by a dozen or more dogs. These dogs are not harnessed in a neat row, for there is no need here to navigate through the closely growing trees of the Boreal forest. Rather, the dogs are tied to individual lines connected to the front of the *komatiq*. The Inuk will change the position of the dogs as he sees fit, for some are better in the areas where there are stretches of open water, as they are somehow able to tell when thin ice will bear the weight of the sled and its supplies. Others are better suited to finding the easiest ways across a series of ice ridges which rise to block the horizon. Yet others can sense the location of a predatory polar bear, and guide the Inuk away from the danger before he even knows it exists.

The land is open but it is not empty. There are many obstacles between the Inuk and his destination. It is in his ability to read the landscape, to select the correct lead dog for the circumstances, that he pins his survival.

The school principal exists in a similarly forbidding terrain. Her or his landscape is full of dangers, both hidden and observed, and there are many obstacles between the place where the school exists *now* and the destination described in the carefully constructed vision statement. The principal pins her or his survival on the ability to read this landscape, to select the correct leadership style for the circumstances, and to guide the *komatiq* which is the school across the wasteland to the safety of the camp.

The sled is loaded with a variety of bundles. Here, in the centre, are the students. At the front, mainly, with a smaller bundle at the back, are the teachers. Pushed to the back are the parents, and along the sides the community, the school board, provincial department of education employees, university professors and other miscellaneous groups. Crammed into all the available nooks and crannies are the resources for the school, possibly not enough for the journey but all that were available when the time to travel arrived. The principal checks the load, makes sure that everything is tied down and scans the horizon through squinting eyes.

The destination is known, for she or he has been there before or has read about it in the books that make up the maps of educational reform and renewal. Yet it is also not known, for her or his travel to there has never been from this place. The destination is over the horizon, and the first part of the journey is across unfamiliar ground. A tentative path is determined, the principal mentally mapping the territory she or he can see in front. She or he selects the leadership style that she or he thinks is most appropriate for this terrain, and harnesses it in the lead position. The other styles are tied on individually, extending in a fan shape from the central hitch. Each will share in the pulling of the sled for as different circumstances arise which require different tactics, so the principal will change the lead style around.

The recognition, indeed prediction, of which contingency variables are likely to be encountered enables the principal to establish a proactive administration. Through this imaginization (Morgan, 1997) of the future, the principal moves beyond the maintenance of the school system and enters into the practice of systems change. As the circumstances change, so does the leadership style employed. In one instance, the principal may face a request from a community group to use the school car park for a Saturday morning pancake breakfast; here she or he employs her or his managerial style and provides a prompt response. Later, she or he is attempting to introduce a new discipline code to the school. Here she or he engages the staff, students and parents in a constructivist discussion to determine the parameters and consequences of (un)acceptable practice.

It is in the ability to predict which style will be appropriate before there is an emergency that the effective principal will make a difficult journey appear quite untoward. This is a search for *sprezzatura*, an Italian Renaissance term implying the 'ability to do something of great difficulty or complexity as if it had cost no effort at all' (Chambers, 1996, p. 96). Such is the image projected by many an admired principal.

With the dogs hitched, the sled loaded and the direction set, the Inuk does not consider his task complete. He does not now climb aboard the *komatiq* and rest. Rather, he runs alongside the sled, urging the dogs to run faster, to slow down for that patch of soft snow, to veer left in order to avoid the widest leads, to stop and huddle in the lee of a ridge so as to avoid an oncoming storm. Sometimes he uses his whip, pushing the labouring dogs to even greater efforts. Sometimes he hauls upon the ice brake, slowing the team from its breakneck pace. Sometimes he jumps onto the edge of the sled and tightens a rope, or rearranges the load for better balance, or shifts an unwieldy bundle to another part of the sled. Sometimes, perhaps, across a rare smooth field of ice, he sits on the back of the *komatiq* and waggles his feet and enjoys the view.

Such reflective moments are equally rare for the principal. For most of the time she or he is scanning the landscape. Is that a storm coming up over the horizon? Is that a problematic pack of wolves following behind in the tracks? Is that a soft spot ahead where special care must be taken? Is the load properly balanced, with the various bundles in a proper relationship to each other? Is the optimum load being carried for the resources available? These are the questions asked by the principal on a daily basis. Although the questions seldom differ, the answers are rarely the same.

## EMERGENT THEMES

In utilizing the metaphor of an Inuit dog-team to explore notions of school leadership, three themes emerge. First, it is apparent that the relationships between the Inuk, the *komatiq* and the dogs are intricate and reciprocal. The Inuk must be able to both lead and follow the dogs; the dogs must be able to both guide and be guided; and, the sled must hold a balanced and moderate load.

Second, and further to the first, the interdependency of Inuk and dogs is such that 'leadership' is difficult to define. Whereas the Inuk selects a certain lead dog for certain conditions (thus practising leadership), he might then help to manoeuvre the sled in the direction the dogs want to go (thus practising followership). As such, the relationship is not dichotomous but rather an example of 'two principles which oppose one another in their actions ... [and simultaneously] produce one another and overcome one another' (Hooker, n.d., p. 2). At any one time, then, the Inuk is both leading and following, although one act has temporary dominance over the other.

The third theme relates to the size and arrangement of the load, which must be such that the sled can be pulled by the dogs. In addition to the cargo being transported, the sled must also carry the resources required for a successful journey. Further, these goods must be arranged in such a way that the sled is balanced and will not be upset should a rough environment be experienced.

These three themes can be reviewed through an educational lens. The leadership–followership relationship has consumed many writers, who strive to understand whether and when teachers might be leaders and principals might be followers. Such discussions often sink into a slough of arguments related to specific aspects, the minutiae of politics, power and so forth. I would suggest that we accept the fluid location of leadership, consider that both it and followership may emerge at different times, to different people, and recognize that there is no one 'correct' interpretation of this relationship. Indeed, the leader in one endeavour might quite logically be the follower in another. Such thinking requires us to break the shackles of hierarchy and position, and to focus on the function rather than the role of leadership.

I would suggest that leadership and followership can be contemplated as opposite principles, the Yin and Yang of educational administration. The cyclical nature of these opposing phenomena means that each will turn into its opposite in a cycle of reversal, that each has within it the seed of its opposite state, and that even if the opposite is not currently visible it is always there, for 'no phenomenon is completely devoid of its opposite state ... This is called "presence in absence"' (Hooker, n.d., p. 2). The use of the dog-team metaphor allows us to better grasp the complexity and interdependency of the leadership–followership relationship.

## CONCLUSION

This, then, is leadership for the new millenium. It is neither static nor discrete, neither bounded nor prescribed. This is contingency theory leavened by the realities of the postmodern era.

There is a growing need for school leaders to recognize that the building is no longer separate from the community. Indeed, I am not sure that it ever was. In the early years of compulsory primary education, one-room schools were very much part of the fabric of the community they served. The post-war baby boom, coupled with the collapse of the agricultural industry and migration to the urban centres, led to a huge increase in children attending school. This, in turn, resulted in a movement towards a factory model of education, where more and more children were crammed into limited space. As the buildings became more crowded and less personal, so the bureaucratic management style became ascendant. It was impossible for principals to individually know all their students, and so in order to maintain the illusion of fairness they pretended to know none.

In these postmodern times we are rediscovering the importance of community. We seek to re-create safe and appropriate spaces wherein effective teaching and learning can take place. We strive to provide a caring environment where individuality is preserved, but not at the cost of cohesiveness and community. Here children can learn not only the academic knowledge required for success in the world beyond school, but can also find spiritual and physical maturity. The membrane between school and community has become translucent to the point of invisibility. As school children perform community service for their citizenship credit, so elections are held in gymnasiums and parents meet every Thursday evening in the art room for their pottery classes. As the school sends notes home to parents, so the parents and the home become part of the school. As the children arrive at classes and the parents volunteer their time in the teachers' room, so the school becomes part of the home.

In the world outside this community, departments and ministries of education issue new edicts related to curriculum and assessment. Daily newspapers describe the latest whereabouts of paedophiles. Companies dominant in the town lay off thousands of employees. Parents claim that the school is unsuitable for their children because it is not preparing them for jobs in the real world.

It is in this landscape that the principal functions. As the Inuk scans the horizon for storms, ice ridges, polar bears and weak ice, so the principal scans her or his landscape. She or he must rely on the contents of the educational *komatiq*, on the students, teachers and resources with whom she or he must work. There is no opportunity, out here on the sea ice, to suddenly replace items with new ones.

Informed by a knowledge of the landscape through which the community must pass, assisted by an ability to read the changing environment, the leader guides the school across difficult terrain towards an established goal. She or he selects different leadership styles as appropriate, but does not discard the ones that are not best suited for the task in hand. Rather, she or he uses their strengths as needed, and keeps the different styles close so that she or he might always be aware of their strengths and weaknesses. The leader cajoles and inspires, threatens and rewards, and sometimes gets the opportunity to rest along the way. At such times the journey becomes worthy of the effort, and there comes a moment to relax and waggle one's feet.

## NOTE

1. An earlier version of this chapter was presented, as a paper, to the Annual Meeting of the British Educational Management and Administration Society, Warwick, England, on 19 September 1998.

## REFERENCES

Barbour, A. (1998) *Louder than Words: Non-verbal Communication*. Available: http://www.minoritycareernet.com

Beck, L.G. (1999) Metaphors of educational community: an analysis of the images that reflect and influence scholarship and practice, *Educational Administration Quarterly*, 35(1), 13–45.

Berg, J.H. (1995) Context and perception: implications for leadership, paper presented to the annual meeting of the American Educational Research Association, San Francisco, California, April.

Bolman, L.G. and Deal, T.E. (1991) *Reframing Organizations: Artistry, Choice, and Leadership*. San Francisco, CA: Jossey-Bass.

Breck's (2002) *Bulbs from Holland Catalogue*. Port Burwell, ON: Author.

Burns, J.M. (1978) *Leadership*. New York: HarperCollins.

Chambers, D. (1996) *Stonyground*. Toronto, ON: A.A. Knopf.

Davis, B., Sumara, D. and Luce-Kapler, R. (2000) *Engaging Minds: Learning and Teaching in a Complex World*. Mahwah, NJ: Lawrence Erlbaum Associates.

Edmunds, R.R. (1979) Some schools work and more can, *Social Policy*, 9, 28–32.

Fiedler, F.E. (1993) The contingency model: New directions for leadership utilization, in M.T. Matteson and J.M. Ivancevich (eds), *Management and Organizational Behavior Classics*, 5th edn (pp. 333–44). Homewood, IL: Irwin. (First published 1974.)

Fiedler, F.E. (1996) Research on leadership selection and training: one view of the future, *Administrative Science Quarterly*, 41, 241–50.

Freire, P. (1970) *Pedagogy of the Oppressed*. New York: Continuum.

Gardner, J.W. (2000) The nature of leadership, in *The Jossey-Bass Reader on Educational Leadership* (pp. 3–12). San Francisco, CA: Jossey-Bass. (First published 1990.)

Goddard, J.T. (1993) *Marxiavellian leadership*, unpublished research paper, Department of Educational Administration, University of Alberta.

Goddard, J.T. (1997) Monocultural teachers and ethnoculturally diverse students, *Journal of Educational Administration and Foundations*, **12**(1), 30–45.

Goddard, J.T. and Foster, R.Y. (2001) Educational leadership in northern Canada: the challenge of diversity, paper presented to Division G of the American Educational Research Association, Seattle, Washington, April.

Greenfield, T.B. (1993) Organization theory as ideology, in T. Greenfield and P. Ribbins (eds), *Greenfield on Educational Administration: Towards a Humane Science* (pp. 75–91). London: Routledge. (First published 1977.)

Greenleaf, R.K. (1977) *Servant Leadership*. New York: Paulist Press.

Hales, C. (1993) *Managing through Organisation*. London: Routledge.

Hajnal, V., sackney, L., Walker, K. and Shakotko, D. (1997) Institutionalization and school leadership: successful and unsuccessful efforts, paper presented to the annual meeting of the Canadian Association for the Study of Educational Administration, St. John's, Newfoundland, June.

Hallinger, P. and Leithwood, K. (1996) Culture and educational administration: a case of finding out what you don't know you don't know, *Journal of Educational Administration*, **34**(5), 98–116.

Hargreaves, A. (1997) From reform to renewal: a new deal for a new age, in A. Hargreaves and R. Evans (eds), *Beyond Educational Reform: Bringing Teachers Back In* (pp. 105–25). Buckingham: Open University Press.

Hart, A.W. (1994) Creating teacher leadership roles, *Educational Administration Quarterly*, **30**(4), 472–97.

Heck, R.H. (1996) Leadership and culture: conceptual and methodological issues in comparing models across cultural settings, *Journal of Educational Administration*, **34**(5), 74–97.

Hersey, P. and Blanchard, K.H. (1977) *Management of Organizational Behavior: Utilizing Human Resources*, 3rd edn. Englewood Cliffs, NJ: Prentice-Hall.

Hodgkinson, C. (1996) *Administrative Philosophy: Values and Motivations in Administrative Life*. Oxford: Pergamon.

Hooker, R. (n.d.) *Chinese Philosophy: Yin and Yang*. Available: http://www.wsu.edu:8080/~dee/CHPHIL/YINYANG.HTM

Hughes, L.W. (1994) *The Principal as Leader*. New York: Macmillan.

Kelley, C. (2000) From policy to performance: weaving policy and leadership strategies to improve student achievement, in B.A. Jones (ed.), *Educational leadership: Policy Dimensions in the 21st Century* (pp. 71–82). Stamford, CT: Ablex.

Lambert, L., Walker, D., Zimmerman, D., Cooper, J., Lambert, M., Gardner, M. and Slack, P.F. (1995) *The Constructivist Leader*. New York: Teachers College Press.

Leithwood, K. (1994) Leadership for school restructuring, *Educational Administration Quarterly*, **30**(4), 498–518.

Leonard, P. (1999) Understanding the dimensions of school culture: value orientations and value conflicts, *Journal of Educational Administration and Foundations*, **13**(2), 27–53.

Lezotte, L.W. (1989) School improvement based on the effective schools research, paper presented at the Annaul Meeting of the International Congress for School Effectiveness, Rotterdam, the Netherlands, January.

Lugg, C.A. and Boyd, W.L. (1993) Leadership for collaboration: reducing risk and fostering resilience. *Phi Delta Kappan*, **75**(3), 253–6, 258.

McGee Banks, C.A. (2000) Gender and race as factors in educational leadership and development, in *The Jossey-Bass Reader on Educational Leadership* (pp. 217–56). San Francisco, CA: Jossey-Bass.

Miklos, E. (1983) Alternate images of the administrator, *Canadian Administrator*, 22(7), 1–6.

Morgan, G. (1997) *Imaginization: New Mindsets for Seeing, Organizing, and Managing*. San Francisco, CA: Berrett-Koehler.

Murphy, J., Hallinger, P. and Mitman, A. (1983) Problems with research on educational leadership: Issues to be addressed, *Educational Evaluation and Policy Analysis*, 5(3), 297–305.

Ogawa, R.T. and Bossert, S.T. (1995) Leadership as an organizational quality, *Educational Administration Quarterly*, 31(2), 224–43.

Patterson, J.L. (1993) *Leadership for Tomorrow's Schools*. Alexandria, VA: Association for Supervision and Curriculum Development.

Simon, H.A. (1960) *The New Science of Management Decision*. New York: Harper and Row.

Simons, G.F., Vazquez, C. and Harris, P.R. (1993) *Transcultural Leadership: Empowering the Diverse Workforce*. Houston, TX: Gulf Publishing.

Smith, L.T. (2001) *Decolonizing Methodologies: Research and Indigenous Peoples*. Dunedin, NZ: University of Otago Press.

Smith, S.C. and Piele, P.K. (1997) *School Leadership: Handbook for Excellence*. Eugene, OR: ERIC Clearinghouse on Educational Management.

Thom, D.J. (2001) *The World Leadership Opportunity: Resolved Christianity and One Education System*. London: Ming-Ai Institute.

Wallace, M. (2000) Integrating cultural and political perspectives: the case of school restructuring in England, *Educational Administration Quarterly*, 36(4), 608–32.

# 2

# Embracing Uncertainty: Organizing and Leading to Enhance the Knowledgeability and Capability of Teachers

RODNEY T. OGAWA

## INTRODUCTION

In this chapter, I consider the institutional and organizational context of teaching, explaining that teachers work as direct agents of the social institution of education. Teachers, thus, stand at the boundary between social order, as defined by institutions and reflected in the structures of school organization, and the potential chaos, or uncertainty, that would result if they failed in their mission. I then explore the complexity and thus uncertainty that teachers encounter in deploying a multidimensional knowledge base. I close by considering how we might conceptualize school organization and leadership in ways that better accommodate the presence of uncertainty in teaching.

## THE INSTITUTIONAL CONTEXT OF TEACHING

Institutional theory provides two opposing accounts of the relationship between organizational structure and technology. The first emphasizes factors that are internal to organizations in explaining that structure is only loosely related to activity. The second emphasizes the institutional environment in explaining how organizational structure constrains technology.

### Decoupling structure from activity

The institutional account that has been most widely aired in the educational administration literature explains that organizations' structural features are only loosely associated with their core technologies. This account emphasizes conditions and agendas that are internal to organizations: the absence of a clear technology and the need to maintain legitimacy.

*Absence of a clear technology*

Institutional theory explains that organizations do not always adopt structures in order to enhance the effectiveness or efficiency of their technical operations. Instead, they sometimes symbolically adopt structural features that mirror institutions (DiMaggio and Powell, 1983; Scott, 1987; Zucker, 1987), which are 'cognitive, normative, and regulative structures and activities that provide stability and meaning to social behavior' (Scott, 1995, p. 33). Some institutions specify appropriate organizational purposes as well as legitimate means for attaining them (Meyer and Rowan, 1977; Scott, 1987; Zucker, 1987).

Most discussions of highly institutionalized organizations begin with the absence of a clear technology (DiMaggio, 1988; DiMaggio and Powell, 1983; Meyer and Rowan, 1977). For, in the absence of technical bases for determining structural efficiencies, organizations develop structures to mirror institutions. By doing so, they can gain legitimacy with stakeholders in their environments without necessarily having to demonstrate the effectiveness or efficiency of their technical operations (DiMaggio and Powell, 1983; Meyer and Rowan, 1977; Scott, 1987; Zucker, 1987).

Scholars of educational administration generally agree that teaching is the core technology of school organizations. And, at least since Cohen, March and Olsen (1972) modelled decision-making in organized anarchies, it has been axiomatic that teaching is an unclear technology: a process whose cause–effect relations are poorly understood (Meyer and Rowan, 1977). Thus, according to this institutional account, teaching is a largely barren seedbed for the structure of school organizations.

*Decoupling to maintain legitimacy*

Institutional theory also explains that highly institutionalized organizations engage in two forms of decoupling (Meyer and Rowan, 1977). First, they decouple structures adopted for institutional purposes in order to respond to competing and even contradictory environmental demands. Second, school organizations decouple administrative structure from the activity of teaching in order to avoid the loss of legitimacy that could result if stakeholders found that teachers were not complying with programmes or policies. As Meyer and Rowan (1977) observe, this would explain the relative infrequency with which administrators supervise teachers to ensure their compliance with the many programmes adopted to conform to environmental demands and explain the widely observed failure of institutionally derived structures to affect teaching and learning. This account, however, does not square with substantial evidence that unambiguous directives from the institutional environment result in organizational structures that influence the work of teachers (Rowan and Miskel, 1999).

## The impact of structure on activity

A second institutional account emphasizes the linkages between the institutional environment, the structure of school organizations and teaching. It begins, as does the first, with school organizations adopting structures to mirror institutions in the environment. But, then the two accounts diverge with the second explaining that these structures constrain and, thus, influence teaching.

Institutional theory was developed, in part, to oppose the dominant orientation of the American social sciences, which emphasize internally derived goals as the motive for action (Meyer, Boli and Thomas, 1987). Institutional theory stresses the influence of external influences, namely institutions, on the behaviour of both individual and collective actors. It is exactly this view on which the second institutional account of the relationship between the structure of school organizations and teaching builds.

### Highly institutionalized organizations

Like the neo-institutionalists cited above, Selznick (1957) explained that organizations are more or less institutionalized. He contrasts 'organization' with 'institution', defining organization 'as an expendable tool, a rational instrument engineered to do a job' and institution as 'more nearly a product of social needs and pressures' (Selznick, 1957, p. 5). Selznick further claims that highly institutionalized organizations – or, simply institutions – are 'infused with value' because they embody or symbolize a community's aspirations and sense of identity.

Clearly, by Selznick's conceptualization, schools are highly institutionalized organizations. They may, in fact, approximate the 'ideal' of institutionality. For, public schools are clearly characterized by the two conditions that contribute to a high degree of institutionalization: ambiguous and contested goals and an unclear technology. This has important implications for the work done in schools.

### Organized agents of a social institution

Stinchcombe (1965) observes that special purpose organizations in modern societies take over much of the function of social institutions. In general terms, social institutions are complexes of roles that fulfil needs or functions of society and thus serve as the building blocks of social integration (Parsons, 1951). Institutions, thus, provide the basis for social order. One such institution is education.

While the institution of education is enacted by many agents, schools in the USA have taken over much of society's knowledge-transmission function (Coleman, 1987). Schools are organizations that contribute to the maintenance of social cohesion, or order, by morally and technically socializing people who are not integrated into existing cultural, political and economic structures (Bidwell, 1965).

Thus, schools adopt structures that mirror society's values to accomplish more than simply gaining legitimacy with external stakeholders, as neo-institutionalists tend to emphasize. Schools are also organized around social values in order to impart them to students. Schools, therefore, respond to institutions by developing structures – including curriculum guidelines, programmes and even job titles – to shape both what is taught and how it is taught. Consequently, social values permeate the technical core of school organizations.

Against this institutional backdrop, teachers are directly involved in socialization and knowledge transmission. They are institutional workers, tending the boundary between the collective order set by institutions and embodied in the structure of school organizations and the uncertainty that lies beyond. Thus, teachers are direct agents of social integration and order.

## TEACHING AS INSTITUTIONAL WORK

This characterization of teaching is consistent with the natural systems perspective from which institutional theory springs, because it treats teaching as a technology, or work, that is socially constructed (Scott, 1992). It is derived not so much from the material contingencies of production, as posited by rational theorists, but from the social and political context of school organizations and their institutional environments.

Organizational politics and the institutional environment constrain pedagogical design and the selection of content. Dominant political coalitions adopt favoured practices and values and embed them in the structure of school organizations. And, the institutional environment, typically in the form of the state or professions, legitimates some pedagogy and curriculum and not others (Scott, 1992).

Teachers, however, do not simply enact the technologies that have been designed or adopted and embedded in the structure of schools. In Giddens's (1984) terms, individual actors are both 'knowledgeable' and 'capable'. They are knowledgeable: They act in ways that they know or believe will produce a particular outcome. Moreover, they are capable: They can and do select from among alternative acts.

This suggests that, to understand the productive processes of highly institutionalized organizations, analysts should tap the knowledge and capability of individuals who are directly involved. This, however, is largely missing in the literature on school organization.

Organizational analysts who characterize teaching simply as an unclear technology approach the study of school organization as outsiders and largely ignore the perspectives of the people who work in schools. This is evident in their failure to cite research on either what teachers do or how teachers view their work. Assuming that, in Giddens's terms, teachers are capable and knowledgeable, examining how teachers view their work may provide important insights to the core technology of school organization.

## TEACHER KNOWLEDGE

Research on 'teacher knowledge' attempts to yield a view of teaching through the eyes of teachers, themselves. Fenstermacher (1994) identifies at least four research programmes on teacher knowledge, which differ conceptually and methodologically. These programmes include bodies of work that examine teacher narratives, pedagogical content knowledge reflective practice and teacher researchers.

Reacting in part to the potential distortions that some critics claim can result from applying theory to research on teaching, one programme of research has sought expressly to uncover the rich and complex knowledge that teachers possess (Clandinin, 1986; Clandinin and Connelly, 1987; Connelly and Clandinin, 1988; 1995; Elbaz, 1983; 1991). Researchers who work from this perspective gain access to teacher knowledge through teachers' narratives and stories and from the images that teachers associate with their work (Clandinin, 1986; Elbaz, 1983).

Another programme of research was initiated to address limitations of research on teaching effectiveness, which ignored such critical features of teaching as classroom context, student characteristics and curriculum content. In an influential essay, Shulman (1987) calls for a thoroughgoing examination of the teaching knowledge base. He suggests that at the intersection of general pedagogical knowledge and subject matter knowledge stands pedagogical content knowledge, which he claims is the special province of teachers. In subsequent research, Shulman and his associates began studying the impact of subject matter knowledge on the planning and instruction of novice secondary teachers (Grossman, 1990; Grossman, Wilson and Shulman, 1989). They found that teachers' content knowledge affected not only what teachers taught, but also how they taught it.

While these two research programmes represent contrasting conceptual and methodological approaches to the study of teacher knowledge, they reveal similar knowledge domains, which demonstrate that teaching is indeed constrained by its institutional and organizational context but also very much the product of teachers' knowledgeability and capability.

### The institutional press on teachers

Research on teacher narrative and pedagogical content knowledge make it clear that teaching is constrained by the institutional environment and the structures that school organizations develop in responding to that environment. For example, Shulman (1987) lists educational contexts as one category of teacher knowledge. He also notes that one of the four major sources of teaching's knowledge base lies in the settings of institutionalized educational processes.

The literature on teacher narrative is even more explicit about the presence of the institutional environment as a backdrop to teaching. It notes that teachers are affected by policies and programmes established by the school, district and beyond (Elbaz, 1983). Clandinin and Connelly (1995) characterize this as the teachers' 'knowledge landscape', which includes sacred and secret stories. Sacred stories emanate from policy-makers and academics. This is consistent with institutional theory, which identifies government and the professions, including the universities which train professionals and provide them with much of their specialized knowledge, as the most powerful institutional agents (DiMaggio and Powell, 1983; Scott, 1987). Teachers tell 'secret stories' about their classroom lives. In between, teachers tell 'cover stories' to obscure inconsistencies between the secret and the sacred.

The presence of cover stories reveals that the account provided by institutional theory regarding the decoupling of structure from activity is incomplete. Institutional theory explains that school organizations decouple structure from the activity of teachers to maintain legitimacy (Meyer and Rowan, 1977). Research on teacher knowledge adds that teachers are left to resolve inconsistencies and even contradictions between the institutions to which school organizations respond and the exigencies of their classrooms, implying one form of capability.

## Teachers as knowledgeable actors

Research on teacher narrative and pedagogical content knowledge also reveal that teachers are knowledgeable: They act in ways they know or believe will produce particular outcomes (Giddens, 1981). This is first evident in teachers' sense of purpose. Inquiry on teacher narrative suggests that teachers possess fairly clear, although not necessarily well articulated, ideas regarding their purposes and intentions in the classroom (Clandinin and Connelly, 1987). Similarly, Shulman (1987) identifies educational purposes as one of the categories of teaching's knowledge base.

That teachers are knowledgeable is also demonstrated by evidence that they know how to attain their purposes. Narratives reveal that teachers have notions about what instructional content will fulfil their purposes (Clandinin, 1986; Clandinin and Connelly, 1987; Elbaz, 1983). Research on pedagogical content knowledge shows that teachers' content knowledge affects their pedagogical choices and the purposes they pursue.

Teacher narratives also disclose the intensely social nature of teaching. They indicate that teachers utilize social relations to accomplish their instructional purposes. Elbaz (1983) indicates that Sarah, an English teacher, used her knowledge to shape a social world in which 'the kids learn from the human experience of being in the classroom and the way an adult reacts to them and helps to create an environment where they react to each other' (Elbaz, 1983, p. 88). Clandinin (1986) similarly reports that social relationships emerged as a basic structure for giving an account of the two teachers in her study, leading her to conclude that teaching is a 'social business'.

Finally, research on teacher narratives and pedagogical content knowledge indicates that teachers possess a complex knowledge base. Taken together, these two bodies of work suggest that the knowledge base of teaching resides in seven domains: 1. ends/purposes/values; 2. self; 3. students/learners; 4. context/milieu; 5. curriculum/materials/development; 6. content/subject matter; and 7. pedagogy/ instruction Shulman and his associates add an eighth domain that lies at the intersection of content and pedagogy, which they characterize as pedagogical content knowledge. The essential point is that teachers draw from knowledge in each of these domains in their work; they are knowledgeable.

## Teachers as capable actors

The literature on teacher knowledge also demonstrates that teachers are capable: They can and do select from among alternative acts (Giddens, 1981). Moreover, the array of options from which teachers make their selections is vast and highly complex.

McDonald (1992) observes that teaching rests at the centre of three points that form a triangle: teacher, students and subject. He posits that the craft of teaching emerges from the uncertainty of joining these three elements. We have seen that it is actually more complex than McDonald indicates. Teachers draw on knowledge in eight, not three, domains.

Teachers not only select from among alternatives in each domain, but condition each choice by the choices they make in other domains. They must take stock of themselves, their purpose, their students or a particular student, the context, curriculum, subject matter and pedagogy, and the mix of these elements. As the teacher in Elbaz's (1983) study found, teaching can be a chaotic activity, with a multiplicity of events, or stimuli, to which the teacher must attend, not serially but simultaneously. Moreover, the findings of research on teacher knowledge suggest that teaching engages the immediate contingencies of the classroom (Clandinin, 1986; Elbaz, 1983; Shulman, 1987). Thus, in acting capably, teachers encounter great complexity and immediacy, two conditions that foster uncertainty.

Citing Dewey (1929), McDonald (1992) warns that we should not view this uncertainty as a problem that must necessarily be eliminated. Rather, he explains that the uncertainty should be acknowledged and even preserved because it 'saves a place for novelty and genuine growth and change' (McDonald, 1992, p. 7); that is, it saves a place for learning.

### The problematic nature of uncertainty

McDonald's admonition confronts a limitation of traditional conceptualizations of organization which emphasize, not the accommodation of uncertainty arising from complexity, but its elimination. Boulding (1956) conceptualized a hierarchy of systems, which range in complexity from the static structures of level one to the social systems of level eight. He lamented that most social science theories operate at level two (simple, clockwork-like systems) and level three (cybernetic, or control systems) while social phenomena actually operate at level eight (multicephalous systems). Building on this point, Pondy and Mitroff (1979, p. 99) argue that leading conceptualizations of organization adopt a control system rather than an open system perspective and thus stress the 'problematic nature of uncertainty for the organizations'.

The treatment of uncertainty as problematic is reflected in the prevailing orientation of the educational profession and policy community toward instructional improvement (McDonald, 1992). Researchers strive to determine the elements of effective teaching and effective schools, seeking generic processes and qualities that underlie instructional effectiveness across settings and teachers (Shulman, 1987). Rationalistic optimism has been buoyed by advances in research on human cognition (Rowan, 1995). Teacher educators sometimes promote sanitized depictions of teaching to ease novices through their first encounters with its uncertainty (McDonald, 1992). Reformers restructure schools to encourage particular changes in teaching (Elmore, 1990; McDonald, 1992).

This perspective is being challenged. The challenge is particularly significant because some of its leading proponents are scholars whose research was grounded in the assumption that instructional improvement would result from the reduction of uncertainty. For example, Clark (1988), whose research once held the promise of revealing how successful teachers think, lamented that research would never produce such definitive results. Citing the many sources and various forms of teachers' implicit theories, he concludes: 'Research on teacher thinking does not promise to discover a generically effective method or set of techniques for dealing with uncertainty, complexity, or dilemmas. By their very nature these qualities defy the quest for a technical fix' (Clark, 1988, p. 10). By acknowledging that to improve teaching will require more than generic fixes because of its complexity and uncertainty, he implies that improvement will mean enhancing the knowledgeability and capability of teachers.

More recently, Elmore, Peterson and McCarthey (1996; Peterson, McCarthey and Elmore, 1996) examine how changes in the structure of three elementary schools affect the instructional practices of teachers. They report that the link is 'weak, problematic and indirect' (Elmore, Peterson and McCarthey, 1996, p. 237) and thus conclude that changing the practice of teachers requires enhancing their knowledge and skills rather than restructuring schools. That is, it requires enhancing knowledgeability and capability. Elmore, Peterson and McCarthey urge researchers to determine how people learn new ways to do established tasks and the organizational conditions that facilitate the acquisition of knowledge and skills.

Elmore, Peterson and McCarthey's (1996) advice places the issue exactly where this chapter began. Given the conceptual arguments that I have raised here, the questions I originally posed should be modified to ask: how can school organizations be structured to enhance the knowledgeability and capability of teachers? How can leadership contribute to organizing for knowledgeability and capability?

## ORGANIZING AROUND TEACHING

In considering how schools might be organized around teaching, we confront the apparent contradiction outlined above: organizing is aimed at reducing uncertainty, while teaching necessarily embraces uncertainty. This suggests a point of departure for exploring how to organize around teaching lies in identifying the types of uncertainty that must be managed for teaching to occur.

Research on teacher knowledge informs the discussion by revealing that teaching is shaped by two sets of constraints: (a) the institutional press on schools and (b) teachers' knowledgeability and capability.

## Organizing in response to the institutional press

Research on teacher narrative and pedagogical content knowledge indicates that teachers are agents of moral and technical socialization (Bidwell, 1965) and, therefore, are constrained by the institutions, or cultural rules, in the environment and by the structures that school organizations develop in response to the environment (Clandinin and Connelly, 1995; Elbaz, 1983; Shulman, 1987). Government and the professions play central roles in shaping institutions (Scott, 1992). This suggests that one dimension of organizing for teaching would include structures for monitoring and responding to educational policies and professional developments.

School organizations are well organized to respond to the governmental influences. School districts, for instance, regularly monitor state and federal legislation. They react to state and federal initiatives by developing structures, or getting organized, to shape what is taught and how it is taught by adopting curriculum guidelines, textbook adoptions, categorical programmes, and the like.

Local interests also shape school organizations. Schools embody or symbolize, as Selznick (1957) observes, a community's aspirations and sense of identity. Local boards of education, whose members adopt policies and programmes that reflect local values, govern public schools. Educational reform in the 1980s took this a step further by 'restructuring' the governance of schools. Site-based management delegated decision-making authority from district boards to school councils, which involve site administrators, teachers and parents. Reformers reasoned that individuals directly involved in schools and the communities they serve are best able to determine personnel, programmes and budgets. Research, however, indicates that the alteration of school and governance structures did little to affect the instructional practices of teachers and, thus, had little impact on the academic performance of students (Elmore, Peterson and McCarthy, 1996). Indeed, research on teacher narrative suggests that teachers conceal and obscure inconsistencies between policies and their classroom lives.

Schools and districts are less well organized to respond to the educational profession, which is represented for the most part by professional organizations and universities. Certainly, school districts are organized to manage relations with unions that represent teachers in negotiating for compensation and work conditions. But, teacher contracts rarely attend to issues of curriculum content or instructional methods. Districts also host professional development activities, often presenting workshops that feature university-based researchers or external consultants who speak on timely instructional topics. Beyond such events, teachers, administrators and other professionals are left largely on their own to learn about recent developments in their respective areas of expertise. They attend university courses, teacher institutes and professional meetings, sometimes with the support and blessing of their school districts but often at their own expense. Unfortunately, research suggests that professional development activities that are not tied to the curriculum that teachers actually teach have little impact on what and how they teach (Cohen and Ball, 1990; Cohen and Hill, 2000; 2001).

The failure of existing governance structures and professional development programmes to affect the instructional practice of teachers marks their inability to enhance the knowledgeability and capability of teachers. State and federal policies and programmes can fail to resonate with local values and sentiments. Consequently, some reformers have called for reducing the regulatory authority of states by exposing schools to market forces through the introduction of vouchers, which families can ply, or the provision of charters, which schools can obtain. However, the market would replace democratic discourse as the vehicle for determining the values that will be reflected in the curriculum and instruction to which students will be exposed and that teachers would enact. Professional development programmes similarly miss the mark with teachers because they often fail to address the immediate context in which teachers work. Thus, many educators argue for professional development that provides teachers with opportunities to study and learn the curriculum that their students will actually use (Cohen and Hill, 2001, p. 2). However, many proponents of this approach link professional development to the implementation of statewide curriculum reform, thus creating the potential gap between centralized regulation and local norms.

Thus, local context is crucial in considering how to structure school organizations to monitor and respond to governmental and professional influences in ways that will contribute to enhancing the knowledgeability and capability of teachers. Educators, including teachers, must join their communities in forming norms and expectations for schools and their students. And, as many scholars suggest, educators must join professional networks both within and outside their schools to define and confront key curricular and instructional issues. Schools must be organized to facilitate such community building and professional networking. Time and other resources must be allocated to enable and encourage this work.

## Organizing to enhance teacher knowledgeability and capability

The literature on teacher knowledge reveals that teaching is also shaped by teacher knowledgeability and capability. That is, teachers act in ways they know or believe will produce particular outcomes and can and do select from alternative acts (Giddens, 1981). Because enhancing both of these capacities would require increasing rather than reducing complexity, traditional conceptualizations of organization, which emphasize uncertainty reduction, may not provide an appropriate framework for considering how to organize to enhance teacher knowledgeability and capability. Thus, I turn to the literature on organizational learning because it focuses directly and expressly on the paradox of organizing for uncertainty.

As so often is the case in organization theory, little consensus has coalesced around the concept of learning. This is reflected in the many definitions that have been proposed (Raitt, 1995). What is salient to the present discussion is that some of these definitions reflect the notions of knowledgeability, capability and the role of social interaction in shaping them. For example, Levitt and March (1991) suggest 'knowledgeability' when they describe learning as the encoding of inferences from the past in routines that guide behavior. Huber (1991) implies 'capability' in explaining that learning occurs when an organization increases the range of its potential behaviors by processing information. And, Raitt (1995, p. 72) suggests the social nature of organizational learning by observing that it occurs when people draw on their combined experiences, capabilities and perspectives to 'acquire information from the environment and generate appropriate responses to organizational issues'. Taken together, these points suggest that organizing to enhance the knowledgeability and capability of teachers, which necessitates learning, must include collective activity. This is wholly in keeping with the current emphasis on learning communities and teacher networks as vehicles for the professional development of teachers (Darling-Hammond, 1994; Darling-Hammond and McLaughlin, 1995; Lieberman, 1995; Talbert and McLaughlin, 1994).

Raitt's emphasis on the social nature of organizational learning foreshadows another key point on which theorists differ: the appropriate level of analysis. Some theorists eschew the individual level, arguing that organization is the appropriate unit of analysis (Huber, 1991). Others emphasize the learning of individuals within organizations (Raitt, 1995). Weick and Westley (1996, p. 442) attempt to resolve the debate by arguing that 'social learning processes have something to teach us about individual learning as well as vice versa'. In advancing their position, Weick and Westley (1996) suggest focusing on organizations' cultures (Cook and Yanow, 1991) to draw inferences about their learning. Specifically, they propose that organizational knowledge, or the content which learning changes, is reflected in language, artefacts and co-ordinated action routines.

Finally, Weick and Westley (1996) make the interesting observation that organizational learning is an oxymoron. Organizing, as I noted above, has been conceptualized as the reduction of uncertainty. Learning, on the other hand, requires the presence of uncertainty. Weick and Westley (1996, p. 441) 'treat occasions which juxtapose order and disorder as social spaces where learning is possible'. This suggests a very different way of conceptualizing organization to enhance the capacity of teachers. Currently, the emphasis is placed on determining 'best practices' and developing effective methods for disseminating information about them. That is, we seek to maximize order. Weick and Westley would have us seek, instead, those social spaces in schools where teachers, administrators and others can wrestle between order and disorder.

The emerging literature on organizational learning, thus, suggests three parameters for organizing to enhance teacher knowledgeability and capability. First, the cultural norms of schools are more likely than formal, organizational structures to provide a sense of order that does not eradicate the uncertainties that characterize teaching and learning. For example, school-wide norms that emphasize academic achievement and equity of educational opportunity leave teachers to draw on their full instructional repertoires, where prescriptive instructional programmes reduce teachers to reciting scripted lessons and students to echoing 'right' answers.

Second, organization that enhances teacher knowledgeability and capability would facilitate the capacity of individuals, such as teachers and administrators, to influence the organizational level, such as school and district. This, in fact, is exactly the point that Elmore, Peterson and McCarthey (1996, p. 239) raise in noting, 'It is just as plausible for changes in practice to lead to changes in structure and vice versa'.

Third, organizing to build teacher capacity would present teachers with both order and disorder, or organization and uncertainty. Most examples that come to mind suggest that order is provided, as noted above, by the institutional environment in the form of government policies, professional norms and/or local community preferences. Uncertainty necessarily arises from enacting these influences in the content and practices of instruction. For example, curriculum standards present teachers with order by specifying common sets of educational outcomes. Disorder, or uncertainty, is introduced when teachers are faced with having to devise instructional practices that will enable diverse students to attain standards. School organizations, thus, might engage groups of teachers to discuss how they are approaching this challenge, sharing what works and what does not, thus building knowledgeability, and broadening instructional repertoires, thus enhancing capability.

These three parameters suggest that schools can be organized around the knowledgeability and capability of teachers by providing conditions that are consistent with the notion of professional communities as vehicles for promoting the professionalism of educators (Darling-Hammond, 1994; Darling-Hammond and McLaughlin, 1995; Lieberman, 1995; Talbert and McLaughlin, 1994). Such communities would engage teachers in sustained, collaborative efforts to confront the intersection of what research on teacher narrative refer to as 'sacred' stories arising in the institutional environment and 'secret' stories of teachers' lives in their classrooms, that is, where teachers wrestle with the uncertainties of enacting the organization imposed by policy, the profession and local communities. Discourse would come to be governed by norms that arise within each professional community. And, the communities would be informed by the experiences of individual teachers, which consequently would shape the cultural norms and even the formal structures of schools and districts.

## Leadership for knowledgeability and capability

Selznick (1957) notes that the conceptualization of leadership is necessarily rooted in the conceptualization of organization. In this chapter, I have begun to develop a conceptualization of organizing around the knowledgeability and capability of teachers. What are its implications for conceptualizing leadership in schools? To answer that question, I turn to the concept of leadership as an organizational quality, which colleagues and I previously reintroduced (Ogawa and Bossert, 1995; Pounder, Ogawa and Adams, 1995).

The concept of leadership as a quality of organizations rather than individuals has a long history. Chester Barnard (1938) implied that any member of an organization might exert leadership by noting that leadership is not confined to executives. Thompson (1967) explained that leadership courses throughout organizations, flowing both up and down the hierarchy. Researchers at the University of Michigan's Institute for Social Research argued explicitly that leadership is an organizational quality and therefore can and should be measured at the organizational unit of analysis.

The view of organizational leadership is consistent with a view of schools as highly institutionalized organizations and, thus, with organizing around the knowledgeability and capability of teachers. As an organization-wide characteristic, leadership affects the performance of organizations by shaping structures, which are the regularized patterns of action of and interaction between participants. As Ogawa and Bossert (1995, p. 238) assert, 'In a word, leadership is organizing'. By developing structures that reflect institutions, or cultural rules, leadership enables organizations to manage relations with external stakeholders and gain social legitimacy. These structures serve as foci for symbolic activities that shape and reinforce shared norms and values, which can produce solidarity that leads to co-ordinated activity. Thus, in another word, leadership is cultural. All members of organizations can draw on individual resources, such as knowledge and skill, or resources to which they have access from their positions in the organization to shape organizational structures. Thus, leadership is not the province of a few individuals in certain parts of the organization. Leadership, instead, is organizational.

This conceptualization of leadership reflects the three parameters that characterize the organization of schools around teacher knowledgeability and capability. Leadership is cultural, developing structures on which symbolic activities focus to shape and reinforce norms and values that guide the relations and interactions that occur in professional communities, both within schools and between schools and the profession. Culture produces group solidarity and, consequently, co-ordinated action. This type of leadership provides organization, or certainty, but does not eliminate the complexity and uncertainty that teaching embraces, enabling teachers to work as members of professional communities in confronting the uncertainties they face enacting curriculum content and instructional practice. Finally, along with other participants in school organizations – including administrators, students and parents – individual teachers and professional communities provide leadership by developing structures that can affect all levels of school organization.

## REFERENCES

Barnard, C.I. (1938) *Functions of the Executive*. Cambridge, MA: Harvard University Press.

Bidwell, C.E. (1965) The school as formal organization, in J.G. March (ed.), *Handbook of Organizations* (pp. 972–1022). Chicago: Rand-McNally.

Boulding, K. (1956) General systems theory – the skeleton of science, *Management Science*, 2, 197–208.

Clandinin, D.J. (1986) *Classroom Practice: Teacher Images in Action*. London: Falmer.

Clandinin, D.J. and Connelly, F.M. (1987) Teachers' personal knowledge: what counts as personal in studies of the personal, *Journal of Curriculum Studies*, 19, 487–500.

Clandinin, D.J. and Connelly, F.M. (1995) *Teachers' Professional Knowledge Landscapes*. New York: Teachers College Press.

Clark, C.M. (1988) Asking the right questions about teacher preparation: contributions of research on teacher thinking, *Educational Researcher*, 17, 5–12.

Cohen, D.K. and Ball, D.L. (1990) Policy and practice: an overview, *Educational Evaluation and Policy Analysis*, 12, 347–53.

Cohen, D.K. and Hill, H.C. (2000) Instructional policy and classroom performance: the mathematics reform in California, *Teachers College Record*, 102, 294–343.

Cohen, D.K. and Hill, H.C. (2001) *Learning Policy: When State Education Reform Works*. New Haven, CT: Yale University Press.

Cohen, M.D., March, J.G. and Olsen, J.P. (1972) A garbage can model of organizational choice, *Administrative Science Quarterly*, 17, 1–25.

Coleman, J.S. (1987) Families and schools, *Educational Researcher*, 16, 32–8.

Connelly, F.M. and Clandinin, D.J. (1988) *Teachers as Curriculum Planners*. New York: Teachers College Press.

Connelly, F.M. and Clandinin, D.J. (1995) Teachers' professional knowledge landscapes: secret, sacred and cover stories, in D.J. Clandinin and F.M. Connelly (eds), *Teachers' Professional Knowledge Landscapes* (pp. 3–15). New York: Teachers College Press.

Cook, S.D.N. and Yanow, D. (1991) Culture and organizational learning, in M.D. Cohen and L.S. Sproull (eds), *Organizational Learning* (pp. 430–59). Thousand Oaks, CA: Sage.

Darling-Hammond, L. (1994) Developing professional development schools: early lessons, challenge and promise, in L. Darling-Hammond (ed.), *Professional Development Schools: Schools for Developing a Profession*. New York: Teachers College Press.

Darling-Hammond, L. and McLaughlin, M.W. (1995) Policies that support professional development in an era of reform, *Phi Delta Kappan*, 76(8), 597–605.

Dewey, J. (1929) *The Quest for Certainty: A Study of the Relation of Knowledge and Action*. New York: Minton, Balch.

DiMaggio, P.J. (1988) Interest and agency in institutional theory, in L.G. Zucker (ed.), *Institutional Patterns in Organizations: Culture and Environments* (pp. 3–21). Cambridge, MA: Ballinger.

DiMaggio, P.J. and Powell, W.W. (1983) The iron cage revisited: institutional isomorphism and collective rationality in organizational fields, *American Sociological Review*, **48**, 147–60.

Elbaz, F. (1983) *Teacher Thinking: A Study of Practical Knowledge*. London: Croom Helm.

Elbaz, F. (1991) Research on teachers' knowledge: the evolution of a discourse, *Journal of Curriculum Studies*, **23**, 1–19.

Elmore, R.F. (1990) Introduction: On changing the structure of public schools, in R.F. Elmore (ed.), *Restructuring Schools: The Next Generation of Educational Reform* (pp. 1–28). San Francisco, CA: Jossey-Bass.

Elmore, R.F., Peterson, P.L. and McCarthey (1996) *Restructuring in the Classroom: Teaching, Learning and School Organization*. San Francisco, CA: Jossey-Bass.

Fenstermacher, G.D. (1994) The knower and the known: the nature of knowledge in research on teaching, in L. Darling-Hammond (ed.), *Review of Research in Education*. Washington, DC: American Educational Research Association.

Giddens, A. (1981) Agency, institution, and time-space analysis, in K. Knorr-Cetina and A.V. Cicourel (eds), *Advances in Social Theory and Methodology: Toward an Integration of Micro and Macro-sociologies* (pp. 161–74). Boston, MA: Routledge and Kegan Paul.

Giddens, A. (1984) *The Constitution of Society*. Berkeley, CA: University of California Press.

Grossman, P.L. (1990) *The Making of a Teacher: Teacher Knowledge and Teacher Education*. New York: Teachers College Press.

Grossman, P.L., Wilson, S.M. and Shulman, L.S. (1989) Teachers of substance: subject matter knowledge for teaching, in M. Reynolds (ed.), *Knowledge Base for the Beginning Teacher* (pp. 23–36). Oxford: Pergamon Press.

Huber, G.P. (1991) Organizational learning: the contributing processes and the literatures, in M.D. Cohen and L.S. Sproull (eds), *Organizational Learning* (pp. 124–62). Thousand Oaks, CA: Sage.

Levitt, B. and March, J.G. (1991) Organizational learning, in M.D. Cohen and L.S. Sproull (eds), *Organizational Learning* (pp. 516–40). Thousand Oaks, CA: Sage.

Lieberman, A. (1995) Practices that support teacher development: transforming conceptions of professional learning, *Phi Delta Kappan*, 76(8), 591–6.

McDonald, J.P. (1992) *Teaching: Making Sense of an Uncertain Craft*. New York: Teachers College Press.

Meyer, J.W. and Rowan, B. (1977) Institutionalized organizations: formal structure as myth and ceremony, *American Journal of Sociology*, **83**, 440–63.

Meyer, J.W., Boli, J. and Thomas, G.M. (1987) Ontology and rationalization in western cultural account, in G.M. Thomas, J.W. Meyer, F.O. Ramirez and J. Boli (eds), *Institutional Structure: Constituting State, Society, and the Individual* (pp. 12–40). Newbury Park, CA: Sage.

Ogawa, R.T. and Bossert, S.T. (1995) Leadership as an organizational quality, *Educational Administration Quarterly*, **31**, 224–43.

Parsons, T. (1951) *The Social System*. Glencoe, IL: Free Press.

Peterson, P.L., McCarthey, S.J. and Elmore, R.F. (1996) Learning from school restructuring, *American Educational Research Journal*, **33**, 119–53.

Pondy, L.R. and Mitroff, I.I. (1979) Beyond open system models of organization, in B.M. Staw (ed.), *Research in Organizational Behavior*, Vol. 1 (pp. 3–39). Greenwich, CT: JAI Press.

Pounder, D.G., Ogawa, R.T. and Adams, E.A. (1995) Leadership as an organization-wide phenomena: its impact on school performance, *Educational Administration Quarterly*, **31**, 564–88.

Raitt, E. (1995) Schools as learning organizations, in S.B. Bacharach and B. Mundell (eds), *Images of Schools* (pp. 71–107). Thousand Oaks, CA: Corwin Press.

Rowan, B. (1995) Learning, teaching and educational administration: toward a research agenda, *Educational Administration Quarterly*, **31**, 344–54.

Rowan, B. and Miskel, C.G. (1999) Institutional theory and the study of educational organizations, in J. Murphy and K.S. Louis (eds), *Handbook of Research on Education Administration* (pp. 359–83). San Francisco, CA: Jossey-Bass.

Scott, W.R. (1987) The adolescence of institutional theory, *Administrative Science Quarterly*, **32**, 493–511.

Scott, W.R. (1992) *Organizations: Rational, Natural, and Open Systems*. Englewood Cliffs, NJ: Prentice-Hall.

Scott, W.R. (1995) *Institutions and Organizations*. Newbury Park, CA: Sage.

Selznick, P. (1957) *Leadership in Administration*. New York: Harper and Row.

Shulman, L.S. (1987) Knowledge and teaching: foundations of the new reform. *Harvard Educational Review*, **57**, 1–22.

Stinchcombe, A.L. (1965) Social structure and organizations, in J.G. March (ed.), *Handbook of Organizations* (pp. 142–93). Chicago: Rand McNally.

Talbert, J.E. and McLaughlin, J.W. (1994) Teacher professionalism in local school contexts, *American Journal of Education*, **102**(2), 123–53.

Thompson, J.D. (1967) *Organizations in Action*. New York: McGraw-Hill.

Weick, K.E. and Westley, F. (1996) Organizational learning: affirming an oxymoron, in S.R. Clegg, C. Hardy and W.R. Nord (eds), *Handbook of Organization Studies* (pp. 440–58). Thousand Oaks, CA: Sage.

Zucker, L.G. (1987) Institutional theories of organization, *Annual Review of Sociology*, **13**, 443–64.

# 3

## Leadership, Learning and Negotiation in a Social Psychology of Organizing

IAN E. MORLEY AND DIAN-MARIE HOSKING

### INTRODUCTION

The purpose of this chapter is to introduce some key themes in a social psychology of organizing, and to show how they relate to recent research linking talk about leadership to talk about communities of practice. Our general approach is one form of social constructionism and attempts to show how a social psychology of organizing is social *because it shows that talk about people and talk about contexts cannot be separated.* We take the view that this is because the relationship between people and contexts is one of mutual creation: so, people create contexts and contexts create people. Furthermore, we suppose that both contexts and persons are created, maintained and changed in practice (praxis), particularly in conversation, and that most of the relevant conversations are best described as a form of negotiation. Leaders enter into this 'mutual construction' process because they have been assigned and/or earned the responsibility to encourage certain kinds of conversations – those that contribute to the construction and maintenance of 'cultures of productivity' (to borrow a term from Akin and Hopelain, 1986). More generally, we define (analytically) leadership acts as those that make a special contribution to the continuing (re)construction of such 'cultures'.

These views are part of our response to both 'new leadership' research (House and Singh, 1987) and what preceded it. To see why such a response is needed it is sufficient to reflect on the large number of commentaries that say, despite years of research on leadership, little progress has been made, and the main research programmes are 'degenerating' (in Lakatos's [1978] sense). This is not the place for us to draw out a detailed critique of the history of leadership research, although we have entered into aspects of this debate elsewhere (e.g. Hosking and Morley, 1988; 1991). Let us say, despite the risk of oversimplification, that too much research on leadership has sought to identify those characteristics that leaders bring as inputs to situations and thereby allow them to influence the output of 'followers' (see Hosking and Morley, 1991, ch. 9). The inputs were conceived as personality traits (such as dominance) or as interaction styles (such as Initiating Structure and Consideration), and much effort was devoted to finding the ideal profile. When it became clear that there was no such ideal profile, heroic attempts were made to find contingency models, saying what kind of profile was needed in what kinds of circumstances. The best known attempts have been those of Fiedler (1967) and Hersey and Blanchard (1969).

Despite some robust defences (e.g. Fiedler and House, 1988) this sort of research and theory can be said to rely on increasingly ad hoc defences against three main sorts of criticism:

1) *If* there is an ideal style (e.g. high Initiating Structure *and* high Consideration), it is one that most people cannot sustain, so identifying such a style has little practical value (Morley and Hosking, 1985).
2) There does not seem to be any such ideal style. Leadership style conceived in this way does not seem to be a key input with respect to high performing groups (e.g. Vaill, 1982).
3) And, perhaps most importantly, there is something fundamentally misguided about this whole approach (e.g. Hosking and Morley, 1991).

We shall try to say, briefly, what we think is most misguided from our own personal points of view (and let us admit freely that some of our views will be controversial). What we shall try to do, explicitly, in a more general critique, is to draw out some of the themes that we have emphasized and that others have not. That is to say, if we have had a distinctive part in any debate about 'new leadership' it has been because, first, we have a general view about the nature of a social psychology of organizing (e.g. Hosking and Morley, 1991; Morley, 1992) and that, second, we have applied this general view to the study of leadership in particular (e.g. Hosking, 1997; 2001).

## A SOCIAL PSYCHOLOGY OF ORGANIZING

Let us then consider further the view that there is something misguided about the whole of the 'traditional' approach to leadership. Our most radical criticism would be that traditional research is misguided because it uses inappropriate models of persons, processes and contexts, and of the relationships between them. Another way of putting this is to say that traditional theories entirely fail to appreciate the necessity for people to:

● make sense of people and things, tasks and events, by placing them in the framework of existing reality constructions, and to use those frameworks to construct appropriate action, meaning action that may be justified in terms of the norms of appropriate reference groups;
● recognize that the most important features of contexts are social relations in which other people voice multiple value-ations including commitments to particular reality constructions;

- engage in disputation and initiate changes acceptable to other members of appropriate reference groups;
- In these ways participants may contribute to the ongoing construction of 'cultures of productivity'.

Let us begin by considering each of these points in more detail.

## 1  Interpreting events

Research on leadership has had little to say about those cognitive processes whereby people make sense of issues, amplify their interpretations, and mobilize them in the ongoing construction[1] of intelligent social action.[2] In contrast, the image promoted by cognitive psychology has been that the human mind is a device that is: 'exquisitely tailored to make sense of the world. Give it the slightest clue and off it goes, providing explanation, rationalisation, understanding' (Norman, 1988, p. 2; also see Hosking and Morley, 1991, p. 20). However, it is important that this image is supplemented by, or possibly subordinated to, one in which interpretation depends on a 'persistent framework of institutions and customs' (Bartlett, 1932, p. 255). At that time Bartlett was concerned with the *constructive* nature of memory. Later, he began to explore the connections between memory and thinking. If memory was constructive, so was thinking, and his research led him to the conclusion that each kind of thinking was 'an extension of evidence, in line with evidence and in such a manner as to fill up gaps in the evidence' (Bartlett, 1958, p. 20). What Bartlett added to his earlier work was a much greater appreciation of the constraints placed by *social interactions* (conversations) and social conventions (norms) on what counted as evidence, on what counted as legitimate inference and on what counted as filling gaps in the evidence. This is part of what we had in mind when we said that contexts and persons are created, maintained and changed in conversations.

With hindsight we may distinguish two aspects to Bartlett's work, and they are both important. Bartlett's first insight was that cognitive processes function to extend evidence, in line with evidence, and to fill gaps in evidence, so that what is said is acceptable to an ordinary member of a reference group. In a similar spirit Hosking and Morley (1991, p. 26) suggested that our:

> evaluative beliefs are much more affected by the context in which they are to be expressed than we would ordinarily suppose. Thus, making sense of the world is social rather than solitary. What we learn, and how we express that learning, is very much affected by those we meet, where we meet them, and by our relationships with them.

Another way of putting this is to say that different kinds of conversations or narratives work to instantiate different kinds of 'cognitive tuning',[3] so that what we say, and how we say it, is tuned to the demands of 'projects' or 'life-tasks' as they unfold in our dealings with different people. Lave and Wenger's

(1991) talk of 'situated learning' as participation in 'communities of practice' expresses closely related lines of argument.

Bartlett's second insight was that different kinds of thinking are guided by different kinds of conversation and by different norms, but that they are all 'fundamentally cooperative, social, and [cannot] proceed far without the stimulus of outside contacts' (Bartlett, 1958, p. 123).[4] He was not the first person to make this kind of point, but his own work, and that of others, notably Asch (1952), influenced subsequent writers to take seriously the message that minds are social rather than individual because they are based on the discursive practices of particular social groups (Billig, 1989; Brown and Duguid, 1991; Harré, 1979; Harré and Gillett, 1994; Hosking and Morley, 1991; Lave and Wenger, 1991; Orr, 1990, Valsinger and van der Veer, 2000).

We have tried to combine these two insights by saying that people may sometimes engage in very limited kinds of conversation, and therefore become too confident that they understand the world and what they are able to do in it. However, many tasks require 'actively open-minded thinking' (Baron, 1988), 'vigilant information processing' (Janis and Mann, 1977), or 'rational analysis for a problematic world'[5] (Rosenhead, 1989). Behind these different terminologies is a recognition that intelligent social action consists in following rules of good thinking, that good thinking should be free from bias and that 'ambiguities and differences between observers' should be considered as 'essential aspects in the evaluative task' (Linstone, 1984, p. 36). Leaders have a primary responsibility for ensuring that such conversations take place.[6] They do so because relational processes feature multiple reality constructions and shifting influence. Skilful leadership processes promote systematic methods that, in turn, promote actively open-minded thinking and a 'culture of productivity' (Akin and Hopelain, 1986).

## 2   Contexts are social because they are relational settings

The most important aspects of contexts are other people and their narratives or local-cultural constructions. This said, one might expect research on leadership to be integrated into the social psychology of groups. However, when this has happened, research on leadership has been integrated into a (North American) paradigm of experimental social psychology that has tended to ignore differences in valuations and influence, to the extent that most researchers would be perfectly willing to define groups in terms of people who *share certain values*.

This is defensible neither in theory nor in practice (e.g. Sarason, 1972). We have stressed that the potential for conflicts of value (or valuation[7]) is inherent in the *ongoing (re-)creation* of social settings. If groups share values about ends and about means that is a collective achievement, it is not something constitutive of groups. Further it is an achievement constructed through power relations. In other words, *politics is essential to an understanding of the activities of organizing* – or the creation of settings. A group, relations between groups or, more generally 'organizing', is constructed in conversations – in multiple narratives that voice different knowledge claims and commitments – in the activities of people engaged in different projects or life-tasks.

We think that it is important to think of social contexts as 'relational settings' in the sense we have outlined (Hosking and Bass, 2001; Hosking and Morley, 1991). We suggest that there are two main consequences of this. The first is the operation of the principle of 'cognitive tuning' identified above. The second is that we may think of organizing as a series of projects (perhaps life tasks) and related identities, linked in various ways. Typically, to carry out such projects we need help from other people, either to complete the projects to standard, or to complete them at all. We have argued that project work of this kind proceeds through a series of negotiations, most explicitly in Morley and Hosking (1985) and Hosking and Morley (1988; 1991). Again, related lines of theorizing can be found using the language of 'communities of practice' although, in our view, the politics of relations within and between communities has been relatively neglected.[8]

### 3 Disputation, negotiation and change

Hosking and Morley (1991) set out four theses:

1) Negotiation begins when someone acts to change the status quo – including narrating the possibility of change.
2) Continuing negotiations will involve simplification and partiality.
3) The process of negotiation may be divided into stages of decision-making.
4) Each stage poses cognitive and political problems.

The first thesis is simply an attempt to find some non-arbitrary way of saying when negotiation in relation to some project begins, so that analysis is possible.

The second thesis has three main aspects: namely, that people have limited capacity to process information, that social actions are inherently ambiguous and have to be made sense of, and that constructions (narratives) are partisan – meaning that they are made from particular points of view; and passed on to others in summary form (Dunsire, 1978; Hosking and Morley, 1991; Morley and Ormerod, 1996).

The third thesis treats negotiations as historical narratives to be decomposed into open-ended stages. The historical element comes in because when people negotiate contracts their major concern is one of accounting. They have to find a rationale, convincing to some referent person[s] or group[s], making sense of what is happening now, in relation to what has happened in the past and to what is likely to happen in the future (Hosking and Morley, 1991; Morley, 1992). The stage element came from the decision-making sequence identified by Snyder and Diesing (1977) in their study of *Conflict Among Nations*. However, there is nothing sacrosanct about their stages.

Others have chosen different descriptions to suit particular purposes (e.g. Friend, 1989). However, whatever descriptions are chosen it seems to us that particular narratives are chosen in relation to particular projects and, once agreed, constrain commitments to particular policies (or lines of action).

Our final thesis is thus that each stage of this 'structure in process' involves cognitive and political aspects (strictly, cognitive-social on the one hand, and social-political on the other). The *cognitive* aspects arise because people have to organize their intellectual activity and think clearly about the issues. The *political* aspects arise because people dispute what count as issues, what count as a sensible lines of development, what count as effective policies and what count as realistic attempts to implement those policies (Hosking and Morley, 1991, p. 7). Both cognitive and political processes are central to leadership when viewed as a certain sort of relational process – as we will shortly outline.

One of the main jobs of a social psychology of organizing is to show how to appreciate the cognitive and political processes through which people create and support various kinds of setting – variously called cultures, rhetorical contexts, formative contexts or 'communities of practice'. Some say that the process of organizing creates orders of value in which different people have different commitments to particular descriptions and to particular actions in particular contexts. Broadly speaking, political actions arise when people think differently and want to act differently. The possibilities for thinking differently arise because social actions are inherently ambiguous, are described from particular points of view and cannot be completely described (Dunsire, 1978; Hosking and Morley, 1991; Morley and Ormerod, 1996). But, once they are described different descriptions differently constrain how the process will 'go on'. (Conversely, once a person is committed to a particular policy, that commitment will mean that certain descriptions are likely to be applied to that policy rather than others.)

As we have said, we think it important to show how to appreciate these cognitive-social-political processes and, in particular, important seriously to explore negotiation as part of the story, joining this line of talk with talk about how such processes may be performed more or less skilfully. In our view, any talk of 'communities of practice' should not overestimate communality, agreement and talk of 'what is' at the expense of multiplicity, disagreement, and what might be. This includes disputation over what counts as knowledge, what counts as maintenance of the community, what counts as change, and what to commit to – if only for a while.

All of this implies that, broadly speaking, *organizing is about commitments and how those commitments are created, mobilized, maintained and changed.* Because of the distinction between two kinds of commitments – to descriptions and to lines of action – approaches of this kind are often called language-action perspectives (see Fikes, 1982; Hosking and Morley, 1991; Morley and Ormerod, 1996; Winograd and Flores, 1986). We believe that some sort of language-action perspective may be used to summarize much of what we have to say about a social psychology of organizing and about the role of leadership in those processes.

## 4  Constructing cultures of productivity

We shall argue that skilful leadership processes promote a 'culture of productivity'. This is defined by relationships in which participants experience the emerging processes as legible, coherent and open-ended. Participants feel the processes to be 'legible' when equivocality is reduced in recognizable and agreeable ways. Processes are 'coherent' when participants experience an integrated structure throughout the process, and processes are 'open-ended' inasmuch as relationships are flexible, i.e., they can create and accommodate change (see Hosking and Morley, 1991). This sort of structure in process supports learning as, for example, argued by Lave and Wenger in their talk of situated learning and 'legitimate peripheral participation' (Lave and Wenger, 1991). We have chosen to emphasize leadership and *skilful processes*. This is rather different from, for example, 'fixing' particular participants as masters or apprentices and different from fixing and putting out of question what counts as skilful performance. We suggest that participants are likely to differ in the extent to which they see themselves and others to consistently influence the legibility, coherence and openness of their culture. Further, participants are likely to see each other as achieving influence in different ways – ways that are more or less acceptable in that culture or community. Finally, some – or indeed all[9] – participants may come to be perceived as making contributions that consistently achieve acceptable influence, and come to be expected to do so. Contributions of this kind we refer to as leadership; those who make such contributions we call leaders (Hosking and Morley, 1991).

### LEADERSHIP IN A SOCIAL PSYCHOLOGY OF ORGANIZING

Within this general framework we can identify four major lines of development with respect to theory and research on leadership. We have made serious attempts to link talk about leadership processes to talk about:

- cognitive and political skills;
- disputation and change (by treating the skills of leadership as cognate with the skills of negotiation);
- task-analysis, and the cognitive and political dilemmas in those tasks;
- social constructionism, organizational learning and the management of organizational learning.

In each case a central part of the point of the enterprise has been to give due emphasis to intelligent social action and to leaders as exercising particular responsibility for its promotion. We shall consider each of these lines of research in turn, although, as we shall see, and as we might expect, they are heavily interdependent.

## 1   The cognitive and political skills of leadership

We have advocated the view that skilful leadership serves to promote social orders in which certain kinds of change are seen collectively to make sense. In other words, we suppose that leadership plays a central part in promoting processes whereby disputation converges onto positions that everyone can live with[10] – because everyone can see that the *process* is transparent, and because everyone can see that the *process* makes sense.[11]

There has been considerable controversy about the meanings of each of these phrases, and we think it is important to consider some of them in more detail. So, when we say that leaders play a central part in promoting certain processes, we do not mean that all leadership is, in the current jargon, 'transformational'. We have more in common with those who suggest that leadership can be viewed as the 'management of meaning' (e.g. Smircich and Morgan, 1992), and that leaders have a central responsibility to organize this *process*. However, this can mean a number of things. In our view it does *not* mean that leaders must impose their visions on others or that they must be more skilful or more successful than their followers. Certainly, leaders may sometimes have to provide 'pictures' or 'frames' or 'visions' or 'principles' or 'scripts' for other people to follow, and people may sometimes rely on them to do so,[12] but it would be a gross mistake to think that they are the only people able to do these jobs (Hosking, 1997). If we have made any contributions to this literature they have tried to show, first, that leaders and followers are much more interchangeable than has been supposed, that leaders engage in trial arguments with themselves and others, and that one of the ways of examining what kind of context (discursive, formative, rhetorical) is involved is to investigate what kinds of input are appreciated, regardless of source (Hosking and Morley, 1988; 1991). Such investigations tell us whether leadership is principled or just self-serving.

Those who have concentrated on visionary aspects of leadership have also tended to forget that leaders cannot simply direct the actions of their 'followers'. Influence has to be acceptable. Part of what this can mean is that 'power over' may not be locally valued as a way of 'creating settings'. In addition, and as we have argued elsewhere (Hosking and Morley, 1991, p. 249): 'To build cultures of productivity, it is essential that differences are articulated through a process of actively open-minded thinking. To build such cultures, ways must be found to respect differences which must be preserved.'

We hope that this is part of what people have in mind when they repeat the 'mantra' that 'leaders lead groups'. This is one reason why we have given such prominence to negotiation. It is in these respects that leaders are just like negotiators. If decisions are to 'stick' they will have to be acceptable to those they represent.

One implication of this is that leaders, considered as negotiators, face two kinds of problem. The first is how to describe change, or the possibility of change, and how to reach a working consensus over the description of this change. The second is how to forge commitments based on these descriptions and to show that they make sense.

## 2 Leadership and the skills of negotiation

Those psychologists who have talked about the skills of negotiation have emphasized the two aspects we have already identified. That is, they have divided skills into intellectual tasks (posing cognitive problems) and influence tasks (posing political problems). As noted earlier, we have tried to stress the social-relational aspects of these 'tasks'.

We have linked talk about leadership both to limitations in cognitive capacity (constrained by the nature of our neural architecture) and to dispositions to engage in rational thinking. In the first case, we have urged that skilled negotiators help others to match their cognitive capacities to the demands of the tasks they face (along the lines outlined by Welford, 1980), mostly by keeping their messages simple and by slowing things down.[13] In the second case, we have argued that leaders need to promote cultures dominated by what Baron (1988) has called actively open-minded thinking (Hosking and Morley, 1991). This means that leadership processes need to be principled in the sense that they encourage 'search that is thorough in proportion to the importance of the question' and 'fairness to other possibilities than the one we initially favour' (Baron, 1988, p. 30). Others, such as Janis have called the process one of vigilant information processing (Janis, 1989; Janis and Mann, 1977).

We, like others, have urged that cognitive and political problems are very much interrelated. However, let us concentrate on political processes for the moment. Here, we have suggested that what leaders do is make particularly influential contributions to a process of change in which all participants negotiate and renegotiate the terms on which they will 'do business'. In such cases the point of the exercise is to establish what changes are possible, and at what cost. The outcome of the deliberations is a set of rules (narratives) defining the terms on which the parties will do business in the future. That is to say, leaders take a major role in a process by which they – and their 'followers' – 'rewrite social history'.

To explain the metaphor we need to explain the written history and the social history. The written history comes from formalized rules and relations such as those characteristic of organization structure. One way to put this is to say that negotiations are conducted in the context of existing rules, and that the effect of negotiation is to change those rules. The social history comes from the fact that changes have to be explained to other people, accepted by them and implemented by them. This is why the most important outcome of negotiation *is an agreed narrative about what has happened, and why, providing a rationale linking what is happening now to what has happened in the past and to what will happen in the future.* If such narratives are not acceptable they will not stick.

## 3  Task-analysis, decision-making and dilemmas

Historically, it is quite remarkable how studies of leadership have tried to avoid any serious analysis of the nature of leadership tasks. But it is impossible to talk about skill, or strategy or tactics, without talking about goals, valuations, bias and other cognate concepts. Such talk ought to follow from the detailed analyses of particular tasks, *even if made from particular points of view.* There has been little such analysis, and we think that this is one main reason why research on leadership has said little about skill, or strategy or tactics or about intelligent social action, and it is one main reason why leadership research has been denigrated in terms of its practical value (Hosking and Morley, 1988; 1991; Hunt *et al.*, 1984).

Fortunately, some recent research has attempted to fill this void and, without attempting to be comprehensive, we shall select some prominent examples:

- Those working within the domain of planning and decision-making within public policy domains have attempted systematically to analyse what it would mean to carry out a rational analysis of alternative policies within those domains (Friend, 1989; Friend and Hickling, 1987; Friend and Jessop, 1977; Levin, 1976). Much of this research has been conducted within the framework of attempts to rethink the nature and effectiveness of operational research (Morley and Ormerod, 1996; Rosenhead, 1999).
- Some have attempted to link talk about planning, talk about decision-making, and talk about negotiation to talk about design (Clausing and Andrade, 1996; Hosking and Morley, 1991).
- Some have attempted explicitly to analyse the skills of negotiation in industrial or international or legal or other contexts (Morley, 1992).
- Others have tried to identify difficulties in managing relationships that may apply wherever there are questions of organizational trust within or between groups (Hosking and Morley, 1988; 1991; Kotter, 1982; Morley, 1992).
- Some have tried to explore what leadership might mean when local-cultural valuations support inclusive relations of equals and distributed leadership (e.g., Brown and Hosking, 1986; Hosking, 2001).
- Others still, have tried to explore problems of cognitive tuning, such as how to influence people without offending them, or how to make public politically sensitive information without provoking damaging responses (te Molder, 1999).

In each case the researchers have tried to identify dilemmas that have application beyond the immediate context of significance. Thus, Friend and his associates have set out an approach to planning under pressure in which dilemmas are linked to various kinds of uncertainty faced by decision-makers. In this framework, dilemmas about the nature, timing and scope of cognitive and political problems come to the fore, as they apply to the core processes of shaping, designing, comparing and choosing.[14] Pugh and Morley have outlined a stage-based approach to design (called 'Total Design') in which they identify dilemmas of commitment within each stage (so that making decisions too soon may be based on an incomplete analysis of intellectual problems, but that delaying decisions too long may be based on an incomplete analysis of political problems). Researchers who have analysed difficulties in managing relationships, have focused on those that implicate the role of the leader (e.g. dilemmas about democracy) and those concerned with the nature of organizational trust within and between groups (e.g. dilemmas about confidentiality). Finally, te Molder (1999) has attempted to explore the nature of various dilemmas posed by defensive reactions to the communication process.

We think that all of this adds up to a view that asserts that: 'the way in which such dilemmas are handled, when working under real-time pressures, can have deep influences not only on the decisions reached, but also on the way the decision process is steered through a labyrinth of possible organizational channels' (Friend, 1989, p. 123). Groups that fail to negotiate an acceptable path through such dilemmas are not likely to be effective in the long run. Leadership that fails to understand the relationships between the different kinds of dilemma is likely to fail.

## 4   Social constructionism and organizational learning

Less than 50 years ago psychology was dominated by the psychology of learning. Yet in Bechtel and Graham's (1998) *A Companion to Cognitive Science* the only chapter that includes 'learning' in its title is a chapter on 'Machine learning'. Part of this shift has been an attempt to provide an integrated view of cognition in which talk about learning is integrated with talk about memory, perception, problem-solving, reasoning and understanding, and other cognate concepts (as in Anderson, 1990). Another part of this shift has been an attempt to link talk about learning to technical issues in mathematics, computer science, and philosophy (as in Glymour, 1999). The former has been welcomed and the latter has not. One result has been that talk about learning has been more obviously geared to work in international relations (e.g. Jervis, 1970; 1976) and to organizations ('learning organizations' and 'organizational learning') (e.g. Cohen and Sproull, 1996; Hosking and Bouwen, 2000) than it has been before. For our part, we would wish to welcome some developments in both fields.

It is both convenient and, we think, important, to consider some of the main issues that have emerged about learning in relation to 'constructionism' and 'social constructionism'. The former embraces all those who, like Piaget, Bruner and others, have emphasized the active role that the mind plays in going beyond the information given – so that learning is a process by which knowledge is constructed. Much of the discussion remains dominated by Piagetian theory, but all modern cognitive psychologists are constructionists in this sense. Despite this, few of them pay sufficient attention to those social processes that subject constructive processes to normative constraints. This brings us to *social* constructionism. One variant could be broadly described as expanding constructionism by giving much more prominence to both local and global principles of cognitive tuning. The former come from conversations, whether formal or informal, and the latter from institutional formulations of knowledge and epistemologies (McCormick and Paechter, 1999). Our own work is both constructionist and social constructionist – in the sense outlined.[15]

In terms of constructionism, we have emphasized that expertise within a given domain requires knowledge within that domain, and that much of that knowledge is tacit. It is not taught explicitly but learned, like craft knowledge, with experience of particular contexts or relational settings. In this respect our own framework is close to those that are usually described as neo-Piagetian (Demetriou, Shayer and Efklides, 1992). However, we have also taken the view that domain-specific learning requires systematic guidance in the form of 'scaffolding', and in this respect our position is closer to that of Vygotsky (see Wood, 1988). Connections can also be seen between our work and the more analytical and critical variants of the 'communities of practice' literature (Lave and Wenger, 1991; Orr, 1990). However, we have paid more attention than most to those systematic methods that attempt legibly and coherently to produce 'structure in process', particularly in the context of engineering product design, and in the context of operational research.

Putting this together, let us say that the relationship between tacit and explicit knowledge is controversial,[16] but that we have emphasized the importance of explicit knowledge more than others. If we were to extend our previous treatments we would agree with Glaser's (1999) statements that 'the value of practice can be increased, if we see it as something to be carefully designed' (*ibid.*, p. 97) so that: 'teaching practice can make apparent the forms of students' thinking, in ways that can be observed, transmitted, discussed, reflected on, and moved toward more competent performance and dispositions for reasoning' (Glaser, 1999, pp. 99–100). Educational leaders, because they are leaders, have a primary responsibility to facilitate such practices.

We hope we have said enough to be clear that this does not mean that such leaders have to be more expert than others. However, they have to be sufficiently knowledgeable to be able to co-ordinate and to encourage 'face to face confrontation and discussion of differences' (Hosking and Bass, 2001, p. 355). They have to be able to organize processes whereby such discussion is constructive rather than destructive, so that there is convergence on policies that all can understand and live with (Clausing and Andrade, 1996; Hosking and Morley, 1991).

## CONCLUSIONS

We have put forward a position on leadership that is both constructionist and social constructionist.[17] The constructionist elements come from consideration of the architecture of the mind and from a consideration of those active processes by which minds create reality. The social elements come from consideration of those principles by which our cognitions are 'tuned' because of interpersonal and institutional constraints. Psychologists have tended to promote the former at the expense of the latter. Sociologists have tended to promote the latter at the expense of the former. Some social psychologists, such as us, have tried to find an appropriate balance between the two. For these and other reasons, we have tried to produce a social psychology that is informed by cognitive psychology (so that we are not criticizing 'straw' people) but remains genuinely social (so that is not just cognitive psychology with some social 'factors' added).

The net effect of all of this is that leaders should participate in relational processes in ways that:

- link their own knowledge and experience intelligently to that of others;
- (help to) organize negotiations within ('internal') and between ('external') groups;
- deal with cognitive and political aspects of the core problems in their (individual and collective) decision-making tasks;
- focus on key dilemmas in their individual and collective tasks.

This line of argument could be said to upgrade the role of 'followers' and to downgrade that of 'leaders'. Leaders do have special responsibilities, but one is not to ignore the talents of their followers.

## NOTES

1. We have deliberately used interchangeably the tools of 'interpretation', 'sense making', and 'construction'. In the present context, these language tools are to be understood, not as references to individual acts, but in relation to our argument that talk about people and talk about contexts cannot be separated.

2. Here we mean to talk of language as both one form of action, and as a tool for talking about and reflecting on action.

3. The term 'cognitive tuning' is taken from Cohen (1961).

4. The particular quotation refers to Bartlett's views about scientific thinking, but we think that he would have been quite happy to generalize these remarks to other kinds of thinking (see Bartlett, 1958).

5. Which *here* means a socially constructed world or worlds.

6. Perhaps it is worth asking, at this point, when do people stop thinking? When do they think a problem has been solved? The halting problem has been an important one for computer science, and perhaps there is an equally important halting problem in psychology. The answer may be slightly more complicated, but it is nonetheless revealing. If Hosking and Morley (1991) are correct, the 'stop rule' is that people will stop

thinking when they have done enough 'to minimize doubts that the policies they have chosen will be certified by competent members of their reference groups. In some rhetorical contexts this may increase the likelihood of biased information processing ... In other rhetorical contexts it may have the opposite effect, producing an increased commitment to interpretive practices based on systematic methods [that] promote actively-open-minded thinking' (Hosking and Morley, 1991, p. 102).

7. The language of 'value' has often been used in the context of a wider thought style that separates 'fact' and 'value' and treats the latter as an 'input from individual' (see our earlier discussion) that 'messes up' rational thinking. We use the term 'valuation' in the context of our social constructionist perspective – emphasizing that social constructions of reality necessarily imply some ordering of value.

8. The issue of power was given more attention in the early literatures on communities of practice but has been relatively neglected in later, more prescriptive and managerialist developments of the concept. The 'critical', analytical emphasis of Lave and Wenger (1991) has been marginalized by treatments that for example, take for granted a unitary and uncontested conception of hierarchy, what counts as 'mastery', who is expert and who novice, and the institutionalized conventions that help to legitimize and stabilize such realities and relations.

9. Although in our experience this is both rare and difficult to do – even when participants are explicitly trying to construct such ways of going on in relation as, for example, in some social movement groups (see, e.g., Brown and Hosking, 1986).

10. Chester Barnard provided the useful concept of 'latitude of acceptance' to indicate that one does not have to accept in the sense of agree but only find for example, some decision acceptable in the sense of falling within one's latitude of acceptance.

11. This point has been elaborated by Morley in the context of engineering product design (Pugh and Morley) and by Hosking in the context of organizational development (Hosking, 2002; Hosking and Bass, 2001).

12. And they may acquire power by doing so.

13. This sort of message is quite general. Some of the skills of negotiation are the skills of socially competent actors. It is not only negotiators who sometimes have to slow things down, and repeat what they have said, so that those in their audience are able to take in what they have to say: so do teachers.

14. In our terminology, the core processes are identification (of issues), development (of possible lines of action), choice (between options) and implementation (of policies). We think that the similarities between the terminologies are much more important than the differences.

15. Another variant, referred to by Steier (1991) as 'second order constructionism', gives serious attention to what follows from recognizing 'observers' (theorist-researchers) to be part of (rather than apart from) the social processes they study. This shifts the focus away from epistemology, collapses the distinction between ontology and epistemology, opens up new possibilities for research, and gives ethics a new prominence (see also Hosking, 2000).

16. Indeed, from one point of view the distinction is very problematic – explicit knowledge is just the visible 'tip of the iceberg' – reliant on tacit knowledge (we cannot say everything we know); see, for example, Dachler and Hosking (1995).

17. As we have remarked elsewhere, there are many social constructionisms. The version we have outlined here is but one. Elsewhere, Hosking has explored a version of social constructionism that 'starts' with construction processes and stays with talk of processes rather than persons – not least because talk of persons is so often misunderstood

as necessarily individualistic! In addition, she has sought to develop a critical variant of social constructionism which (reflexively) includes the 'scientist'/narrator in her own narrative (see, for example, Hosking, 2000).

## REFERENCES

Akin, G. and Hopelain, D. (1986) Finding the culture of productivity, *Organizational Dynamics*, **14**, 19–32.

Asch, S.E. (1952) *Social Psychology*. Englewood Cliffs, NJ: Prentice-Hall.

Baron, J. (1985) *Rationality and Intelligence*. Cambridge: Cambridge University Press.

Baron, J. (1988) *Thinking and Deciding*. Cambridge: Cambridge University Press.

Bartlett, F.C. (1932) *Remembering: A Study in Experimental and Social Psychology*. Cambridge: Cambridge University Press.

Bartlett, F.C. (1958) *Thinking: An Experimental and Social Study*. London: Unwin University Books.

Bechtel, W. and Graham. G. (eds) (1998) *A Companion to Cognitive Science*. Oxford: Blackwell.

Billig, M. (1989) *Arguing and Thinking: A Rhetorical Approach to Social Psychology*. Cambridge: Cambridge University Press.

Brown, H. and Hosking, D.M. (1986) Distributed leadership and skilled performance as successful organizing in social movements, *Human Relations*, **39**, 65–79.

Brown J.S. and Duguid, P. (1991) Organizational learning and communities of practice: toward a unified view of working, learning, and innovation, *Organization Science*, **2**(1), 40–57.

Clausing, D. and Andrade, R. (eds) (1996) *Creating Innovative Products Using Total Design: The Living Legacy of Stuart Pugh*. Reading, MA: Addison-Wesley.

Cohen, A. (1961) Cognitive tuning as a factor affecting impression formation, *Journal of Personality*, **29**, 235–45.

Cohen, M.D. and Sproull, L.S. (eds) (1996) *Organizational Learning*. Thousand Oaks, CA, London and New Delhi: Sage.

Dachler, H.P. and Hosking, D.M (1995) The primacy of relations in the social construction of organizational realities, in D.M. Hosking, H.P. Dachler and K. Gergen (eds), *Management and Organization: Relational Alternatives to Individualism*. Aldershot: Avebury.

Demetriou, A., Shayer, M. and Efklides, A. (1992) *Neo-Piagetian Theories of Cognitive Development: Implications and Applications for Education*. London: Routledge.

Dunsire, A. (1978) *The Execution Process Volume 1: Implementation in a Bureaucracy*. London: Martin Robertson.

Fiedler, F.E. (1967) *A Theory of Leadership Effectiveness*. New York: McGraw-Hill.

Fiedler, F.E. and House, R.J. (1988) Leadership theory and research: a report of progress, in C.L. Cooper and I. Robertson (eds), *International Review of Industrial and Organizational Psychology*. Chichester: Wiley.

Fikes, R.E. (1982) A commitment-based framework for describing informal cooperative work, *Cognitive Science*, **6**, 331–47.

Friend, J. (1989) The strategic choice approach, in J. Rosenhead (ed.), *Rational Analysis for a Problematic World: Problem Structuring Methods for Complexity, Uncertainty, and Conflict*. Chichester: Wiley.

Friend. J. and Hickling, A. (1987) *Planning Under Pressure: The Strategic Choice Approach*. Oxford: Pergamon.

Friend, J. and Jessop, W.N. (1977) *Local Government and Strategic Choice* (2nd edn). Oxford: Pergamon.

Glaser, R. (1999) Expert knowledge and processes of thinking, in R. McCormick and C. Paechter (eds), *Learning and Knowledge*. London: Paul Chapman Publishing, published in association with the Open University.

Glymour, C. (1999) The hierarchies of knowledge and the mathematics of discovery, in P. Millican and A. Clark (eds), *Machines and Thought: The Legacy of Alan Turing, Volume 1*. Oxford: Oxford University Press.

Harré, R. (1979) *Social Being: A Theory for Social Psychology*. Oxford: Blackwell.

Harré, R. and Gillett, G. (1994) *The Discursive Mind*. Thousand Oaks, CA, London and New Delhi: Sage.

Hersey, P. and Blanchard, K.H. (1969) Life-cycle theory of leadership, *Training and Development Journal*, 23(5), 26–34.

Hosking, D.M. (1997) Organising, leadership, and skilful process, in Grint, K. (ed.), *Leadership: Classical, Contemporary and Critical Approaches*, Oxford: Oxford University Press.

Hosking, D.M. (2001) Social construction as process: some new possibilities for research and development, *Concepts and Transformation*, 4(2), 117–32.

Hosking, D.M. Leadership processes and leadership development: Reflections from a social constructionist paradigm. http://www.geocities.com/dian_marie_hosking/ldrship.html

Hosking, D.M. (2000) Ecology in mind: mindful practices, *European Journal of Work and Organisational Psychology*, 9(2), 147–58.

Hosking, D.M. (2002) *Constructing changes: A social constructionist approach to changework (and beetles and witches)*. Tilburg: Tilburg University.

Hosking, D.M. and Bass, A. (2001) Constructing changes in relational processes: introducing a social constructionist approach to change work, *Career Development International*, 6(7), 348–60.

Hosking, D.M. and Bouwen, R. (2000) Guest editors of special issue on: Organizational learning: relational constructionist approaches. *European Journal of Work and Organizational Psychology*, 9(2), 129–303.

Hosking, D.M. and Morley, I.E. (1988) The skills of leadership, in G. Hunt, B.R. Baliga, H.P. Dachler and C.A. Schriesheim (eds), *Emerging Leadership Vistas*. Lexington, MA: Lexington Books.

Hosking, D.M. and Morley, I.E. (1991) *A Social Psychology of Organizing: People, Processes and Contexts*. New York: Prentice-Hall.

House, R.J. and Singh, J. (1987) Organizational behaviour: Some new directions fo I/O Psychology. *Annual Review of Psychology*, 38, 669–718.

Hunt, J.G., Hosking, D.M., Schriescheim, C.A. and Stewart, R. (1984) *Leadership and Managers: International Perspectives on Managerial Behavior and Leadership*. Elmsford, NY: Pergamon.

Janis, I.L. (1989) *Crucial Decisions: Leadership in Policymaking and Crisis Management*. New York: Free Press.

Janis, I.L. and Mann, L. (1977) *Decision-Making: A Psychological Analysis of Conflict, Choice and Commitment*. New York: Free Press.

Jervis, R. (1970) *The Logic of Images in International Relations*. Princeton, NJ: Princeton University Press.

Jervis, R. (1976) *Perception and Misperception in International Politics*. Princeton, NJ: Princeton University Press.

Kotter, J.P. (1982) *The General Managers*. New York: Free Press.

Lakatos, I. (1978) *The Methodology of Scientific Research Programmes: Philosophical Papers Volume 1*. Cambridge: Cambridge University Press.

Lave, J. and Wenger, E. (1991) *Situated Learning: Legitimate Peripheral Participation*. Cambridge: Cambridge University Press.

Levin, P.H. (1976) *Government and the Planning Process*. London: Allen & Unwin.

Linstone, H.A. (1984) in H.A. Linstone, A.J. Meltsner, M. Adelson, B. Clary, P.G. Cook, S. Hawke, R.-E. Miller, A. Mysior, J.S. Pearson Jr, J. Schuman, L. Umbenstock, D. Wagner and S.J. Will, *Multiple Perspectives for Decision-Making: Bridging the Gap Between Analysis and Action*. New York: North-Holland.

McCormick, R. and Paechter, C. (1999) *Learning and Knowledge*. London: Paul Chapman Publishing in association with The Open University.

Morley, I.E. (1992) Intra-organizational bargaining, in J. Hartley and G.M. Stephenson (eds), *Employment Relations*. Oxford: Blackwell.

Morley, I.E. and Hosking, D.M. (1985) Relationships between Consideration and Initiating Structure: two causal relationships rather than one?, *Current Psychological Research and Reviews*, 4(2), 119–32.

Morley, I.E. and Ormerod, R. (1996) A language-action approach to operational research, *Journal of the Operational Research Society*, 47, 731–40.

Norman, D.A. (1988) *The Psychology of Everyday Things*. New York: Basic Books.

Orr, J.E. (1990) Sharing knowledge, celebrating identity: community memory in a service culture, in D. Middleton and D. Edwards (eds), *Collective Remembering*. London: Sage.

Rosenhead, J. (ed.) (1989) *Rational Analysis for a Problematic World: Problem Structuring Methods for Complexity, Uncertainty, and Conflict*. Chichester: Wiley.

Sarason, S.B. (1972) *The Creation of Social Settings and the Future Societies*. San-Francisco, CA: Jossey-Bass.

Smircich, L. and Morgan, G. (1992) Leadership: the management of meaning, *Journal of Applied Behavioral Science*, 18, 257–73.

Snyder, G.H. and Diesing, P. (1977) *Conflict Among Nations: Bargaining, Decision-Making and System Structure in International Crises*. Princeton, NJ: Princeton University Press.

Steier, F. (1991) *Research and Reflexivity*. London: Sage.

te Molder, H.F.M. (1999) Discourse of dilemmas: An analysis of communication planners' accounts, *British Journal of Social Psychology*, 38, 245–63.

Vaill, P. (1982) The purposing of high performance systems, *Organizational Dynamics*, Autumn, 23–39.

Valsinger, J. and van der Veer, R. (2000) *The Social Mind: Construction of the Idea*. Cambridge: Cambridge University Press.

Welford, A.T. (1980) The concept of social skill and its application to social perfor-mance, in W.T. Singleton, P. Spurgeon and R. Stammmers (eds), *The Analysis of Social Skill*. London: Plenum Press.

Winograd, T. and Flores, F. (1986) *Understanding Computers and Cognition: A New Foundation for Design*. Norwood, NJ: Ablex.

Wood, D. (1988) *How Children Think and Learn*. Oxford: Blackwell.

# 4

---

# Distributing and Intensifying School Leadership[1]

PETER GRONN

Early in the new millennium, an informed understanding of the leadership of schools requires an appreciation of two interrelated phenomena: the distributed pattern of leaders' work and the intensification of work practices. The purpose of this chapter is to discuss each of these features and the ways in which they are reconstituting school leadership. I begin with a review of leadership and then suggest why leadership practice has taken a distributed or dispersed form. Next I consider intensification and its connection with leadership. Finally, I address briefly some implications of distribution and intensification for the recent predilection of policy-makers for regimes of designer-leadership.

## ON LEADERSHIP

Leadership is one of a family of terms in both academic and common usage, which is invoked to designate modes of human conduct and engagement. Historically, other close family members have included power, authority, influence, manipulation, coercion, force and persuasion. Within this discursive family, leadership has always been the favourite offspring. None of its siblings command anything like the reverence and respect with which leadership is adorned. But this hallowed status is puzzling, for leadership shares some of the defining attributes of its family members, more, in fact, than is normally credited. Unfortunately, however, there exists no ideal schematic arrangement with which to represent the connections between the meanings of this family of terms. It is difficult to conceive of them as positioned along a continuum, for example, for such an apparatus presupposes a linear set of relationships partitioned between two end-points or extremities, but then one has to ask: extremes of what, and should the spaces between the concepts be equi-distant or uneven? In his short, but much quoted, discussion Lukes (1974, p. 32) inserted this family of terms into an L-shaped conceptual space. Interestingly, Lukes excluded leadership but included inducement and encouragement. Let us begin slightly arbitrarily, then, with power which, along with influence, is the closest leadership family relative.

It is not uncommon to hear power spoken of in the following ways: power structure, concentrations of power, powerful persons, empowerment, power elites or pluralities of power. There is some similarity here with authority, in that we also refer to such phenomena as authority structures, authority figures or authoritative persons. On the other hand, authority is usually thought of as a more constitutive term than power in the legitimation of human conduct, because authority establishes a legal framework or an order for action, although, perhaps slightly confusingly, an authority structure also confers 'powers' on office-holders, such as legislators or the judiciary. During the radical critique of behaviourist and liberal social theory during the 1970s and early 1980s, disputes about power oscillated between claim and counter-claim that it was a capacity or attribute of persons, or was evident in relationships between persons and the social structures that framed their actions. In the 30 Years' War (or thereabouts) between the paradigms, the relational view has prevailed. But this was not so in the case of leadership where, until recently, a mostly underdetermined agency view of leadership has held sway. Briefly, an underdetermined view of agency is one which downplays the constraints on an individual's actions, while exaggerating the individual's capacities and opportunities for action. Leadership has this much in common with power: while power has become a term of critique over the last 25 or so years (thanks largely to Lukes), leadership is usually associated with the targets of that critique: the powerful. The actions of the powerful are legitimated by authority, including legally sanctioned armed force in the defence of the nation and coercion by the state.

Oddly, the thing about leadership is that it is too immature a sibling to stand on its own feet, for it requires a fellow sibling, influence, to provide support. That is, when commentators try to define leadership, almost invariably they have to invoke influence to help them. Typical here is Rost (1993, p. 102, original text italicized) who, in his exhaustive conceptual review, defines leadership as 'an influence relationship among leaders and followers who intend real changes that reflect their mutual purposes'. But this definition begs some questions: if leadership is a type, or part, of influence does that not make 'leadership' unnecessary? That is, if it is influence we are really talking about, then why not stay with that word? Why must influential conduct be elevated to the status of leadership? Rost's definition introduces a binary or dualism between leaders and followers. So strong is the attributed symbiosis between these two analytical constructs that they are like the horse and carriage in the song about marriage: you cannot have one without the other. But why not? Why are organization members automatically assumed to fit into either of these binary categories? And why has the claim that there can be no leadership without followers become a truism? If we consider the other siblings, it is apparent that, with the possible exception of power, no other family member is portrayed in binary terms. In the case of power, the dualism of the powerful and the powerless is the closest one gets to anything as conceptually hard and fast as leaders and followers, and yet this power dichotomy has never been anywhere near as thoroughly embedded in the public or academic consciousness as the leader–follower binary.

## ON DISTRIBUTED LEADERSHIP

The main reason why the leader–follower dualism retains its academic currency, as Calder (1977) pointed out, is less because 'leadership' describes a recognizable and agreed-upon form of behaviour, than because its symbolic force resonates powerfully with the lay public. Indeed, people have been shown to retain a strong romantic attachment to leadership and the research of numerous leadership theorists trades on that preference. An important corollary of this affection for leadership is a pervasive assumption that parallels the leader–follower binary, namely, that followers vastly outnumber leaders. That is, there is a belief that leaders are genuinely special individuals and few in number. This may be described as a focused view, in which leadership is seen as being monopolized or concentrated in one or a few hands.

Suppose we consider the possibility, first raised by Gibb (1969) that, while it may be focused, organizational leadership is equally likely to be distributed. In the case of power, it is standard practice for political scientists to research patterns of power distribution in political and social systems. Indeed, in *Who Governs?*, a classic account of power in a US city, Dahl (1975, p. 90) described his focus as 'the distribution of influence' in his case study community. While Dahl did not use the expression 'distributed leadership', his investigation provides what is effectively an account of distributed leaders, in the sense that community influence was dispersed amongst a number of influential groups, rather than concentrated in one small elite and, from time to time, was expressed directly and indirectly by leader and sub-leader groups across a range of community-wide issues. But what about organizations? Are there patterns of organizational leadership corresponding to the dispersal of power and influence across a society? Gibb's (1969, p. 215) claim was that, in organizations, 'leadership is probably best conceived as a group quality, as a set of functions which must be carried out by the group'. But as a group function or set of operations, leadership could either be focused or distributed, and there was no 'force in the nature of the leadership relation itself', he said, 'making for "focused" rather than "distributed" leadership' (Gibb, 1968, p. 94). This idea of a dispersal of functions has been well captured by Spillane, Halverson and Diamond's (2000, p. 6, original emphasis) idea of leaders' practice as '*stretched over* the social and situational contexts of the school'.

## PATTERNS OF DISTRIBUTION

A distributed view of leadership demands that we de-centre 'the' leader, a requirement that contradicts the ruling scholarly illusions of the last two decades or so which have privileged high-profile, vision-driven individuals who, allegedly, engineer transformational turnarounds. As I have pointed out elsewhere (Gronn, 2002b; 2002c), there are two main ways of thinking about de-centred, stretched leadership: as numerical sharing or dispersal and as conjoint agency. In the former case, the unit of analysis becomes 1+ or $1^n$ leaders, i.e., potentially the entire organizational membership and, in the case of conjoint agency, it means plural-member work units. Until recently, with some notable exceptions (e.g., Sayles, 1964), the fondness of management and organization theorists for 'the lone chief atop a pyramidal structure' (Greenleaf, 1977, p. 61) has mostly veiled the realities of these working dynamics in a pall of ignorance. With the recent 'discovery' of distributed leadership, however, this cloud has begun to dissipate.

As vehicles for concertive action, plural-member work units range from partnerships between two or more persons through to conventionally understood teams or even numerically larger groupings. They operate informally or their existence may be formalized and routinized. These units may either co-perform or collectively perform their work. In the former case, the individuals will be located together and work in shared time, whereas in the latter they may be separated in time and space, and be linked by asynchronous means of communication. There are three main types: spontaneous collaboration, intuitive working relations, and institutionalized and quasi-institutionalized practices.

## Spontaneous collaboration

From time to time in organizations such as schools, colleagues with shared skills, interests and backgrounds come together deliberately in twos and threes to address a temporary difficulty. Equally, colleagues possessing different attributes may find themselves 'thrown together' inadvertently to attack common problems. These experiences provide opportunities for brief bursts of synergy which may come to nothing but which, because the individuals discover previously untapped work capacities, may stimulate further collaboration. The effect of colleagues' co-ordinated effort is to facilitate conjoint agency through their cognitively aligned plans and reciprocally experienced influence patterns. A good illustration is the way the 'morning round' evolved between Audrey Proctor, a nursery-infant school head, and Julie Harris, her deputy (Nias, 1987, p. 39).

## Intuitive working relations

Another form of concertive action is the intuitive understanding that emerges over time when two or more organization members come to rely on each other to accomplish their work. Examples are chief executives (CEOs) and their personal assistants (PAs) or school principals and their deputies. Here, joint leadership is evident in their shared role space. The working partnership becomes the focal unit that is attributed with leader status, by the members themselves and by their colleagues. This effective role sharing occurs when the members capitalize on their dependence on one another by balancing each other's skills or, perhaps, because they are constrained to do so due to overlapping role responsibilities. Intuitive working relations are analogous to intimate interpersonal relations (e.g., friendships) in which the members trust one another unconditionally and blend their actions within an implicitly understood framework. Such an intuitive level of understanding explains how, for example, at a school assembly Julie Harris 'fed Miss Proctor a cue which enabled her to comment on care in the use of crayons' (Nias, 1987, p. 37).

### Institutionalized and quasi-institutionalized practices

Distributed leadership may also occur in two, three, four or more multi-member work units or even larger units such as teams. An example is the threesome comprised by Hodgson, Levinson and Zaleznik's (1965) role constellation of senior hospital executives. Another is the couple formed by an Australian headmaster and the head of a new school campus (Gronn, 1999). Perhaps the most interesting recent example of institutionalized distributed leadership is the concept of partner principals. The models documented by Court (2001) include: split-task specialization (i.e., one principal for administration and one for curriculum); emergent split-task specialization (i.e., the division of labour is negotiated); alternating co-principals (i.e., turn-taking or simultaneous 50–50 job-sharing); and, rotation of responsibilities within a collective teacher leadership executive group (i.e., no-principal schools).

Each of these patterns of distributed leadership rests on a changed set of assumptions about the rearticulation of work as part of a changing division of labour (see Gronn, 2002c, pp. 428, 432–4). Briefly, at the heart of a division of labour is an inherent tension between an imperative of differentiation, as tasks proliferate through increased specialization, and an imperative of integration, as these specialisms have to be rearticulated and combined in new work designs. The rearticulation of patterns of work alters existing forms of employee interdependence and the co-ordination of work activities. Interdependence concerns the fulfilment of role responsibilities. While some formal responsibilities may be discrete, others may overlap or complement one another. In practice, the degree of complementarity and overlap may be greater than is commonly acknowledged. Nias (1987, p. 31), for example, notes that 'interdependence was a characteristic of the whole staff' at her case study school and not just confined to the relationship between Proctor and Harris. Role complementarity and overlap suggest that the accomplishment of workplace responsibilities depends on reciprocal actions rather than solo performance. Co-ordination, on the other hand, refers to the alignment and management of the activities which, taken together, constitute particular work projects or the totality of ongoing work. Co-ordination is facilitated by a variety of scheduling, sequencing and control mechanisms. As part of the recent wave of school reform and restructuring in many countries, the introduction of new accountability policies has resulted in significant changes in the division of labour in schools. The adoption of policies of self-managed schooling, for example, has altered existing co-ordination patterns and interdependent relationships, and has also dramatically intensified the work of school leaders.

## INTENSIFIED WORK

As with distributed leadership, there are numerous references to the intensification of school leaders' work, particularly in the literature critiquing the recent wave of school reform. Intensification represents a strategic policy outcome that results in the de-professionalization or proletarianization of the work of school personnel (Blackmore, 1996).

The phenomenon of intensification refers to new work practices which entail significantly increased levels of output, with expectations of output enshrined in employment contract-based performance indicators and productivity targets, with satisfactory target attainment rewarded through incentive bonus payments, and with contract renewal potentially prejudiced by non-attainment of targets. Adherence to these new effort norms requires amounts of physical, cognitive and emotional energy expenditure not contemplated previously. At the same time as these role demands and associated expectations increase, the scope for institutional-level autonomy and discretion is circumscribed by externally imposed budgetary and other resource constraints as part of a lean and mean policy rubric of 'doing more with less'. In these circumstances, life 'at the pointy end' for those school leaders who mediate national- and state-level policies to local communities, such as principals, for example, is experienced as extremely demanding and stressful. Clarke and Newman (1997, p. 74) note how competing in the managerial career stakes has come to mean being able to demonstrate 'commitment through long (often excessive) hours of work and being able to cope with high stress': 'Such intensification, linked to career uncertainty and occupational fragility, has a profound effect on both men and women, with implications for their children, partners and parents as well as their own quality of life.'

Data on intensification has been procured as part of the Monash University Readiness for Leadership project.[2] One of the informants, a newly appointed principal, looks back over the 12 months since she assumed responsibility for a metropolitan primary school with an enrolment of about 270 children: 'I've done 62 hours a week this week already without today [a Friday morning]. I was in last Sunday for 12 hours.'

In this lengthy extract, the new prinicipal describes her normal working day:

When I get in here in the morning, which is normally between 7.30 and 7.45, I have to open my e-mail ... I can't read off the computer because I've got bad eyes so I download all the e-mails. Most of them have got attachments. METRO region so far this year [May: four months into the school year] have sent me and every other principal [indicates three ring binders] 426, 554, 120 e-mails ... Now, that's before I start. Any given morning I can have between six and eight e-mails with attachments that I have to open, read, take in, absorb, print and put in folders. That's before I start a day. Then I have curriculum. I have to drive student welfare at this school. I drive it. All the change implementation, leadership team meetings, making sure that people are doing what they are supposed to be doing in classes. I don't actually look at work programs because I don't have time. The new ETWR [Experienced Teacher With Responsibility] process which is the new career structure, I interviewed all of my sub-12s, all of my Level-12 teachers who thought they were eligible for this thingo, for this promotion position. I had to read all the applications, there's eight of them. We had to have meeting after meeting to decide our criteria etc. And then we had our interviews and we've had to look at all their documentation. Then *I* have to do all the bookwork for that which is all computer-generated. We've advertised teacher vacancies this year. We've got to do all of that. It just doesn't end. And that's the paper warfare. And then the dealing with the people stuff, like at the moment I am pushing aside. I'm, I'm, I'm keeping myself above the water level by staying in the office and ploughing through the paperwork. When I have finished that I can get back out and put most of my time into the people and children. But it's just never ending. It's just, and you have always got to respond, fill in pro formas and, drives you nuts. The workload is massive ... And then you've got all this stuff you have to deal with like the unhappy parent, the parents' club who want to talk to you about this, the school council president who wants to talk to you on the phone just to chat and, you know keep, keep up, be informed, and teachers who say 'keep us informed'. It just goes on and on and on.

Immediately following this description, however, the newly appointed principal confessed: 'But I love it'.

## COPING WITH INTENSIFICATION

The newly appointed principal's reflections graphically encapsulate a dualistic feature of role intensification: work pressures are experienced as both a challenge and a burden; a challenge to keep up and to meet their demands while wanting to do so ('But I love it'), and wanting to be seen to be doing so, yet simultaneously feeling oppressed by the weight of them. There are also clear affinities between the newly appointed principal's description and the characteristics of brevity, variety, fragmentation and interruption that Mintzberg (1973) claimed were intrinsic to managerial work, but there are also discontinuities, for the new performativity and accountability requirements that now frame leaders' work have introduced significantly different qualitative demands.

School leaders now have to mediate the prescriptions of policy while trying to respond to immediate contextual pressures and new division of labour imperatives pulling them towards greater levels of the aforementioned task interdependence and new modes of co-ordination. While the scope for creative agency might appear limited in such circumstances, documentation of a range of negotiated responses is beginning to accumulate. Alexiadou (2001) found that, with the introduction of quasi-market reforms to the UK Further Education (FE) sector, for example, institutional managers' professional identities shifted in one of three directions: some were able to accommodate pragmatically to marketization while clinging to professional educational values, others chose to actively engage with market values and practices, while yet others became gung-ho entrepreneurs. When confronted by circumstances similar to those described by the newly appointed principal, some school leaders, like Boyle and Woods's (1996) 'Chris', have reconstructed themselves as superleaders. Others, typified by Riseborough's (1993) 'Stan D. Fast', have managed to immunize their schools from the intrusion of reform. Still others, despite the competitive marketized environment, have actively resisted through inter-school collaboration or outright policy subversion (Wallace, 1998). Next, while Reay and Ball's (2000, p. 153) four female London comprehensive heads were (willingly) 'conscripted into competitive ways of operating', a commitment to feminist values, and contextual opportunities for their expression, enabled three New Zealand women secondary heads to craft strategies combining resistance, agreement and policy appropriation, thereby ameliorating the institutional impact of post-1989 neo-liberal reforms (Strachan, 1999). Finally, prospective school leaders have been disengaging. Older mid- and late-career teachers, for example, are starting to eschew institution-wide responsibilities beyond their classrooms (Gronn, 2003).

## ACCOUNTING FOR DISTRIBUTED AND INTENSIFIED WORK

But why does leadership practice take a distributed and intensified form, and is there a link between these two phenomena?

To the extent that commentators connect the two phenomena, they tend to answer these questions in one of two main ways. First, it is claimed that distributed work practice heightens the intensity of the work experience. In this explanation, distributed leadership *per se* is not mentioned, but vehicles for the dispersal and sharing of leadership, such as teams, are highlighted. The most benign version of this claim is that the team experience is cognitively stretching for the membership, because team-based work increases the 'salience of the task demands by providing members with a broader perspective on their own work' (Donnellon, 1996, p. 221). A more sinister version is that, in return for greater participation in decisions about work targets and operations, higher productivity is demanded of organization members for which they are expected to 'give more time, to give more energy, to identify strongly with the goals and needs of their organization, and to learn how to collaborate effectively with coworkers' (Barker, 1999, p. 11). Fully extended, the argument is that team-based work is controlled through an intimidating regulatory regime of panoptican-like peer discipline and surveillance.

A second explanation links the emergence of distributed leadership to the consequences of new public management (NPM) accountability policies. As Court (2001, p. 21) notes, an assumption which informs NPM is distrust, i.e., that public sector professionals are motivated by 'acquisitiveness and a desire to increase their own power and status' and, consequently, 'provider capture'. In parallel with these allegations, as part of a reassertion of the need for 'leadership', NPM's proponents have also demonized management, especially corporate middle managers, tiers of which were 'hollowed out' through downsizing in numerous organizations over the last decade and a half. Thus, with better educated workforces, organizations allow workers to manage their own work and then 'downsize their unneeded managers' (Barker, 1999, p. 7). A consequence, according to Grey (1999, p. 572), is that 'we are all managers now', because the possibility is opened up that management as a function ceases to be the monopoly of a cadre of elite career specialists. But displaced middle managers are antithetical to distributed structures such as teams, notes Donnellon (1996, p. 155), because they see these as infringing their traditional authority and control. Another consequence of NPM's proponents framing of 'management' and 'managers' (as traditionally understood) as part of the problem of inefficiency, is that the survivors (i.e., existing and potential managers) feel betrayed. One response to distrust and their alleged redundancy is the aforementioned disengagement. With the expansion of individual role space under NPM-style accountability, therefore, and with expectations of higher productivity as part of performance-based work contracts, school managers, particularly principals, have had to find creative ways of accomplishing their work by delegating the task load. It should be noted, however, that delegated authority is not necessarily synonymous with distributed leadership, for those to whom tasks are delegated may not be perceived as leaders when performing them. The effect of delegation is to create a range of formal and informal working arrangements which may or may not entail democratic power-sharing and opportunities for dispersed or shared leadership, and which are intended at least partly to compensate for role intensification.

Both of these explanations foreground social changes in the division of school leadership labour. But for the sake of completeness, these need to be linked with developments in the technological side of the division of labour. Thanks to the introduction of information and communication technology (ICT) systems, schools, like many corporate and human service organizations, are located in complex data-rich, information-saturated task environments. The increased adoption of networked ICT by school leaders, for example, is both a medium and an outcome of changes in the technical component of the division of labour. On the one hand, ICT is an outcome of change, in that schools are now computer-networked to local authorities, regions, central offices and service providers. These links facilitate e-mail connections, Internet access and data search capabilities that are intended to enhance student learning. As a medium, on the other hand, the provision of ICT has altered the division of labour by imposing numerous new official accountability demands on schools. In Victoria, for example, schools are required to record an extensive amount of student cohort performance data in English and Mathematics, along with survey data on school management, environment and resources, onto a central database where, for purposes of a triennial review process, it is benchmarked against state-wide and Like School Group norms. These kinds of accountability demands intensify work because of the scale and scope of the information required, and the telescoping of the deadlines for their transmission. Thus, networked ICT transforms schools into simultaneous beneficiaries and victims. On the one hand, students are provided with potentially expanded access to infinite information space and flexible learning environments and, for school leaders, ICT facilitates improved co-ordination across campuses, in the case of multi-site schools, and between institutional partners, in the case of school clusters. On the other hand, school leaders are at the mercy of highly intrusive, remote and speedier information control systems which generate the kind of message volumes engulfing the newly appointed principal, thereby augmenting the constraints on schools and limiting their discretion for independent action.

## IMPLICATIONS OF DISTRIBUTED AND INTENSIFIED LEADERSHIP

As yet, the full implications of this changed work order have yet to be fully catalogued. To the extent that the social and institutional costs of NPM reform are experienced as de-professionalization, then work intensification may be fuelling leadership disengagement and corroding the willingness of teachers to be good organizational citizens. A sense of de-professionalization is likely to result when the scope for independent individual and collective agency in workplace decision-making is dramatically circumscribed. De-professionalization is experienced as the diminution of previous policy autonomy and discretion. It is likely to have long-term effects in that career identities are being reconstructed in the direction of increasing workplace servility rather than empowerment. That is, school personnel under self-managing schooling are experiencing externally imposed controls as evidence of highly demanding and greedy systems, in which they are required to work increasingly at the beck and call of remotely located external officials, rather than their immediate school peers. Intensification may be central to the reworking of teachers' professional identities, therefore, because it automatically implicates them in a revised understanding of their commitments as work colleagues, and a reassessment of their overall career trajectories and plans.

At a personal level, both intensification and distribution call forth whole new sets of leadership attributes. One early prototype of leadership under conditions of distribution, in a study which took the division of labour as its analytical focus, but in an era preceding intensification, is found in Sayles's (1964) *Managerial Behavior*. Here, following extended fieldwork, manager-leaders were shown to be less the hierarchically defined occupants of roles who initiated ordered sets of relations in accordance with the fine-grained legalisms of their employment contracts, than role incumbents who were immersed in problem-solving amidst workflows and processes. In the absence of similar recent detailed empirical studies of changes in the division of labour and their impact, but with the imperatives of interdependence and co-ordination which were mentioned earlier in mind, the following brief list of attributes is necessarily indicative. With contemporary distributed leadership, the successful development of new employee synergies, for example, would appear to require a capacity to articulate previously invisible and tacit dimensions of role performance. Distributed leadership also seems to demand a new forbearance for reciprocity and interdependency, the ability to cope with a sense of impermanence, a willingness to continually restructure procedures in the search for successful operational formulae, a finely tuned tolerance for ambiguity and uncertainty, and heightened negotiation skills. Emotionally, school leaders need to be willing to withstand acute personal pressures, display a capacity for emotional containment, and acquire a sense of how events coalesce, fuse and flow. They are also likely to find themselves constantly repositioning and aligning themselves and their schools in response to market pressures and movements, and working in increasingly multicultural work environments requiring cultural sensitivity and understandings of cultural norms.

The earlier lengthy extract from the newly appointed principal shows a principal grappling with some of these new tensions. On the one hand, we witness an individual whose actions, in her endeavour to get across all of the detail, as it were, seem to be evidence of a focused, rather than a distributed, pattern of work. This is indicated by her constant use of 'I'. On the other hand, this extract is not about leadership and whether the newly appointed principal is perceived as a leader, for the focusing in question is the focusing of responsibilities on her as the accountable school-level manager. That is, all of the external and situational constraints to which she alludes in the extract come to her by virtue of the way school-level accountability works, for as the principal, the newly appointed principal is answerable for the entirety of school operations.

## DESIGNS FOR LEADERS

Despite the confluence of factors that produce intensified and distributed leadership, the latest wave of school reform has generated an entirely new discourse for legitimating the roles of school leaders. This new mandate for the leadership of schools is a system of 'designer-leadership' (Gronn, 2002a), with designs for leaders embodied increasingly in national, normative sets of competency standards, for which the UK's NPQH, LPSH and HEADLAMP schemes, and the ILLSC standards in the USA are prototypical.

Designs for leaders intrude significantly into the domain of school leaders' work because they operate through highly structured and externally imposed regimes of assessment and accreditation, the intention of which is to license or authorize the initial appointments of education professionals and to guarantee their continuing engagement in professional practice in conformity with sets of desired norms. For this reason, the adoption of designer leadership represents a new weapon in the armoury of professional governance and control. This trend is significant for at least two reasons. First, standards entail a new discursive and regulatory apparatus for legitimating new understandings of professional practice, which shifts control of that definition away from the profession to various auditing bodies. Second, standards introduce a new mode of leader formation in which the production of leaders is customized to the needs of user-systems rather than in accordance with the stipulations of traditional providers (e.g., universities). The outcome of customization is a reprofessionalization (or perhaps de-professionalization or even proletariani-zation) of the production of occupational identities. In this way, historic patterns of voluntarist, pluralistic identity construction are yielding to centralized, monocultural norm imposition and forms of standardization that de-legitimate and minimize variations in personal career passage.

The realities of distributed leadership are at odds with leader design speci-fications, for the latter embody, explicitly or implicitly, a heroic or focused leader prototype. As to the intensification of practice, this means, as we have seen, subjecting oneself as a leader to a self-imposed regime of disciplined work performance. It also entails manoeuvring within potentially infinite information space and greatly expanded role space, being constrained by mas-sively increased task demands and tightly telescoped time frames, being sub-jected to heightened external surveillance through auditing and monitoring regimes, and having to internalize possible values dissonance and absorb the costs of emotional stress. Standards-based designs for school leaders, with their extensive bullet-point lists of performance norms, are likely to exacer-bate the experience of an intensified work order and consolidate teachers' leadership disengagement. This is because, by 'raising the bar' of heroic per-formance expectations even higher, standards provide yet another strong dis-incentive for teachers to aspire to leadership as a career goal. Despite this possibility, intensification is now part of a calculated game of identifying heroic leaders. The structured interview technique forming part of the Gallup profile for the identification and assessment of leadership potential (cited in Tomlinson and Holmes, 2001, p. 113), for example, asserts that 'talented people' use 'more intensifiers and have more emotional commitment'. Moreover, the life themes recorded over 30 years in Gallup's library of 'highly effective performers' focus on: 'the intensity of the performer's drive for task completion, based on a keen awareness of the leader's strengths, which are underpinned by a values system and a determination to help others achieve quality'.

With intensification now considered by many to be a virtue, it remains to be seen whether potential school leaders will eschew the opportunity to pro-vide the exceptional performance now associated with leadership.

## CONCLUSION

In this chapter, I identified two contemporary features of school leadership, distributed and intensified work. While intensification was shown to be a creature of the reconstitution of leadership under NPM-style accountability and performativity policy frameworks, regimes of intensified work are also facilitated and consolidated by networked ICT systems. And while distributed leadership has surfaced as many school leaders seek to compensate for the effects of intensified work by expanding the critical mass of organizational leadership, it has also become more prevalent as a result of new electronic communications systems. The possibility was also raised, however, by reference to an earlier generation of studies, that distributed leadership has not so much been 'discovered' as 'rediscovered', due to the awareness that interdependence, rather than follower-dependence, provides the empirical foundation for leadership. Finally, it was shown that recent leadership development policies, far from acknowledging the distributed realities of practice, tend to contradict them, and that these policies take for granted the reality of intensified work as a desired norm. Faced with the unintended consequence of impending leader disengagement, however, these design assumptions may be unlikely to prove sustainable in the long term.

## NOTES

1. I wish to thank Dr Felicity Rawlings for her helpful comments on an earlier version of this chapter.
2. I am grateful to the Monash Small Grants Scheme for funding this project.

## REFERENCES

Alexiadou, N. (2001) Management identities in transition: a case study from further education, *Sociological Review*, **49**(3), 412–435.

Barker, J.R. (1999) *The Discipline of Teamwork: Participation and Concertive Control*. London: Sage.

Blackmore, J. (1996) Doing 'emotional labour' in the education market place: stories from the field of women in management, *Discourse*, **17**(3), 337–49.

Boyle, M. and Woods, P. (1996) The composite head: coping with changes in the primary headteachers' role, *British Educational Research Journal*, **22**(5), 549–68.

Calder, B.J. (1977) An attribution theory of leadership, in B.M. Staw and G.R. Salancik (eds), *New Directions in Organizational Behavior* (pp. 179–204). Chicago, IL: St. Clair.

Clarke, J. and Newman, J. (1997) *The Managerial State: Power, Politics and Ideology in the Remaking of Social Welfare*. London: Sage.

Court, M. (2001) Collaborative or managerial? Reviewing studies of co-principalships and shared teacher initiatives. Paper presented to the annual conference of the British Educational Research Association, Leeds.

Dahl, R.A. (1975) *Who Governs? Democracy and Power in an American City*. New Haven, CT: Yale University Press.

Donnellon, A. (1996) *Team Talk: The Power of Language in Team Dynamics*. Boston, MA: Harvard Business School Press.

Gibb, C.A. (1968) Leadership: psychological aspects, in D.L. Sills (ed.), *International Encyclopedia of the Social Sciences*, vol. 9 (pp. 91–101). New York: Free Press/ Macmillan.

Gibb, C.A. (1969) Leadership, in G. Lindzey and E. Aronson (eds), *The Handbook of Social Psychology*, vol. 4 (2nd edn) (pp. 205–83). Reading, MA: Addison-Wesley.

Greenleaf (1977) *Servant Leadership: A Journey into the Nature of Legitimate Power and Greatness*. New York: Paulist Press.

Grey, C. (1999) 'We are all managers now'; 'we always were': on the development and demise of management, *Journal of Management Studies*, 36(5), 561–85.

Gronn, P. (1999) Substituting for leadership: the neglected role of the leadership couple, *Leadership Quarterly*, 10(1), 41–62.

Gronn, P. (2002a) Designer-leadership: the emerging global adoption of preparation standards, *Journal of School Leadership*, 12(5), 552–78.

Gronn, P. (2002b) Distributed leadership, in K. Leithwood and P. Hallinger (eds), *Second International Handbook of Educational Leadership and Administration*, (pp. 653–96). Dordrecht: Kluwer.

Gronn, P. (2002c) Distributed leadership as a unit of analysis, *Leadership Quarterly*, 13(4), 423–51.

Gronn, P. (2003) *The New Work of Educational Leaders: Changing Leadership Practice in an Era of School Reform*. London: Sage/Paul Chapman Publishing.

Hodgson, R.C., Levinson, D.J. and Zaleznik, A. (1965) *The Executive Role Constellation: An Analysis of Personality and Role Relations in Management*. Boston, MA: Harvard University, Graduate School of Business Administration.

Lukes, S. (1974) *Power: A Radical View*. London: Macmillan.

Mintzberg, H. (1973) *The Nature of Managerial Work*. New York: Harper and Row.

Nias, J. (1987) One finger, one thumb: a case study of the deputy head's part in the leadership in a nursery/infant school, in G. Southworth (ed.), *Readings in Primary School Management* (pp. 30–53). London: Falmer.

Reay, D. and Ball, S.J. (2000) Essentials of female management: women's ways of working in the education market place. *Educational Management & Administration*, 28(2), 145–59.

Riseborough, G. (1993) Primary headship, state policy and the challenge of the 1990s: an exceptional story that disproves total hegemonic rule, *Journal of Educational Policy*, 8(2), 155–73.

Rost, J.C. (1993) *Leadership for the Twenty-First Century*, Westport, CT: Praeger.

Sayles, L.R. (1964) *Managerial Behavior: Administration in Complex Organizations*. New York: McGraw-Hill.

Spillane, J.P., Halverson, R. and Diamond, J.B. (2000) Towards a theory of leadership practice: a distributed perspective. Working paper, Institute for Policy Research, Northwestern University.

Strachan, J. (1999) Feminist educational leadership in a New Zealand neo-liberal context, *Journal of Educational Administration*, 37(2), 121–38.

Tomlinson, H. and Holmes, G. (2001) Assessing leadership potential: fast track to school leadership, *Journal of Educational Administration*, 39(2), 104–17.

Wallace, M. (1998) A counter-policy to subvert education reform: collaboration among schools and colleges in a competitive climate, *British Educational Research Journal*, 24(2), 195–215.

# SECTION 2

# THE PERSPECTIVES IN PRACTICE

# 5

## Challenging Circumstances: The Role of Distributed and Intensified Leadership

### MEGAN CRAWFORD

### INTRODUCTION

Individual views on leadership have the power to stimulate strong debate. For example, there are many dangers inherent in the aggrandizement of leadership, one being that potentially good leaders in education may be daunted by the view of leadership that they see being offered as exemplars for them. In Chapter 4 in this book, Gronn calls this the heroic or focused leader prototype. Different perspectives do need to be explored carefully in order to try and understand the helpfulness and explanatory power of those perceptions. It is most important to look at Gronn's chapter in this volume with the current burdens of expectation about leadership from policy-makers firmly in mind. My research relates to schools in challenging contexts, for which a heroic leader is often seen, by the popular press as *the* answer. Gronn begins with the suggestion that an informed understanding of the leadership of schools requires an appreciation of two interrelated phenomena: the distributed pattern of leaders' work and the intensification of work practices. In order to explore these further, this chapter looks at one particular situation, that of an English primary school subject to 'special measures' as a result of its inspection by the national inspectorate, and reanalyses some of the empirical data from the perspective of distributing and intensifying school leadership. The initial research was inspired by Conger and Kanungo (1998), who have researched extensively into the area of charismatic leadership in the business sector. They reiterate the finding that leaders and their contexts are intertwined in a complex and intimate fashion. During a time of crisis, they propose that any environment is more receptive to leadership in general, and likely to be open to proposals for radical change.

The chapter asks if this research provides some further or complementary insights into the relationship between leadership and the process of creating effective educational organizations, especially in the context of challenging circumstances. In particular, I ask whether Gronn's viewpoint provides extra illumination into our understanding of the nature of leadership in such schools. First, the circumstances of one particular school in challenging circumstances are discussed and the key issues for the leadership of that school. Secondly, I shall use the metaphor of the leadership family to explore participants' perceptions about what constitutes effectiveness as a leader in such a situation, whilst at the same time discussing distributed leadership. Finally, Gronn's ideas about the nature of leadership will be related to the empirical data.

## SCHOOLS SUBJECT TO SPECIAL MEASURES

The Office for Standards in Education (OFSTED) (1996) defines schools found to be 'in need of Special Measures' as 'Schools where the inspector concludes that the school is failing to give its pupils an acceptable standard of education'. The core concerns that OFSTED (1996) has identified across schools in special measures are:

- the under achievement and low levels of attainment of the pupils;
- a high proportion of unsatisfactory teaching;
- ineffective leadership.

Special measures include the submission of an Action Plan, which identifies how the key issues will be dealt with for approval by the Secretary of State for Education and Employment, monitoring by Her Majesty's Inspectors (HMI) of the implementation of the Action Plan, and regular reports to the Secretary of State on the school's progress. Schools must demonstrate that the necessary steps are being taken to address the key issues identified in the inspection report. In general terms a failing school is expected to improve and be close to providing an acceptable standard of education within two years of being deemed to need Special Measures.

Ferguson *et al.* (2000) suggest that schools in disadvantaged areas are more likely than those in stable communities to be judged harshly. They also note (*ibid.*, p. 103) that only one in a hundred schools with a high proportion of socially disadvantaged children receive 'very good' inspection reports compared with one in five of those with only a small proportion of such children. Past histories of such schools (Gray *et al.*, 1999, p. 73) are spelt out in writings in this area:

> All experienced significant changes in the composition of their catchment areas, problems with the local communities, difficulties in managing falling pupil numbers, budget restraints and the threat of closure. In addition, they have been characterized by low staff morale, general developmental apathy, and low levels of pupil performance ... improvement from such a baseline represents a formidable challenge.

The office for Standard in Education, in their publication *Lessons Learned from Special Measures* (OFSTED, 1999), concludes that: 'no single solution will serve as a panacea to remedy all the ills that befall schools' (*ibid.*, p. 2). Law and Glover (1999) also suggest that OFSTED has a reluctance to recognize success even when the school is judged on value-added measures or presents evidence to show that it has improved considerably since the last inspection. This special measures context is important to note as it provides a particular framework within which Gronn's chapter can be discussed.

## THE RESEARCH

The research was a three-year, single-site case study. It was predicated on the assumption that a contemporary phenomenon such as special measures can be investigated in depth, and over time. By using multiple sources of evidence for triangulation (interviews, participant observation, HMI reports, and documentary study), the school was investigated in some detail. Semi-structured interviews were carried out once a term with all the headteachers involved, all governors meetings were observed and recorded, in order to verify each head-teachers' account of the events. School documents (minutes of meetings, HMI/local education authority [LEA] monitoring reports) were also consulted in order to avoid as much as possible anecdotalism or subjectivity. In order to triangulate further, interviews were also held with other key respondents (deputy heads, Key Stage co-ordinators, two LEA officials, a cross-section of staff). This type of research allows very close access to the feelings and actions of participants at all levels within what was at times, an emotionally charged environment. Over the time the school was studied there was almost total staff change. Only two of the original staff remained over the three years of the study, and there were (at differing times) four deputies, two for short periods only. These changes were not all caused by the situation of the school, and the majority of them occurred during the first two years in special measures. At the start of the research the main priority for both the school and the researcher, was to preserve the anonymity of the school, and especially not to add in any way to the pressure already on the staff. The original emphasis of the research was, first, the nature of leading in terms of a primary school that was deemed to require special measures. Secondly, it asked how useful the Conger and Kanungo conceptualization of charisma in business settings is to an 'acting' head in special measures situations.

## THE CONTEXT

Almond Tree Combined School[1] was formed in 1995 by the amalgamation of two established schools, a 5 to 8 first school and an 8 to 12 middle school. Upon amalgamation, the middle school headteacher, Michael Cresswell became the head of the combined school (ages 5–12). The school was located on the edge of a large city, and served an established local authority housing estate. There were seven classes with an average class size of 29.7 (LEA average 28.2). It had a greater than average number of pupils with learning difficulty (36 per cent, LEA average 19 per cent), and many of these had behavioural and emotional problems as well. Forty-six per cent of children were entitled to free school meals (LEA average 15 per cent), and 11 per cent had English as a second language (LEA average 4 per cent). Annual pupil turnover was 40 per cent, as compared with an LEA average of 11 per cent. There was a large budget deficit at the time of the original OFSTED inspection. The school was inspected in February 1997, and placed under special measures. Roll at the time was about 200. They reported that there were significant weaknesses: 'Leadership is weak in all respects. There is no firm direction established by the Headteacher. Too much time is spent dealing with day-to-day crises.'

There were many other issues, including poor quality teaching, poor behaviour and failure to fully implement the National Curriculum. The HMI commented of Almond Tree School (Monitoring report, 1999): 'The contextual factors of this school are worthy of note ... these challenges add to those of a school population with generally poor learning skills on entry'.

Almond Tree needed to recover from the recognized failure of being in special measures. The pressure for fast action from the various agencies (LEA and central government) was intense. The LEA, because of the effect having failing schools might do to its reputation, needed to demonstrate a bias for action, and that change had to be as visible to all the stakeholders (OFSTED, Department for Education and Employment [DFEE]) as soon as possible. An official from OFSTED asked the headteacher on the phone when he would 'find the exit window'. To begin to tackle these concerns, the LEA appointed an experienced 'mentor' head from a local middle school, David Simmons. His brief was to help the headteacher and the senior management prepare the post-OFSTED Action Plan. He then became acting headteacher when Mr Cresswell became ill and took extended sick leave in the summer term of 1997. There was uncertainty for almost a year whilst Mr Cresswell debated whether his future lay within the school or elsewhere. David Simmons was in post for two terms, leaving at Easter 1998 because his own substantive school was due to have its own OFSTED inspection. Another experienced headteacher, Mike White, was seconded from Easter 1998 to December 1998. A substantive head, Jane Davis, was finally appointed in January 1999. Almond Tree was removed from the list of schools subject to special measures in the summer of 2000.

## THE LEADERSHIP FAMILY AND ITS FORMS AT ALMOND TREE

As Gronn (p. 60, this volume) perceptively writes:

> Leadership is one of a family of terms in both academic and common usage, which is invoked to designate modes of human conduct and engagement. Historically, other close family members have included power, authority, influence, manipulation, coercion, force and persuasion. Within this discursive family leadership has always been the favourite offspring.

He contends that power and influence are the closest leadership family relatives. This intriguing metaphor allows me to look again at some of the classifications already given to forms of leadership at the school. In particular, in my original analysis, I had paid considerable attention to the idea of charisma, and its role in the creation of 'leadership' as a crucial factor in school success. Charisma might well be seen as power and influence's spin-doctor. Grint in his work on leadership as art (Grint, 2000, p. 419) suggests that we can visualize leadership as a talisman that we use instinctively, but we can never be sure whether it works or not. The idea of charisma is talismanic, and is deftly woven into popular perception in England through the idea of a 'Superhead' who can be sent in to rescue a school from difficulties. Weber (1947) identified charismatic authority as one of the three main methods of claiming legitimacy in social settings. He describes it as a form of authority based on perceptions of an extraordinary individual. The importance of Weber's critique to the argument here is that he developed the idea that the leader derives his or her role from the belief the followers have about his or her mission.

Charismatic leadership has been the centre of considerable methodical empirical study. Studies have focused on the transformational (Bass and Avolio, 1993), behavioural (House and Howell, 1992), and attribution aspects of charismatic leadership (Conger and Kanungo, 1987; 1988). Howell (1997) suggests that there is general accord among writers in the leadership field that charismatic leaders often emerge during times of instability, crisis and turmoil. She puts it succinctly when she states that any challenging circumstance: 'Increases the likelihood that people will feel helpless, agitated, anxious and frustrated and will therefore eagerly accept the authority of charismatic leaders who appear to be uniquely qualified to lead them out of their acute distress'. (ibid., p. 2).

This longing for certainty and security is not surprising, given very difficult circumstances. Bass (1990) also proposes that differences in charisma can be attributed not only to the exceptional individual, but also to the exceptional situation and to the interaction between them. The Conger–Kanungo model (1998) suggests that it is the organizational members that attribute charisma to those in leadership positions. Conger and Kanungo's research sees charisma as not dependent on the outcome, but on the actions taken by the leader. They conceptualize that a charismatic leader is primarily concerned with influencing the followers to accept and own a vision and to work together towards its realization. The leader uses strategies and techniques to make followers feel empowered within a situation. They perceive charisma as attributed by followers to the leader and based on the premise of the leader giving empowerment to the followers. They argue that empowering organizational members can achieve transformational effects. Bass and Avolio (1993) emphasize the role of charisma in enabling the leader to influence followers by arousing strong emotions and identification with the leader – emotional arousal creating a sense of excitement about what has to be done. They suggest that charismatic leaders also use language to align the followers to the mission. This language may be laced with a strong, convincing delivery, conveying pride and confidence.

This seems particularly relevant when analysing leadership in special measures where morale was low, and motivation ebbing away. It appears that charismatic leaders have their major effects on the emotions and self-esteem of followers – the affective motivational variables rather than the cognitive variables.

Gronn suggests that leadership is too immature a sibling to manage without influence (p. 61, this volume) to help it out. Charisma can be conceptualized as a very close relation of influence, and thus also a sibling of leadership. It may be that certain situations do require what Gronn calls the leader design specifications that personify either explicitly or implicitly a heroic leader prototype. If uncertain situations need leadership certainties, the role of influence, as Gronn notes, calls in the dualism of the powerful and the powerless. But even in what appears to be a clear-cut situation where such dualism may figure particularly strongly, this is not always the case. So, in the case study school, I had originally looked at the role of charisma, especially as perceived by the staff in terms of the three headteachers. This concurs with Gronn's description of leadership's symbolic force that has a particular resonance with the lay public.

## DISTRIBUTING SCHOOL LEADERSHIP

If a distributed view of leadership demands that we de-centre the leader, what does my data say about it? Looking again at the original material in terms of distributing and intensifying school leadership has uncovered a number of new aspects. Overall, the single most popular theme that emerges is the role of the headteacher, particularly in terms of morale and confidence building. This was particularly true during the early stages of the research. This chimes with Gronn's description of intensification and will be returned to later. Gronn suggests that for leadership to be distributed, plural-member work units are needed (p. 63, this volume). He identifies three main types of such work units: spontaneous collaboration, intuitive working relations, and institutionalized and quasi-institutionalized practices. In my data, the latter has the most relevance over time, with the head and the two deputies forming institutionalized practices. The theme of the deputy headteacher and Headteacher as centres for the changes that took place in the school late on, can also be seen as linked to Ogawa's argument (Chapter 2) that leadership is about allowing the development of teacher knowledge and capability. However, it is important to note this sincerely felt need to have *someone to lean on*. It is seen strongly in the responses from teachers:

> The children, teachers and parents felt better when David was here.
>
> (Teacher KS2)

> He would say 'you know what you're doing – get on with it', which gave confidence and was positive, especially for the nursery.
>
> (Teacher KS1)

He was effective because people needed a strong leader at that time.

(Teacher KS2)

The findings of the first monitoring inspection by HMI in January 1998 states: 'It is evident that the present acting Headteacher has done much to move the school forward, to raise morale, and give the staff a sense of purpose'. This leads to a paradox. Staff seemed to demand a figurehead to whom they could pin their hopes of recovery, and this enabled them, and the LEA to begin to feel that the school was moving forward. This links to the research above on the charismatic leader and reflects that need in times of crisis to have the talisman of a strong leader (Grint, 2000). On the other hand, this leads to a state of dependency, which may have contributed to the time the school spent subject to special measures. In particular, over the three years different members of the senior management team (SMT) (two of the Heads and one deputy) spoke of the *lack of ownership* by the staff of what was happening to them:

No one takes responsibility for anything – the dinner times, the state of the buildings. It's as if they have been kept in the dark for a long time and patronized, although it was probably done for the best of motives.

(Jane Davis, Head, 1999)

I said to them 'What are *you* going to do about it?'

(Mike White, Head, 1998)

The staff when I arrived were spending money on Lifebuoy, washing their hands and standing back!

(Deputy head, 1999)

This dependency also has its downside for the heroic leader figure.

## INTENSIFICATION OF LEADERSHIP

Gronn calls it life 'at the pointy end' for those school leaders who mediate national- and state-level policies to local communities. They see it as extremely demanding and stressful. From the point of view of the heads in my case study, there was a great intensification in what they did. Acting headship in special measures was much more challenging than their substantive headships, right from the start of their tenure. Even Jane, the new substantive head, found it much more demanding than her previous position, due, she felt, to the juxtaposition of special measures and social challenge. She found the first term particularly gruelling. Sustaining this type of leadership behaviour required an intense emotional labour. David, the first acting head stated:

It's very tiring, the paperwork and the waking up at 5:15 am and thinking about things – like today there was planning that needed my attention. It takes a huge amount out of you, and there is only so much energy and amount of time you can put in, the high profile for the behaviour round school, paperwork. It's a huge task … I found myself crying at something on television and I am not a crier.

This inner struggle was not obvious to the staff, as the upbeat nature of his public face was most commented on. As mentioned earlier, statements about him invariably contained references to his upbeat mood, and positive aspect. It is debatable, however, how long this perceived invulnerability would have lasted. By the end of two terms, his old back problems had returned, necessitating days off. In contrast, Jane Davis, was perceived in the following terms: 'Tranquillity is strength of her character' (deputy head); 'Jane is calm with an underlying forcefulness'. (teacher KS2). She felt that this perception was due to the phenomenon she described as 'ducks' – calm on the surface with a great deal of paddling going on underneath. Certainly she found herself vulnerable to intestinal ailments and feelings of exhaustion that at times threatened to overwhelm her. This is where she found the value of having others on the team more prepared, as time went by, to take on challenges themselves, and not rely just on her.

Hochschild's (1983) concept of emotional labour is the most useful explanatory device that I have discovered for this. She suggests that emotion should be seen as any other sense, as a way of knowing about the world, and testing for reality in any given situation. Her key premise is that we need emotional awareness in order to reflect on our external or 'objective' world as well as our inner one. She develops this into the concept of 'emotional labour'. 'Emotional labour' requires you to bring to public sight or suppress feeling in order to sustain the outward expression that produces the state of mind that you want others to have. It means that the person has to work very hard at co-ordinating mind and feeling. A leader in challenging circumstances would need a great deal of emotional labour, as, like acting, such a position does require being on the stage full time. Hochschild says that emotional labour takes place when the work involves face-to-face contact with the public, where the person is required to produce emotional states in others, e.g., fear, courage, and where the person has to exercise a degree of control of the emotional activities of staff. This connects with the emotional commitment suggested by Conger and Kanungo, and may be one of the outward ways that charisma can be expressed.

As Gronn suggests, if this sort of intensification is considered a virtue, will school leaders want to provide it, as the long-term rewards for them may lie in loss of physical or mental well-being? My research agrees with him that the current accountability and policy frameworks facilitate and consolidate intensified work practices. As he says, 'these policies take for granted intensified work as a desired norm … these design assumptions are unlikely to be sustainable in the long term'. This was certainly the reality in my case study.

## A PARADOXICAL TRUTH?

How is this apparent paradox to be reconciled? Is charisma a false hope, and distributed leadership the way forward? The answer to this probably lies in emphasizing the truth of the paradox, by viewing the school's leadership journey in *three* distinct stages. In the first stage, or 'heroic leader', staff define the headteacher as charismatic (using Conger and Kanungo's identifiers), and this seems to give hope, and build necessary morale in a difficult situation. Conger (1989) speculates that the more favourable the existing conditions to charisma, the less magnitude or the fewer the number of charismatic attributes are required for the leader to be perceived as charismatic by the followers. Thus, David Simmons was perceived as having these attributes, being someone who raised morale, clearly tied into his grasp of the necessity of fast response, and what several staff described as his 'outgoing' personality. The latter characteristic, which might be viewed as a lucky personal fit to the school, should be viewed in the light of Simmons's conscious desire to be positive, often mentioned during interviews. In the second stage, 'false institutionalization', it may appear that the heroic leader was enough to effect transformation, but this is a false effect. Conger and Kanungo (1998) also characterize charisma as an unstable phenomenon, particularly in terms of leadership succession. and draw attention to the point that charismatic leadership, in particular, is seldom, if ever, institutionalized successfully. Conger and Kanungo (1998, p. 21) also suggest that a dilemma builds up for many followers because, as the followers' self-worth is increasingly defined in their relationship to the leader, a 'precarious dependence' is built. This may help explain some of the comments of some teaching staff concerning the second replacement headteacher, of which the following is a clear example: 'When David left there was another void' (senior teacher KS2).

Jones and Webber (2001, pp. 4–5) argue that when leaders come in from outside the school culture, they can experience an increased vulnerability and a decrease in trust, often because of the successor's willingness to challenge the norms of the organization. This did not happen with the first headteacher, perhaps because the norms had already been challenged so effectively by the OFSTED inspection. The second headteacher, Mike White commented:

> I've tried to get to know staff. In meetings with staff, I have taken the opportunity to revisit some of the areas that we need to develop this term, and probably beyond and I've prepared quite detailed action plans. We've discussed the outstanding issues, and got them agreed with staff. There's now quite a clear timetable in terms of the issues that we're going to tackle. I recognize that my style of management is very different to Dave's and I have to give a little bit of time for staff to adjust to me.

However, because of the school's special measures situation time was the one thing that White did not have. Two HMI monitoring visits took place during this period, and although the school was seen to be making reasonable progress, this was judged: 'to be having limited impact within the classroom'.

Special measures calls for a turnaround within a specified time limit, and this affects the behaviours adopted by those in all leadership positions, but it is specifically the Headteacher who has to be seen to act by the LEA, the local community and, often, demoralized staff. The special measures context also lends itself to according the headteacher disproportionate effectiveness in school turnaround situations. In his conceptualization of organizational context Conger (1989) draws on the *outer* context, beyond the organization, and the *inner* context of culture, structure and power. For quick removal from special measures, the external context – how the school is viewed – becomes more crucial. This perception management was a particular strength of David Simmons. Structure is also amenable to some quick change, but the failing school's culture and power distribution will take longer. The third stage, 'long term leadership', equates with Louis and Miles (1992), i.e., that improving schools develop successful long-term strategies for cultural change. For consistent improvement to flourish, leadership as an organizational quality had to emerge (Ogawa and Bossert, 1997). As the substantive headteacher, Jane Davis, comments: 'For me it was all about longer terming and taking responsibility'.

Developing teacher capability from 1999 onwards was helped by the LEA, which allowed the school to have two deputies in place in order to free up the headteacher to concentrate on more strategic tasks. One of these two deputies, Paul, describes his first impression of the school when he arrived in 1999.

> It seemed to me horrendous, very little policy and if there was, little adherence to it. I'd say that they [*the staff*] were wallowing in special measures. It was as if any problems there were for someone else to sort out. There was no ownership and the kids were getting a poor deal. Lots of old guard thinking and behaviour – the outlook that had failed the school. My approach was to say to them 'Look, it's not as bad as you think.' There was no point in them being miserable, vegetating, or sitting in judgement. They weren't expending their energy to give the kids a good deal. When I came they tried to make me fire fight and I just kept throwing it back. I saw it as standing Jane's [the head] corner and putting ownership back – you know, what have you done about x? I don't think it made me the easiest guy to work with.

This echoes the state of the dependency the staff were in, perhaps caused by charismatic leadership, focused in the heroic prototype. The other deputy at that time, Diana, said that apart from the head's leadership the most important factor in moving the school forward was: 'Without a doubt having stable staff in place. At that point as well we were able to make permanent appointments of many staff'.

One member of staff who had been away from the school through illness for almost half a year also gave an interesting insight into teacher capability. She said, commenting on the latter part of 1999: 'Things seemed to be moving forward when I returned. There was a new management team of head and deputies and I felt like a newcomer ... we also got extra training with the LEA, and that extra was good for everyone'.

## CONCLUSION

In this chapter, I have looked at Gronn's observations on the nature of distributed leadership and the intensification of work, by re-examining empirical data from a small-scale case study. The high performer's drive for excellence, as shown by the leadership of the three heads in the study, did lead to intensification of work that was not desirable in the long term. However, some of the intensification did seem to be necessary, particularly in stage one, in order to raise morale and move forward. Others then had to develop capability in dimensions of their role performance, not just as teachers, but also as leaders. This aligns with Gronn's characterization of distributed leadership as having to have a finely tuned tolerance for ambiguity. If school leaders are to 'acquire a sense of how events coalesce, fuse and flow' (p. 70) then they need to be able to develop synergies within the whole school, so that work intensification does not become a hindrance to distributed leadership practices, but an impetus for them.

## NOTE

1. All the names in this chapter are pseudonyms.

## REFERENCES

Bass, B.M. (1990) *Bass and Stodgill's Handbook of Leadership: Theory, Research and Managerial Expectations*. New York: Free Press.

Bass, B.M. and Avolio, B. (1993) Transformational leadership: a response to critiques, in M.M. Chemers and R. Aymar (eds), *Leadership Theory and Research: Perspectives and Directions* (pp. 49–90). New York: Academic Press.

Conger, J. and Kanungo, R. (1998) *Charismatic Leadership in Organizations*. Thousand Oaks, CA: Sage.

Conger, J.A. (1989) *The Charismatic Leader: Behind the Mystique of Exceptional Leadership*. San Francisco, CA: Jossey-Bass.

Ferguson, N., Earley, P., Fidler, B. and Ouston, J. (2000) *Improving Schools and Inspection: The Self-Inspecting School*. London: Paul Chapman Publishing.

Conger, J.A. and Kanungo, R.N. (1987) Toward a behavioural theory of chrismatic leadership in organizational settings, *Academy of Management*, 12, 637–47.

Conger, J.A. and Kanungo, R.N. (1988) Conclusion: patterns and trends in studying charismatic leadership, in J.A. Conger and R.N. Kanungo (eds), *Charismatic Leadership: The Elusive Factor in Organizational Effectiveness*. San Francisco, CA: Jossey-Bass.

Gray, J., Hopkins, D., Reynolds, D., Wilcox, D., Farrell, S. and Jesson, D. (1999) *Improving Schools: Performance and Potential*. Buckingham: Open University Press.

Grint, K. (2000) *The Arts of Leadership*. Oxford: Oxford University Press.

Hochschild, A.R. (1983) *The Managed Heart: Commercialization of Human Feeling*. Berkeley, CA: University of California Press.

House, R.J. and Howell, J.M. (1992) Personality and charismatic leadership, *Leadership Quarterly*, 3, 81–108.

Howell, J.M. (1997) Organization contexts: charismatic and exchange leadership. *KLSP: Transformational Leadership: Working Papers*. College Park, MD: Academy of Leadership Press.

Jones, J.C. and Webber, C.F. (2001) Principal succession: a case study. Paper presented to the Annual Meeting of the American Educational Research Association, Seattle.

Law, S. and Glover, D. (1999) Does OFSTED make a difference? Inspection issues and socially deprived schools, in C. Cullingford (ed.), *The Inspector Calls*. London: Kogan Page.

Louis, K.S. and Miles, M.B. (1992) *Improving the Urban High School: What Works and Why*. London: Cassell.

OFSTED (1996) *From Failure to Success*. London: OFSTED.

OFSTED (1999) *Lessons Learned from Special Measures*. London: OFSTED.

Ogawa, R.T. and Bossert, S.T. (1997) Leadership as an organizational quality, in M. Crawford, L. Kydd and C. Riches (eds), *Leadership and Teams in Educational Management*. Buckingham: Open University Press.

Weber, M. (1947) *Max Weber: The Theory of Social and Economic Organization*, trans A.M. Henderson and T. Parsons. New York: Free Press.

# 6

## From Singular to Plural? Challenging the Orthodoxy of School Leadership

ALMA HARRIS AND CHRISTOPHER DAY[1]

### INTRODUCTION

Effective school leadership has become a dominant theme in contemporary educational reform. Effective leaders are needed to sustain innovation and are at the heart of capacity building for school improvement (Harris and Lambert, 2003). Research findings from different countries and diverse school contexts have revealed the powerful impact of leadership on processes related to school effectiveness and improvement. (Hopkins, 2000; Jackson, 2000; Van Velzen *et al.*, 1985; West *et al.*, 2000). Of those factors that contribute to effective subject performance and effective schools, leadership takes a prime position (Busher and Harris, 2000; Sammons, 1999). Similarly, in securing enhanced school and student performance, leadership plays a key and vital role (Mitchell and Sackney, 2001; Mortimore, 2000; Southworth, 1995; Stoll and Fink, 1996). The evidence from the international research base is unequivocal – effective leaders exercise an indirect but powerful influence on the effectiveness of the school and on the achievement of students (Leithwood and Jantzi, 2000). Whilst the quality of teaching has a powerful influence upon pupil motivation and achievement, the quality of leadership determines the motivation of teachers and the quality of teaching in the classroom (Fullan, 2001; Sergiovanni, 2001).

It is for this reason that 'leadership' has generated an enormous amount of interest among researchers and practitioners. A vast literature on school leadership and leadership theory exists (see Hallinger and Heck, 1996). Most of this literature is derived from North American and European sources with, it has been argued, an overreliance upon commercial and business views of leadership (Day *et al.*, 2000). Yet, despite a substantial research base, a singular, overarching theory of leadership has proved to be elusive. While researchers in many countries continue to produce a steady stream of empirical evidence about school leadership this endless accumulation of findings still has not produced a consensus about effective leadership practice. As Bennis (1993, p. 259) reflected almost a decade ago: 'Of all the hazy and confounding ideas in social psychology, leadership theory undoubtedly contends for the top nomination. Probably more has been written and less is known about leadership than any other topic in the behavioural sciences'.

Little it seems has changed. A major problem with the contemporary leadership literature is the sheer proliferation of leadership theories, styles or approaches that appear there. There seem to be as many versions of school leadership as there are those who write about it. Goddard (Chapter 1, this volume) has identified 14 different styles of leadership with many premised upon the leadership capabilities and capacities of one person. The complex, competing and sometimes contradictory messages within the leadership field only serve to heighten the fact the research findings are not always accessible or helpful to those in schools (Harris, 2003). Constructions and understandings of the term 'leadership' vary in subtle and numerous ways. It is difficult to discern how 'instructional leadership', 'learner centred leadership' and 'pedagogical leadership' differ. Do they simply offer alternative labels for the same leadership approaches or are they distinctively different theoretical interpretations or positions?

There is also a growing recognition that much of the leadership literature fails to reflect contemporary leadership practice in schools (Morrison, 2002: Owens, 2001; Razik and Swanson, 2001). Traditional notions and models of leadership and organizational change are being disputed and challenged (Foster, 2001; Goleman, 2002; Harris, 2002). Much of the literature omits the importance of the contexts in which people construct social events and share meaning (see Morley and Hosking, Chapter 3, this volume). Also, certain assumptions are reinforced within the literature: first, leaders and followers are not interchangeable; secondly the leadership actions and abilities of one individual are of paramount importance; thirdly, leadership resides in the role of the headteacher or senior management team.

It is only relatively recently that the potential of students to be leaders in schools has been acknowledged (Rudduck, 2001) and the importance of networks of shared leadership practice and devolved leadership responsibilities highlighted (Lambert, 1998). In their recent review of successful school improvement efforts, Glickman, Gordon and Ross-Gordon (2001, p. 49) construct a composite list of the characteristics of what they term the 'improving school', a 'school that continues to improve student learning outcomes for all students over time'. At the top of this list appears 'varied sources of leadership, including teacher leadership'. This work directly challenges assumptions about where leadership is located within a school because it views leadership as agency, a force for change within a school (Day et al., 2000; Riley and Louis, 2001). However, as most of the empirical evidence concerning school leadership has been derived from primarily from headteachers' accounts and descriptions, there are relatively few rich descriptions of alternative models of leadership or accounts of leadership from those who do not occupy designated leadership positions within the school. Hence, the primacy of individual leadership is reinforced and the hierarchical view of leadership firmly maintained.

While contemporary studies of successful leadership from the perspective of all stakeholders do exist, they remain somewhat rare (Foster, 2001; MacBeath 1998). Consequently, this chapter outlines the empirical evidence from a study that took a multi-perspective view on successful school leadership. It explored successful school leadership from the perspectives of all stakeholders both within and outside the school. Parents, governors, pupils, teachers, headteachers, deputies and support staff were all involved in the data collection process. The findings from the study provide a contemporary insight into the tensions and dilemmas facing leaders in schools in the twenty-first century. They also point towards the need to 'challenge the orthodoxy or orthodoxies of school leadership' in favour of a form of leadership that is inherently reflective, collaborative and shared.

## THE RESEARCH

In 1999 the National Association of Headteachers (NAHT) in England commissioned research to identify, examine and celebrate good leadership practice in schools. This project became a means of identifying from those 'closest to the action' the nature and practice of effective leadership in schools in England. The project aimed to examine how existing theories of effective leadership, 'purposeful leadership', 'transformational' or 'moral' leadership, matched up to the successful leadership practice in times of change. The research involved in-depth case studies at 12 schools and interviews were conducted with parents, pupils, teachers, governors, senior managers and headteachers at each school. A full account of the research methodology and outcomes can be found in NAHT (2000) and Day et al. (2000).

The empirical evidence from the study provided a 360-degree perspective on successful leadership in action. It allowed different stakeholders to offer their views on the form and nature of leadership at each school. Inevitably, the head became a focus for discussion as the 'formal leader' but it quickly became evident that the approach to leadership adopted by heads was far from autocratic. From the study, it became clear that although heads were viewed as the main leaders and decision-makers within the school, leadership responsibility did not rest solely with them. The heads were considered to be key but not exclusive leaders within the school. The evidence pointed towards a form of leadership that was distributed through collaborative and joint working. These heads had deliberately chosen to distribute leadership responsibility to others and had put in place systems and incentives to ensure this happened. In all cases, they remained important gatekeepers to change and development, guiding their schools in a clear and purposeful direction. Their leadership was underpinned by a set of core personal values that included the modelling and promotion of respect (for individuals), fairness and equality, caring for the well-being and the development of students and staff. Their commitment to the development of their staff was reflected in their leadership actions insofar that they decentralized and devolved leadership responsibilities to others.

> Over the years I have learned that it is impossible for one person to run a school single-handed. I now know that unless teachers take on leadership roles, the school is unlikely to flourish and they are unlikely to develop and grow.
>
> (Head[2] S1)

> The head believes in giving teachers and pupils a chance to lead. That doesn't mean taking over his job – it means taking responsibility for leading new initiatives and leading teams. Most teachers welcome the opportunity.
>
> (Teacher S7)

Ever present in the actions of the headteachers in the study was a firm belief in teachers as the key to successful school improvement. There was a strong emphasis upon staff development in order to maximize the potential of all teachers. All the heads in the study vigorously promoted staff development whether through in-service, visits to other schools or peer support schemes. Their principal concerns were maintaining teacher morale and motivation in order to build the capacity for change. It was particularly noticeable that staff development did not only focus upon needs which were of direct benefit to the school, but also those which were of direct benefit to the individual.

The heads invested a great deal of time in creating positive working relationships among teachers. Opportunities were provided for teachers to work together, to work across teams and within teams and to take on leadership roles and responsibilities. In one school teachers were asked to take responsibility for writing a whole-school policy, in another they took the lead on a whole-school review of assessment strategies and in another they formed a group responsible for internal change and development. These groupings or teams were always voluntary, permeable and non-permanent. The heads' stated intention in creating such groupings was to create flexible working arrangements within the school that allowed teachers to lead at different times and for different purposes. In this sense the heads operated a distributed form of leadership as responsibilities were dispersed within the organization. But more importantly there was evidence of what Gronn (2000) calls 'conjoint agency', where teachers worked together in partnerships, clusters or formal groups to undertake certain activities that positively affect organizational change and development. 'Conjoint agency' is central to building leadership capacity in schools and requires attention to two areas: structures and processes for involvement and opportunities for teachers to become skilful participants in school development (Harris and Lambert, 2003).

When I first came to this school the teachers looked to me for leadership, they were dependent and in many ways powerless. I've tried to change that by providing them with chances to lead and develop their skills and abilities. The dependency culture has shifted as a result, they now need me less which is a good thing.

(Head S5)

By working together in the assessment team I've felt more involved in the school. It has helped me to see that we are all leaders in this school.

(Teacher S7)

It was considered important by the heads that teachers were given the time and opportunity to collaborate. Opportunities and new approaches to professional development such as mentoring, coaching and peer review were put in place. Where teaching practices were poor, improvements were achieved through investing in forms of professional development and collaboration that raised teachers' knowledge base and skills. Providing groups or teams of teachers who had not worked together before with a specific task or an area for improvement resulted in major benefits to the schools and the individuals involved.

One of the first things the head did was to set up cross-subject teams so that people had the opportunity to work together outside their subject areas. The problem is that departments can become very insular and you never talk to other teachers or work with anyone else. The cross-subject team changed this and allowed us to work on whole school themes and issues together.

(Teacher S4)

I am involved in a team that is exploring the issue of pupil access to the curriculum. This feels quite a responsibility but the team seem to be working well together and staff are responsive to the messages because it's us and not 'top-down'.

(Teacher S9)

It was acknowledged that while this 'distributed' approach to leadership was generally desirable, at certain times in a school's development it was neither feasible nor appropriate. All the heads had adopted autocratic and 'top-down' leadership approaches at critical times in their school's development. However, they all agreed that this leadership approach was least likely to lead to, generate or sustain school improvement. The heads recognized that in order to improve their school they needed to build organizational capacity at a personal and interpersonal level. Hence, whenever possible they sent positive messages to others about their competence and capabilities. They reinforced how much they valued staff and pupils by focusing upon the emotional needs of others through empathy, caring and reassurance. The heads focused their attention primarily upon building relationships with others and encouraging others to take responsibility for making things happen.

I wanted to change the 'dependency culture' that pervaded this school when I arrived. Teachers, pupils and parents expected me to make all the decisions so I involved them wherever I could and delegated whenever I could.

(Head S7)

I see my leadership as enabling other people to take over, to do things … It's being able to trust other people. To be confident in your own ability … to delegate tasks and know they will be done … to allow people to do things and not to try and control it all.

(Head S10)

While the head is the designated leader within this school, we are all leaders and he reinforces this by ensuring we have a voice and some involvement in running the school.

(Teacher S6)

The most important aspect of leadership for all the heads concerned working successfully with people. Being a head was not a 'desk job', though it involved organizational and administrative tasks. It was centrally concerned with building relationships and encouraging others to lead. The heads in this study adopted highly creative approaches to tackling the complex demands of implementing multiple changes. The decision to work with and through teams as well as individuals was a common response to the management of change. They delegated responsibility and authority to their senior management and to middle-level leaders. In many ways, they demonstrated what Goleman (2002) has described as 'resonant leadership', where there is an emphasis on synchrony among those within the group or organization. Goleman (2002, p. 53) suggests that 'resonance stems from whole sets of co-ordinated activities' that comprise a particular leadership style where others are invited to take on leadership roles. This position reflects the work of Stoll and Fink (1996) who describe 'invitational leadership' as a form of leadership where a high premium is placed upon emotional intelligence and interrelationships with others. The heads in the study used a number of strategies for developing leadership skills in others. These strategies included involving others in decision-making processes, mentoring those in leadership positions and offering a wide range of professional and personal support.

From the different vantage points of stakeholders in the study, the heads did reflect many of the facets of invitational and resonant leadership. They quite clearly placed an emphasis upon people rather than systems and invested heavily in staff development. At the core of their leadership practice was a belief in empowering others by allocating real tasks and responsibility for delivery. While the heads emphasized the contingent nature of many of the decisions they made, the central set of democratic values driving their practice did not alter. Their leadership approach was premised not on the basis of power and control, but upon the ability to act with others and to enable others to act. It was primarily concerned with generating 'conjoint agency' (Chapter 4, this volume) and stimulating purposeful collaboration between individuals. Several forms of collaboration existed in the schools to promote shared leadership. There were action research groups, ad hoc groups in which all teachers served at least once, subject-level groups and interdisciplinary teams. In addition, collaboration was promoted and developed through a wide variety of professional development opportunities, e.g., observation, guided practice, coaching, skill-focused dialogue (talking through strategies and approaches) and peer mentoring.

Within all the schools in the NAHT study a climate of collaboration existed among staff in the schools and there was a collective commitment to work together. However, this climate was the result of lengthy discussion, development and dialogue amongst those working within the school. It had been deliberately orchestrated by the head through the provision of opportunities to build social trust. In summary, this study revealed that the successful heads had adopted a shared or 'distributed' approach to leadership which was demonstrated in several important ways. First, they gave central attention to involving teachers in decision-making and setting priorities. Secondly, they kept issues of teaching and learning at the forefront of innovation and change within the school and in doing so provided opportunities for teachers to take an active role in development work. Thirdly, they created 'resonance' by consistently expressing the norms and values of sharing and collaboration that defined the school's vision. Fourthly, they promoted 'conjoint agency' by providing opportunities for stakeholders to work together. Finally, and most importantly, they placed an emphasis upon people over systems and created a climate of enthusiasm, flexibility and social trust where people felt valued and respected.

## CHALLENGING THE ORTHODOXY?

New approaches to organizational change and development are inevitable in a world that is increasingly complex and rapidly changing. Morrison (2002) advocates that the self-organizing schools of the future will require democratic, person-centred and relational styles of leadership. He contends that the 'command and control mentality of bureaucratic organisations where compliance is the watchword' (*ibid.*, p. 32) is anachronistic. In contrast, Morley and Hosking (Chapter 3, this volume) offer us a view of leadership that rests on a much more informal interpretation of organizational change and development that emphasizes diffused and fluid leadership. They suggest that there is 'something misguided about the whole of the "traditional" approach to leadership' because it fails to recognize the necessity for people to construct social events through interaction and dialogue. The findings from this study reinforce this view by highlighting the importance of socio-cognitive processes in organizational change and development. The empirical evidence suggests that successful leaders are those who understand relationships and recognize the importance of reciprocal learning processes that lead to shared purposes (Harris and Lambert, 2003). Essentially, they are more connected to people and networks than the 'traditional' forms of leadership – 'the lone chief atop a pyramidal structure' (Greenleaf, 1996, p. 61) – would suggest.

The overarching message about successful leadership from this study is one of distributing leadership and building the community of the school through developing and involving others. What characterized each of the heads in the study was their commitment to sharing decision-making and authority with others. A number of writers (Shakeshaft, 1996) and Gronn (2000) have argued for a paradigm shift in conceptions of leadership which start not from the basis of power and control but from the ability to act with others and to enable others to act. This model of leadership implies a redistribution of power and a realignment of authority within the school as an organization. It suggests that leadership is a shared and collective endeavour that engages all teachers within the school (Lambert, 1998). It also implies that the context in which people work and learn together is where they construct and refine meaning leading to a shared purpose or sets of goals. Taking this perspective, leadership is a fluid and emergent rather than a fixed phenomenon. It implies a different power relationship within the school where the distinctions between followers and leaders tend to blur. It opens up the possibility for all teachers to become leaders at various times.

Recent research by Silins and Mulford (2002) has shown that student outcomes are more likely to improve where leadership sources are distributed throughout the school community and where teachers are empowered in areas of importance to them. Empowering teachers in this way and providing them with opportunities to lead, they suggest, is based on the simple but profound idea that, if schools are to become better at providing learning for students, then they must also become better at providing opportunities for teachers to innovate, develop and learn together. Louis, Marks and Knese (1996) found that in schools where the teachers' work was organized in ways that promoted professional community, there was a positive relationship with the academic performance of students. Recent research has similarly shown that giving others real responsibility and developing others is the best possible way of moving the organization forward (Harris, 2002). Thus the emphasis is shifted from creating and managing structures as means of control to a view of structure as the vehicle for building the learning cultures and through these the learning and achievement capacities of others in the organization (Gronn, 2000).

Yet the orthodoxy of school leadership that promotes the 'cult of the individual' stubbornly prevails. Fuelled by a view of organizational change that is inherently rational, stable and predictable, it persists because it offers the seductive possibility of prescribing neatly packaged leadership solutions. It also persists because it reinforces the status quo of the leadership–follower relationship, creating dependency cultures and an ownership divide. It is easier, far easier, to point the finger of accountability in the direction of one person than to acknowledge that leadership is collective, shared and distributed throughout the organization. However, in the business world leadership excellence is rapidly being redefined in interpersonal terms. The days of the indispensable, singular leader are numbered as those in multinational corporations embrace a new form of leadership that strips out bureaucracy and fosters collaboration. The old-fashioned 'lead-from-the top' figures of authority who led by virtue of power of their position are no longer tenable. A new model of leadership is emerging, one that recognizes the limitations of an approach to organizational change and development premised upon the efforts of just one person.

This new model of leadership is one that ultimately empowers those within the organization to take leadership responsibility. It requires emotional intelligence, the ability to trust in others to lead and vast amounts of empathy. Here leadership is a shared commodity owned by those who work within the school and by those who work on behalf of the school. Consequently, challenging the orthodoxy of school leadership requires an inevitable and radical shift in our understanding of school development and change. If schools are to be true learning communities this cannot be achieved by clinging to outdated models of leadership. To cope with the unprecedented rate of change in education requires not only challenging the current orthodoxy of school leadership and relinquishing models suited to a previous age, but also establishing new models of leadership that locate power with the many rather than the few.

## NOTES

1. Alma Harris is Professor of School Leadership at the University of Warwick. Christopher Day is Professor of Education, University of Nottingham. Correspondence: Professor Alma Harris, Institute of Education, University of Warwick, Coventry, CV47AL alma.harris@warwick.ac.uk

2. The NAHT study focused on 12 effective headteachers. S1–12 indicate their respective schools.

## REFERENCES

Bennis, W. (1993) *An Invented Life: Reflections on Leadership and Change*. Reading, MA: Addison-Wesley.

Busher, H. and Harris, A. (2000) *Leading Subject Areas, Improving Schools*. London: Paul Chapman Publishing.

Day, C., Harris, A., Hadfield M., Tolley, H. and Beresford, J. (2000) *Leading Schools in Times of Change*: Buckingham: Open University Press.

Foster, R. (2001) Constructivist leadership in high school. Paper presented to the *Annual Meeting of the American Educational Research Association*, Toronto Ontario.

Fullan, M. (2001) *Leading in a Culture of Change*. San Francisco, CA: Jossey-Bass.

Glickman, C., Gordon, S. and Ross-Gordon, J. (2001) *Supervision and Instructional Leadership: A Developmental Approach*. Boston, MA: Allyn and Bacon.

Goleman, D. (2002) *The New Leaders: Transforming the Art of Leadership into the Science of Results*. London: Little Brown.

Greenleaf, R.K. (1996) *On Becoming a Servant Leader*. San Francisco, CA: Jossey-Bass.

Gronn, P. (2000) Distributed properties: a new architechure for leadership, *Educational Management and Administration*, 28(3), 317–38.

Hallinger, P. and Heck, R. (1996) Reassessing the principal's role in school effectiveness: a critical review of empirical research 1980–1995, *Educational Administration Quarterly*, 32(1), 5–4.

Harris, A. (2002) Leadership in schools facing challenging circumstances. Paper presented at *International Congress of School Effectiveness and School Improvement*, Copenhagen.

Harris, A. (2003) Teacher leadership: a new orthodoxy? in B. Davies and J. West-Burnham (eds), *Handbook of Leadership and Management*. London: Pearson.

Harris, A. and Lambert, L. (2003) *Building Leadership Capacity for School Improvement*. Buckingham: Open University Press.

Hopkins, D. (2000) *School Improvement for Real*. London: Falmer Press.

Jackson, D. (2000) The school improvement journey: perspectives on leadership, *School Leadership and Management*, 20(1), 61–79.

Lambert, L. (1998) *Building Leadership Capacity in Schools*. Alexandria, VA: Association for Supervision and Curriculum Development.

Leithwood, K. and Jantzi, D. (2000) The effects of transformational leadership on organisational conditions and student engagement, *Journal of Educational Administration*, 38(2), 112–29.

Louis, K., Marks, H. and Knese, S. (1996) Teachers' professional community in restructuring schools, *American Educational Research Journal*, 33(4), 757–89.

MacBeath, J. (ed.) (1998) *Effective School Leadership: Responding to Change*. London: Paul Chapman Publishing.

Mitchell, C. and Sackney, L. (2001) *Profound Improvement: Building Capacity for a Learning Community*. Lisse: Swets and Zeitlinger.

Mortimore, P. (2000) *The Road to School Improvement*. Lisse, Swets and Zetlinger.

Morrison, K. (2002) *School Leadership and Complexity Theory*. London: Routledge Falmer.

NAHT (2000) *National Association of Headteachers' Final Report*. Day, C., Harris, A., Tolley H., Hadfield, M. and Beresford, J. *Effective Leadership: Final Report*. School of Education, University of Nottingham, England.

Owens, R. (2001) *Organisational Behaviour in Education: Instructional Leadership and School Reform*. Needham Heights, MA: Allyn and Bacon.

Razik, T. and Swanson, A. (2001) *Fundamental Concepts of Educational Leadership*. Upper Saddle River, NJ: Prentice-Hall.

Riley, K. and Louis, K.S. (eds) (2001) *Leadership for Change*. London: Routledge Falmer.

Rudduck, J. (2001) Students and school improvement: transcending the cramped conditions of time, *Improving Schools*, 4(2), 7–15.

Sammons, P. (1999) *School Effectiveness: Coming of Age in the Twenty-First Century*. Lisse: Swets and Zeitlinger.

Sergiovanni, T. (2001) *Leadership: What's in it for Schools?* London: Routledge Falmer.

Shakeshaft, C. (1996) *Women in Educational Administration*. Newbury Park, CA: Unwin.

Silins, H. and Mulford, B. (2002) Leadership and school results, in *Second International Handbook of Educational Leadership and Administration*. Kluwer.

Southworth, G. (1995) *Talking Heads: Voices of Experience*. Cambridge: University of Cambridge Institute of Education.

Stoll, L. and Fink, D. (1996) *Changing our Schools: Linking School Effectiveness and School Improvement*. Buckingham: Open University Press.

West, M., Jackson, D., Harris, A. and Hopkins, D. (2000) Leadership for school improvement, in K. Riley and K.S. Louis (eds), *Leadership for Change*, London: Routledge Falmer.

Van Velzen, W., Miles, M., Elholm, M., Hameyer, U. and Robin, D. (1985) *Making School Improvement Work*. Leuven: Belgium AC.

# 7

## Developing Alternative Conceptions of Leadership and Organizations through Restructuring[1]

### LYNNE M. HANNAY

Secondary school change is considered problematic by many scholars and practitioners. Perhaps the compartmentalized or balkanized (Hargreaves, 1994) structure and the hierarchical leadership practices of most secondary schools contribute to the difficulty associated with substantial change within these organizations. Yet, imposing new structures is insufficient to counter this lack of change impetus; it is the process of participating in the restructuring that might facilitate deep change to the culture or the mindsets within secondary schools. Further, to achieve these goals, the restructuring process itself must generate alternative conceptions of leadership and organizations.

Educational organizations are primarily professional bureaucracies with some elements of a machine bureaucracy (Mintzberg, 1989). In Canadian secondary schools, the subject-based nature of the defined entry requirements compartmentalizes individuals as well as configuring leadership in terms of established formal positions. Together the unquestioned subject-based structure and resulting leadership practices perpetuate a collective tacit and explicit knowledge grounded in past practice, making significant change problematic. Yet, authentic restructuring can challenge assumptions through requiring participants to question their taken-for-granted tacit knowledge of leadership practices and organizational structures.

This chapter explores the relationships created and exposed when a secondary school staff engaged in restructuring over a six-year period because of their school district's mandate to create alternative and contextually based organizational structures. Through their involvement in restructuring, the participants gradually developed a more institutional (Ogawa and Bossert, 1995) or distributed (Gronn, 2000) conception of leadership and perceived the nature of an organization to be more fluid. This was a complex change process that unfolded in a dynamic and rather unplanned process which can best be described through employing the tenets of chaos theory. The research question explored is, how can involvement in restructuring facilitate a reconceptualization of leadership practices and organizational structures? The chapter first outlines a conceptual framework then shares data from the six-year study and concludes by exploring the emerging conceptions as to the nature of organizations.

## CONCEPTUAL FRAMEWORK

Understanding tacit and explicit knowledge (Polanyi, 1962; 1967) is central to the argument in this chapter. Lam (2000, p. 490) maintains that explicit knowledge can be acquired, codified and transferred through logical deduction, and 'can be aggregated at a single location, stored in objective forms, and appropriated without the participation of the knowing subject'. In contrast, she argues that tacit knowledge is 'intuitive and unarticulated', 'personal and contextual' and acquired through practical experience. Jarvis (1997, p. 28) maintains that tacit knowledge is 'pragmatic, i.e., it is accepted because it is known to work. But because it is known to work practitioners are loathe to change it, and so it is essentially conservative'. Often this individual tacit knowledge can become collective explicit knowledge which 'is the accumulated knowledge of the organization stored in its rules, procedures, routines, and shared norms which guide the problem-solving activities and patterns of interactions among members' (Lam, 2000, p. 491). The high potential for individual tacit and collective explicit knowledge being conservative, as Jarvis suggested, might result in problems being perceived as procedural as opposed to uncertain (Reid, 1978). Yet as Ogawa argues in Chapter 2 of this volume, organizational learning requires uncertainty.

Perhaps here lies the difficulty in implementing and sustaining substantial change in secondary schools, as new innovations will be interpreted through past tacit and explicit knowledge. This knowledge is derived from the traditional organizational structure which is typically a hierarchical professional bureaucracy (Mintzberg, 1989). Thus in professional bureaucracies, entry into the organization is determined by formal education and training (Lam, 2000), and the accrued 'knowledge of rationality' (Nonaka, 1994) dominates both the preparation and experience of teachers and school administrators. In Canada, provincial government legislation mandates a university degree for a teaching or a school administrative position. This history creates collective tacit and explicit knowledge supportive of the status quo thus decreasing the possibility of substantial change. As Lam (2000, p. 494) argues, 'professional experts have a tendency to interpret specific situations in terms of general concepts and place new problems in old categories', or as Schwab (1978, p. 602) suggests, without new ways of thinking, 'the best choice among poor and shopworn alternatives will still be a poor solution to the problem' and problems 'cannot be well solved by apparently new solutions using old habits of mind and old ways of doing things'. Thus problems will be defined as procedural as opposed to uncertain, thereby curtailing the possibility of innovation.

The pervasiveness of past collective tacit and explicit knowledge is compounded in secondary schools because of the unquestioned acceptance of the subject-based organizational structure. Siskin (1994) argues this structure shapes the perceptions of the individual teachers and these perceptions can define appropriate, desirable or possible actions. According to Lam (1997, p. 977), the structure can define 'how knowledge and skills are distributed and used'. In secondary schools, the professional bureaucracy and the subject department creates the 'individual specialization and job differentiation' described by Lam. Typically, the structure and resulting practices are more aligned with maintenance of the status quo and managerial tasks (Brown and Rutherford, 1998; Dellar, 1996; Hannay, Smeltzer Erb and Ross, 2001a) than in promoting innovation and collaboration.

The subject-based and professional bureaucracy organizational structure has also defined the practice of educational leadership in secondary schools. Leadership has been designated to a position or role with formal educational requirements aligned with past practice. In Canadian secondary schools, the leadership role is performed by the principal, the vice-principal and sometimes department heads, and these individuals are all products of the entry requirements of the professional bureaucracy. As Ogawa and Bossert (1995) suggest, this perpetuates a technical-rational perspective of leadership. Leadership is defined in terms of past knowledge and possibly restricted to a formal position which, becomes the lens through which innovations are implemented.

A conceptual premise in this chapter is the need to rethink and broaden the concept of leadership in secondary schools through contextual organizational restructuring. In our research, we call this flat-lined or shared leadership but perhaps this is better represented by Gronn's (2000) concept of distributed leadership. He contends that leadership needs to be distributed throughout the organization and not just assigned to fixed positions. Gronn (2000, p. 333) suggests: 'the (tacit and codified) knowledge required to solve complex problems is dispersed throughout organisations. Hence, perhaps, the recent rise in the popularity of teams as vehicles for harnessing collective expertise'. Further, Gronn argues that leadership needs to be considered in terms of activity thus dispelling the leader–follower dichotomy. This is related to Ogawa and Bossert's (1995, p. 225) assertion that leadership needs to be considered 'as a quality of an organisation – a systemic characteristic' and they contend 'how we conceptualize organizational leadership is necessarily rooted in how we conceptualize organizations' (ibid., p. 227).

The combination of organizational leadership and practices within a collective history help explain why secondary schools are notorious for resisting substantive change. If the collective tacit knowledge is primarily reminiscent of past experiences and practices, it can be problematic for practitioners to engage in developing tacit knowledge, either collectively or individually, which challenges past practice (Hannay, Smeltzer Erb and Ross, 2001b). If leadership is only viewed as a formal and contained position, it is unlikely that the sustained and embedded energy to promote change or build change capacity can be internalized. This does provide a glimpse into the difficulty in promoting significant changes in secondary schools and does advance the need for deep restructuring efforts which question taken-for-granted assumptions.

I argue in this chapter that engaging in authentic restructuring requires that individual teachers and administrators question their taken-for-granted tacit and explicit knowledge concerning secondary school organizational practices and purposes. First, only through such questioning and reflection can secondary schools move beyond just being a professional or machine bureaucracy to develop alternative organization forms and thereby foster innovation. Second, deep and sincere engagement in restructuring forces participants to address uncertain, not procedural, problems. Third, only when the vision of leadership changes from a contained to a distributed conception of leadership will the organization be able to support innovative communities of practice.

## RESEARCH PARAMETERS

This chapter reports the experiences of one school out of nine involved in a longitudinal research study. The research study began when an Ontario, Canada[2], school district mandated that all of its secondary schools restructure the middle management of their schools. Further, these schools were given the authority to develop organizational models reflective of the contextual needs of their schools and were expected annually to review and revise these models as warranted. No model was presented to the schools, but it was clearly delineated that the subject department status quo was unacceptable. School-based restructuring committees were formed and these teams gradually developed new organizational models which replaced the traditional subject department model. Department head positions were contractually replaced with positions of responsibility (PORs).

The programme of research attempted to understand both the emerging process and the impact of the mandated restructuring on the participating schools. To accomplish this, qualitative data were collected through yearly interviews (1995–2000) with all individuals in the new positions of responsibility in each school. As warranted other participants were interviewed, individually or collectively through focus groups, including senior school district administrators, school administrators, elected union officials, and members of school-based restructuring committees.

All interviews were audio-taped and transcribed verbatim. Those data were subjected to analysis for emerging patterns and then all data were moved to data displays of the identified patterns. This permitted the researchers to consider the strength of the pattern and also to determine which patterns were dominant in each of the participating schools. Annual reports were prepared based on the data collected.

In this chapter, the investigation is limited to a reanalysis of the experiences of Borden Secondary School[3] staff from 1995 to 2000. Consequently, only qualitative data collected in this one school are reported. These restrictions were made in order to delve deeper into the relationships between leadership practices and organisational restructuring. The school is a mid-size rural school of approximately 800 students enrolled in Grade 9–12.

## FINDINGS

As documented elsewhere (Hannay and Ross, 1997; 1999; 2001; Hannay, Smeltzer Erb and Ross, 2001a; 2001b; Ross, Hannay and Brydges, 1998), the changes experienced in the schools participating in this programme of research were substantive and complex. Further, the experienced process could not be planned, promoted nor reported in a linear fashion. The tenets from chaos theory provide means of retrospectively analysing the dynamic relationship between engaging in restructuring, forging new conceptions of leadership and shaping alternative conceptions of organizations. Key considerations derived from chaos theory include identifying decisions supporting the change pattern (Caine and Caine, 1997), the organizational support for a flexing and emergent change process (Daft, 1998) and individuals affected by decisions need to be involved in the decision-making (Garmston and Wellman, 1995; Goff, 1998). All of these tenets interact within any complex change initiative (Garmston and Wellman, 1995) and they guide the examination of the research question.

## FOUNDATIONAL DECISIONS

Four early decisions shaped the district-wide restructuring efforts: the new school organizational models were to be designed to meet the needs of the individual school context and were to be programme driven; school committees (comprising of teacher volunteers) were to develop and then review their models annually; professional learning was to be provided for the participants; and maintaining the status quo organizational structure was unacceptable (Hannay, Smeltzer Erb and Ross, 2001b). In retrospect, the decisions that the contextually based models were to be developed by school restructuring committees, not only by the school administrators, and the models were to deviate from the status quo provided a fertile basis through which to question tacit organizational knowledge and create new conceptions of leadership.

## MOVING TOWARDS DISTRIBUTED LEADERSHIP

In Borden Secondary School, the early reaction to the restructuring process was one of anger and frustration. While many teachers were angry about the challenge to the status quo, individuals responded to the request by the school district to form school-based restructuring committees. Their initial organizational model mirrored the departmental organizational structure with one significant change which reallocated some money from department head stipends to a time-bank[4]. Yet, further substantial changes were limited by a traditional hierarchical principal who failed to share leadership and authority with the teacher members of the restructuring committee. A participant described the decision-making and leadership practices that existed early in the restructuring process at Borden Secondary School:

> A lot is already decided before a department head meeting occurs and it is basic-
> ally a dissemination of information and they [department heads] just take it back
> to their own department meetings ... I think the morale of the staff would be a lot
> higher if they felt that they had a lot more input and if their input was listened to
> and respected, at the moment I don't think they feel that way.
>
> (Int95: C1)[5]

Further, the history of interaction at Borden Secondary School was one of isolation, as described by a participant: 'at this school the classrooms are very isolated, the teachers are isolated in their classrooms, and not a lot of sharing goes on between teachers' (Int95: C1). In the early years of the restructuring process, the principal was disengaged, unsupportive of staff members involved in the process and failed to assist in implementing organizational change. Consequently, the teacher participants lacked the decision-making space to enact any significant change to the leadership practices or organizational structure. For some staff members this was just fine as they did not want the responsibility, nor did they want to challenge the department status quo. Thus restructuring was perceived as a procedural problem undertaken only to address the school district mandate.

When this principal was transferred, the new principal at Borden Secondary School began slowly to engage the staff in thinking about restructuring and change. The initial school district decision to encourage staff members to share the decision-making and responsibility for the creation of the new organizational models could now impact on the school, and with the new school administration came a gradual distribution of leadership roles and responsibility. Staff members were expected to be involved in restructuring decisions with their input valued. Thus, individuals affected by the decisions became involved in making the decisions. A participant in the fourth round of interviews explained: 'I think that's the one part that I think really was powerful, that people are going, "You mean that meeting that we had selected our priorities, you actually listened to that?" We've had more staff members talk about that the change was generated by consensus' (Int98: C14).

Partnership and team work gradually became the norm which Gronn (2000) argues is necessary to harness collective expertise. A participant talked about the importance of the emerging teamwork: 'There's more dialogue that is occurring among shared positions ... there's a tremendous emphasis on partnership and working as a team ... [with] teachers and administrators talking about being a team and being partners' (Int99: C15).

Through the restructuring process, distributed leadership was practised at various levels of the school's operations. Certainly, there was ample evidence to indicate that leadership was shared at the whole-school level. For instance, a participant explained how this was actualized in school communications:

You have to make certain that the information is not only provided from the top down, but you also have to have the flow of information going from the teachers up to the administration. You definitely need to have some dialogue. If you have the administration saying we're going to do this without any input from the teachers in the classroom, it's not going to work.

(Int98: C11)

This meant that the teacher members of the restructuring committee took active and front-centre leadership roles within the school. Distributed leadership was enacted in the daily practices of the school as described by a school administrator:

What the committee decided was when we go to the staff, everyone, every member of the school planning team is going to have a part in the presentation to the staff. So that it is not going to be seen as one or two people presenting it. I definitely took a role, a non-involved role. I didn't present any part of it. I was part of the team, but it was all the members.

(Int97: SA2)

The emerging school organizational model was based on clusters, not subject departments, and distributed leadership became the norm in this new structure. A school administrator stated: 'Particularly, when you see the kinds of things that are happening with the new clusters. They're working extremely well. They're taking over the leadership of all the staff meetings, any of the professional development in the school, there's a team' (Int97: SA2).

Combined, the increased emphasis on teacher input and teamwork enacted two key tenets in the chaos literature: individuals affected by the decisions were involved in making the decisions and collaborative teamwork was becoming the norm. This set the conditions which enabled a reshaping of the school culture. A participant simply stated 'we went from a culture where we took no risks. You didn't open your mouth' to a culture where 'we are more professional. We talk more professionally' (Int98: C8). A school administrator described the key cultural change as a shift for more decision-making involvement as 'Even at the committee level and at the staff meetings, people are talking more than they used to' (Int97: SA2).

Yet just distributing leadership by itself would have been ineffective in supporting the significant changes documented. Through a combination of distributed leadership and the mandate to challenge the status quo, participants were required to challenge their collective tacit and explicit knowledge about the organization of a secondary school. Restructuring became perceived as an uncertain problem and this was not an easy task as reported by a participant: 'How we were going to organize the school. We had a hard time envisioning something that was totally different. We didn't understand, if you weren't going to have department heads or department facilitators, whatever you call them, we just couldn't see what this was going to look like' (FG98: C1).

The school was reorganized several times over the course of this programme of research with a general move away from subject departments determining both the structure and the middle management positions. Whole-school needs became more important. Through participation in restructuring the process, emerging organizational concepts meant that activity determined the formal leadership positions and that these positions could be adapted as the activity changed. In turn, the increased professional dialogue involved in the restructuring process resulted in new individual/collective tacit and explicit knowledge. Combined, the distributed leadership and new knowledge were reshaping the perceived purpose of an organization – the relationship explored by Ogawa in Chapter 2 in this volume. School organizations became perceived as flexible and responsive. Time, for instance, was less of a fixed variable: 'because we had the time pool and we were restructured, we had the ability here at the school of freeing people up … We had teachers working together, new teachers working together on curriculum, new teachers working with experienced teachers. So that wouldn't have happened in a traditional system' (Int99: C16).

The needs of the school context shaped the organizational structure as opposed to the pre-determined structure curtailing innovation, as explained by a teacher: 'As a school planning team … we are refining to look at what the needs are that are presenting themselves now … we've been able to look at making some changes and we can make some changes again in a few years' (Int99: C16).

Conceivably, the most significant mindset change from the restructuring process was a general acceptance of, and the development of, a process to address continual change. A participant described the impact: 'It's very exciting to be part of an evolving, and I'm not going to say part of change, 'cause it's evolution. To see how, hopefully, it can survive change. We've built something that can adapt. I think that's what I get excited about. That I have seen people working together' (Int99: C13).

There was also acceptance that managing change requires a questioning of past knowledge and structures. The taken-for-granted assumptions were questioned as described by a participant 'If we continue to look at things the way we've always looked at them, then there may be barriers' (Int00: C5).

The increased collaboration impacted on teachers. In a rather poignant comment, a teacher new to the school and the profession explained the context for this impact:

> I found that this school has helped me become a better teacher because I found that there's more shared dialogue with teachers, more opportunity for new innovations to occur. I find, particularly with our administration, that any new idea is welcomed. There is that receptiveness and that openness … helped me learn to be a better teacher.
>
> (Int99: C15)

Perhaps how deeply institutionalized the emerging collective tacit and explicit knowledge about conceptions of organizations and distributed leadership became is best represented by the reactions of some participants, in the last year of this study, to the issues that emerged when the Ontario government forced the amalgamation of school districts and, consequently, of their teacher union affiliates. The new union affiliate advocated the same model in each secondary school, which meant a return to past organizational structures and past knowledge. The inherent challenge to distributed leadership within schools and the school–district–union partnership was met with strong resistance from Borden Secondary School staff who, five years earlier, had originally vehemently resisted challenging the status quo! In our last interviews, this theme was dominant as exemplified by a teacher participant:

> We really believed in those positions. Losing them meant a great deal of frustration for our staff ... It was so important to our staff, it seemed to be the one thing that brought us together as a whole group. It seemed to be something so wonderfully positive that we all agreed on. Then to have a top-down decision made about those positions being eliminated was really disconcerting.

(Int00: C15)

All of this impacted on the conceptions of leadership. Ongoing structural change, broadening the parameter of leadership, questioning the 'givens' and collaborative interaction, all seem reflective of Gronn's comments earlier in this volume (p. 70):

> Distributed leadership also seems to demand a new forbearance for reciprocity and dependency, the ability to cope with a sense of impermanence, a willingness to continually restructure procedures in the search for successful operational formulae, a finely tuned tolerance for ambiguity and uncertainty, and heightened negotiation skills.

Borden Secondary School moved dramatically over the course of this programme of research. The school staff entered the restructuring process as an isolated culture which cherished past practices and which willingly defined leadership in terms of a formal position within the defined professional bureaucracy. Yet, partially because a new administrator sought to share leadership practices, and through involvement in the restructuring process, the school staff gradually supported an organizational structure hinting of some characteristics reminiscent of Mintzberg's (1989) innovative or adhocracy organizational structures and practised distributed leadership grounded in activity as described by Gronn (2000).

## DISCUSSION

The changes experienced in Borden Secondary School since 1995 are complex and provide a venue through which to explore the dialectical relationship between leadership and organizational structures. As noted earlier in this chapter and elsewhere (Hannay, Smeltzer Erb and Ross, 2001b), chaos literature provides a useful means of reanalysing the process experienced in this school. In retrospect, two initial decisions by the school district set the conditions that encouraged the dynamic relationship between emerging conceptions of their organizational structures and leadership practices. The two key decisions were: the status quo organizational structure was unacceptable, and the restructuring process would involve teachers not just school administrators.

The key to understanding the process in Borden Secondary School is the relationship between these two decisions, as it is questionable whether either decision by itself could have facilitated the complex change achieved in this school. It is unlikely that active participation only in restructuring could have facilitated the deep changes documented through the longitudinal study. The restructuring process inherently required that participants frame the problem as an uncertain, rather than as a procedural problem in order to challenge their tacit and explicit knowledge. Even with this need, data collected in the first two years of this study failed to indicate any significant questioning of past knowledge. This suggests that the invitation to challenge past structures was insufficient by itself to foster deep innovation. Only when a school administrator was willing to distribute leadership could the invitation to change be fully accepted because the teachers were given the decision-making space to participate fully in restructuring their school. Yet, possibly, distributed leadership also might have been insufficient to foster significant change because new leadership roles might fail to question past assumptions. Thus restructuring might remain a procedural problem.

We return to the research question addressed in this chapter: how might involvement in organizational restructuring challenge conceptions of the nature of an organization and of leadership practices within secondary schools? Our findings suggests it was the combination of reconceptualizing the organization along with the active engagement through distributed leadership that provided the conditions supportive of substantive change. The questioning of past practice, in conjunction with the distributed leadership, promoted alternative means of interaction in the school. Dissimilar to most secondary school subject departments, the new clusters in Borden Secondary School furthered the distribution of leadership, promoted the deep questioning of past practice, supported deeper collaboration and facilitated innovation. Through the process, over time, the new clusters thus supported the development of communities of practice with a more fluid interaction pattern designed to support innovation (Wenger and Snyder, 2000).

Yet, there is a need to delve deeper into the dialectical relationship between organizational norms and leadership practices to further understand the difficulties associated with sustaining significant change in secondary schools. Mintzberg (1989) outlines different organizational models, three of which are pertinent to our discussion: professional bureaucracy, innovative or adhocracy and J-form (Japanese) organizational structures. Lam (2000) provides a useful lens to understand the nature of knowledge, both apparent and prized, in these different organizational forms. She describes four types of knowledge as embrained, embodied, encoded and embedded, and argues that these forms of knowing are dominant in different organization forms. Lam defines the different forms of knowledge as:

> Embrained knowledge (individual-explicit) is dependent on the individual's conceptional skills and cognitive skills. It is formal, abstract or theoretical knowledge ... Embodied knowledge (individual-tacit) is action oriented it is practical, individual type of knowledge ... Encoded knowledge (collective-explicit), sometimes

referred to as 'information', is conveyed by signs and symbols ... Embedded knowledge is the collective form of tacit knowledge residing in organisational routines and shared norms.

(Lam, 2000, pp. 492–3)

Organizationally, professional bureaucracies tend to promote embrained knowledge through the formal educational requirements and machine bureaucracies focus on encoded knowledge in order to 'formalize operating skills and experience into objective knowledge through codification' (Lam, 2000, p. 495). Lam (2000) argues that innovative organizations raise individual tacit knowledge to collective explicit knowledge through such alternative organizational models as operating adhocracy and the J-form. These organizational models focus respectively on embodied and embedded knowledge, both of which are more likely to foster innovation through creating a dialectical relationship between tacit and explicit knowledge, thus enhancing the willingness to accept an uncertain problem.

Lam's topology of organizational knowledge further clarifies the connection between organizational restructuring and distributed leadership. Secondary schools are professional bureaucracies, with elements of a machine bureaucracy, with embrained knowledge coming from similar educational requirements and with encoded knowledge emanating from school operations and traditions. The subject-department structure symbolizes the resulting individual and collective knowledge and the combination of structure and collective knowledge can prohibit creative problem-framing and solutions. Deep restructuring challenges these mindsets because changing their organizational model becomes an uncertain problem. When the school district involved in this programme of research made the early decision that the status quo was not acceptable, the foundation was laid through which this knowledge could be questioned. Developing new organizational models necessitated that the staff members challenge their deeply held tacit and explicit encoded knowledge about the functioning and structure of their school. Yet, deep questioning was only possible when leadership was distributed in the school. When this occurred, the staff raised that knowledge for collective retrospection and this process permitted the emergence of elements of Mintzberg's (1989) innovative or adhocracy organizational structure. The credo that the status quo was unacceptable created the reason to engage in the deep questioning of tacit and explicit knowledge, and without such questioning it is highly improbable that the existing tacit and explicit knowledge would have fostered innovation. Distributed leadership provided opportunities for enacting communities of practice (Wenger and Snyder, 2000) and without this collective retrospection, collaboration and reculturing were highly improbable.

## CONCLUSION

It is problematic to envision schools as something other than professional bureaucracies. However, without a reconceptualization of organizations as more porous and responsive, it is also questionable whether schools can meet emerging societal demands. As this study has demonstrated, such an evolution requires distributed leadership in which those affected by the decision both participate and accept responsibility in making decisions and taking action. Further, participants must be challenged to deeply question and rebuild their individual and collective tacit knowledge. The difficulty in secondary schools is that tacit knowledge is a product of embrained or encoded knowledge (Lam, 2000) which tends to support 'best practices' which often are defined in terms of past practice. For innovation to occur in secondary schools, it might be necessary to stimulate new collective tacit and explicit knowledge which challenges past practice. This process could trigger reculturing in a secondary school, and some scholars argue that reculturing will be required to facilitate significant change (e.g., Fullan, 1999). The interactive relationships between restructuring, distributed leadership and reculturing provide a glimpse into the difficulties with fostering and sustaining significant change in secondary schools. Yet, as the experiences of the school investigated in this chapter suggest, such change is possible if the conditions support an internal challenge to taken-for-granted assumptions and provide a means through distributed leadership to permit participants to become deeply engaged in and to own the process.

## NOTE

1. This Research Program was funded by grants from the Social Science and Humanities Research Council of Canada and the Ontario Ministry of Education and Training with support from the Kawartha Pine Ridge District School Board and District #49 Ontario Secondary School Teachers' Federation.

2. Ontario legislation gives the jurisdiction of determining the organisational structure of schools to the local school district with the middle-management positions legally defined as Positions of Responsibility.

3. A pseudonym.

4. The time-bank was money allocated to cover supply teachers to allow regular faculty to work together on a school initiated project.

5. Throughout this longitudinal study, we have consistently coded the source of all data by the year the data were collected, the school [alphabet] and by the individual. 'Int' identifies the data were from an individual interview while 'FG' means the data were from a focus group.

## REFERENCES

Brown, M. and Rutherford, D. (1998) Changing roles and raising standards: new challenges for heads of department, *School Leadership & Management*, 18(1), 75–88.

Caine, R.N. and Caine, G. (1997) *Education on the Edge of Possibility*. Alexandria, VA: ASCD.

Daft, R.L. (1998) *Organization Theory and Design*. Cincinnati, OH: South-Western College Publishing.

Dellar, G. (1996) The nature of secondary school organization and site specific restructuring, *International Journal of Educational Reform*, 5(4), 463–71.

Fullan, M.G. (1999) *Change Forces: The Sequel*. London: Falmer.

Garmston, R. and Wellman, B. (1995) Adaptive schools in a quantum universe, *Educational Leadership*, 52(7), 6–12.

Goff, K.E. (1998) Chaos, collaboration, and curriculum: a deliberative process, *Journal of Curriculum & Supervision*, **14**(1), 29–42.

Gronn, P. (2000) Distributed properties: a new architecture for leadership, *Educational Management andAdministration*, **28**(3), 317–38.

Hannay, L. and Ross, J. (1997) Initiating secondary school reform: the dynamic relationship between restructuring, reculturing, and retiming, *Educational Administration Quarterly*, **33**, Supplement, 576–603.

Hannay, L. and Ross, J. (1999) Department heads as middle managers? Questioning the black box, *School Leadership & Management*, **19**(3), 345–58.

Hannay, L. and Ross, J. (2001) Internalizing change capacity in secondary schools through organizational change, *Alberta Journal of Educational Research*, **47**(4), 325–40.

Hannay, L., Smeltzer Erb, C. and Ross, J. (2001a) To the barricades: the relationship between secondary school organizational structures and the implementation of policy initiatives, *International Journal of Leadership in Education*, **4**(2), 97–113.

Hannay, L., Smeltzer Erb, C. and Ross, J. (2001b) Building change capacity within secondary schools through goal-driven and living organisations, *School Leadership & Management*, **21**(3), 271–87.

Hargreaves, A. (1994) *Changing Teachers, Changing Times: Teachers' Work and Culture in the Postmodern Age*. Toronto: Ontario Institute for Studies in Education of the University of Toronto.

Jarvis, P. (1997) Learning practical knowledge, in L. Kydd, M. Crawford and C. Riches (eds), *Professional Development in Educational Management* (pp. 26–36). Buckingham: Open University Press.

Lam, A. (1997) Embedded firms, embedded knowledge: problems of collaboration and knowledge transfer in global cooperative ventures, *Organization Studies*, **18**(6), 973–96.

Lam, A. (2000) Tacit knowledge, organizational learning and societal institutions: an integrated framework, *Organizational Studies*, **21**(3), 487–513.

Mintzberg, H. (1989) *Mintzberg on Management*. Toronto: Free Press.

Nonaka, I. (1994) A dynamic theory of organizational knowledge creation, *Organization Science*, **5**, 14–37.

Ogawa, R.T. and Bossert, S.T. (1995) Leadership as an organizational quality, *Educational Administration Quarterly*, **31**(2), 224–43.

Polanyi, M. (1962) *Personal Knowledge: Towards a Post-critical Philosophy*. New York: Harper Torchbooks.

Polanyi, M. (1967) *The Tacit Dimension*. New York: Anchor Day Books.

Reid, W. (1978) *Thinking about the Curriculum: The Nature and Treatment of Curriculum Problems*. London: Routledge and Kegan Paul.

Ross, J., Hannay, L. and Brydges, B. (1998) District-level support for site-based renewal: a case study of secondary school reform, *Alberta Journal of Educational Research*, **44**(4), 349–65.

Schwab, J. (1978) The practical: a language for curriculum, in J. Gress and D. Purpel (eds), *Curriculum: An Introduction to the Field* (pp. 586–607). Berkeley, CA: McCutchan.

Siskin, L.S. (1994) *Realms of Knowledge: Academic Departments in Secondary Schools*. London: Falmer.

Wenger, E.C. and Snyder, W.M. (2000) Communities of practice: the organizational frontier, *Harvard Business Review*, **78**(1), 139–45.

# 8

---

# Collaboration in Communities of Practice

### JANE MCGREGOR

## INTRODUCTION

Leadership is invoked as a desirable and necessary condition for improving education, in much the same way as collaboration is taken to be a virtue. Yet there is a wide spectrum of definitions for both concepts, reflecting a variety of ideological positions, understandings and practices. Further slippery theoretical constructs include 'culture', 'community' and 'learning'. This chapter explores the relationship between certain of these formulations through revisiting an empirical study on teacher workplace cultures in secondary schools.

The impact of social relations with colleagues on teacher practice is increasingly considered in educational literature, whether evidenced through studies of organizational structures such as teams, teacher cultures and subcultures or professional learning communities. These perspectives on forms of association and their reciprocal impact on teacher learning and development, and thence pupil experience, have important insights to contribute to an understanding of leadership as a dimension of schools as workplaces.

The form and pattern of interactions which collectively help to construct 'the school' are commonly approached through binaries, such as the influence of structure or culture on teachers' work (Bennett, 2001) or whether the whole school or groupings like subject departments are the most important foci. The perspectives offered on change within the school as an organization can be similarly dichotomized into a cultural or micropolitical standpoint (Wallace and Hall, 1997) with leadership frequently presented in terms of leaders and followers (Gronn, Chapter 4 in this volume). A relational and process-oriented view of workplace association provides a more holistic and synthesizing understanding of what brings people together, sustaining productive and satisfying work relationships, and the role of leadership in this.

School effectiveness writing often associates leadership with strong and charismatic individuals – the headteacher as hero – implicit in the notion of 'superheads' parachuted into 'failing schools' to turn them around. 'Leadership' can be presented as a simplistic solution to complex layered problems rather than the means to agreed educational ends (Blackmore, 1999). School improvement literature has also focused on leadership as invested or embodied in a person, albeit through the role of the transformational leader in facilitating change (Leithwood and Jantzi, 1990). However, leadership is here explored more as process than person, focusing on relationship rather than role. In such a conception, leadership practices are spread throughout the school as a workplace. Leadership is seen as 'a function to which many staff contribute rather than a set of responsibilities vested in an individual '(Hopkins, Ainscow and West, 1994, p. 165).

In this volume the orthodoxies of leadership are challenged. However, while acknowledging leadership as multidimensional and dynamic, Goddard's contingency typology (Chapter 1) still locates and embodies leadership *in* an individual (e.g. the 'head' ). It also maintains the androcentric perspective of much of the existing literature on leadership. (Blackmore, 1999; Reay and Ball, 2000). Gronn suggests activity theory as a promising approach for reconceptualizing leadership as distributed within 'jointly performed and tool-mediated activity' (Gronn, 2000, p. 322) and in this volume (Chapter 4) he outlines different modes of interdependence. Morley and Hosking (Chapter 3) also describe a relational view of leadership, emphasizing the importance of the construction of context.

In suggesting the utility of relational and practice-based theorizing, the particular focus of this chapter is on communities of practice, a concept which is gaining currency in education (Harris and Bennett, 2001; Little, 1999), drawing particularly on the work of Lave and Wenger (1991). This emphasizes the social and negotiated character of learning, where practice is created by members of the grouping *through* the making of meaning together, which reciprocally then brings into existence the community (Wenger, 2000). This evolving conceptualization of a network of relations as dynamic and constructed through practice has much in common with the understanding of spatiality. The spatial and the social are reciprocally constructed through materially embedded practices and performances that create and maintain everyday social relations, and these are relations of power (Massey, 1999; Rose, 1999).

Gronn (2000) suggests that leadership as a concept needs to be scrutinized in conjunction with influence which links with a Foucaultian understanding of power as a constellation of (often productive) relations shaping action rather than a reified possession (Foucault, 1982; Paechter, 2000) – 'power to' rather than 'power over', or perhaps, 'power with'. Distributed leadership then does not entail distributed roles but (reciprocal) interactions. In this way, collaboration, negotiation, persuasion and so on may be seen as modalities of power within communities of practice. The empirical study on which this chapter is based suggests the importance of tracing where, when and how collaboration occurs and how leadership influences and is expressed through it.

## TEACHER WORKPLACE CULTURES
## AND COMMUNITIES

In the school as a workplace for adults, interactions with colleagues as well as students create possibilities for, or constraints on, learning and improving practice. What goes on 'outside' the classroom may be as important for school development and learning as what goes on within in (Louis and Kruse, 1995; McLaughlin, 1993).

Workplace cultures of teaching typically have been framed in the opposing binaries of individualism and collaboration (Hargreaves, 1993). Collaboration and collegiality (terms which are frequently, and mistakenly, conflated (Fielding, 1999) are actively advocated as means of encouraging professional dialogue and learning (Fullan, 1999).

While collaboration and collegiality are increasingly interrogated (Brundrett, 1998; McGregor, 2000a) it has become a given that strong forms of joint work within collaborative cultures can help frame creative responses to, and capacity to deal with, change (Hopkins, 2001; Nias, Southworth and Yeomans, 1989). Little's work on the social organization of the workplace, on which this empirical study is based, concluded that staff and school development was supported by 'norms of collegiality and experimentation' (Little, 1982, p. 325). Professional learning communities were likely to be built when teachers adopted 'critical practices of adaptability' such as engaging in concrete talk about teaching, and planning, researching and evaluating together. Such robust and reciprocal forms of collaboration are important conditions for progressive school reform, particularly if they generate core common values which are constitutive of and spread throughout the school, manifested in relationships with students (Fielding, 1999; Gitlin, 1999). It is perhaps here that leadership processes may be most clearly visible in encouraging joint work and learning and the structures which support it.

Over the last decade there has been increasing interest in the concept of professional communities, identified as critical contexts of teaching in secondary schools (Louis and Kruse, 1995; McLaughlin and Talbert, 2001) although the suggested scale, boundaries and characteristics differ. Such a community where teachers come together may be actor networks 'within', or more extensively, reaching 'beyond' the school and may be congruent with organizational and cultural units such as the department, or reflect issue-based groupings .

This research highlights the importance of the subject department in secondary schools as the most significant work location for teachers, providing a particular nexus of interaction, practice and identity where the external forces such as curriculum change and professional development are mediated (Ball and Lacey, 1995; Siskin, 1994). Louis and Kruse (1995), in contrast, look to the unit of the institution and use the term *professional community* to describe school-wide assemblages. This maps best onto concepts of collegiality. There are then tensions between the existence of multiple and overlapping subcultures and the whole school coherence seen as necessary for school improvement (Hannay and Lum, 2000; Sammons, Thomas and Mortimore, 1997). It is here that practice-based, relational models such as communities of practice can inform ideas about workplace interaction, distinguishing boundaries between formal and informal work groupings, learning and leadership.

## PRACTICE AND ACTIVITY-BASED THEORIES

The growing importance of interactive, practice-based theorizing parallels the increasing use of relational approaches in the social sciences such as actor network theories and situated learning (Gherardi, 2000). These perspectives move away from a structural analysis of behaviour in terms of pre-existing systems and contents to a focus on actors' contributions to the social order. There is a correspondingly evolving view in education on the critical influence of *context*, which is conceptualized as a nested hierachy of influences, from the classroom to the policy environment. New conceptions of spatiality (McGregor, in press) suggest more effectively, that rather than being a physical container *within* which social relations take place, space is reciprocally constituted *through* the social. In this book, Morley and Hosking note that *'the relationship between people and contexts is one of mutual creation'* (Chapter 3). Space is thus itself enacted (Massey, 1999), made and remade through social relations which are also relations of power. Spatiality is hence, more than context, a series of trajectories extending in space-time beyond the school as an institution. Framing context in this way then foregrounds the importance of leadership as a practice or series of qualities.

These conceptions articulate with new theories of situated learning. In traditional cognitive learning theory, knowledge is located in the heads of individuals; it pre-exists their knowing and can be appropriated, transmitted and stored. This is similar to the way in which power has been conceptualized, as a zero-sum possession (Lukes, 1974). Practice-based perspectives, on the other hand, take knowledge as created through practice, so learning is social and participative rather than cognitive, which parallels relational understandings of power (Sharp *et al.*, 2000). Activity theorists such as Engstrom, Miettinen and Punamaki (1998), locate learning in the social and communal, but in *activity systems* rather than communities of practice.

## SITUATED WORKPLACE LEARNING

The opportunity for teachers to engage in workplace learning is already seen as crucial to the development of schools' capacity for problem solving and improvement (Darling-Hammond, 1998). The professional development of teachers is increasingly closely linked with the context of situated joint work (Retallick, 1999), where 'collaborative cultures turn individual learning into shared learning' (Hargreaves, 1995a, p. 15).

According to Lave and Wenger (1991), learning is an activity situated in social participation, in communities of practice, taking place particularly at the periphery or boundary, absorbing new members, in colliding with other communities or linking with influences from outside. When crossing boundaries there are particular opportunities for reinterpretation which can lead to new knowledge. We might speculate that this may happen particularly in schools where communities of practice overlap with departments as subject subcultures as well as organizational units. How, then, may these notions help interpret patterns of association and leadership in schools?

## COMMUNITIES OF PRACTICE AND
## TEACHER WORKPLACE GROUPINGS

A community of practice, as described by Lave and Wenger (1991), comprises individuals bound by shared practice related to a set of problems or tasks, sharing and creating knowledge through participation. The process of learning is described as 'legitimate peripheral participation', an apprenticeship model where what is learned is that which is entailed in access to participating roles in the community. Knowledge, is then also a dynamic process rather than an object or thing, with communities as emergent social structures in/ through which knowledge is reciprocally created (Wenger, 1998).

Communities of practice are groups of people sharing similar goals and interests, forming around a skill, professional discipline, a skill or issue, employing a shared repertoire of common practices, artefacts, routines and language, and held together by a common sense of purpose. *Through* common activity and collective learning then they come to hold similar beliefs and values and cultural practices. Communities of practice are also important sources of identity where individuals may define themselves through the communities to which they belong, or do not (Wenger, McDermott and Snyder, 2002).

What, then, distinguishes communities of practice from teams, organizational units and subcultures, such as subject departments? Departments as teams are defined organizationally, usually within line management structures, and in time and space by the timetable of lessons. Subject classrooms are often grouped in close proximity and individuals are likely to spend significant time in interactions with their departmental colleagues, particularly where there are departmental offices and strong social ties. Thus subject subcultures tend to develop with their distinctive spatial dimensions, curricula, practices, language, beliefs and values (McGregor, in press; Siskin and Little, 1995). Conceptions of culture (and community) are commonly predicated on homogeneity, security and what is known, rather than the uncertainty that necessarily accompanies learning at the limits of one's competence ('outside the comfort zone') or forging knowledge that is completely new (Ogawa, Chapter 2).

The cognitive apprenticeship model, in its early formulations, lays most emphasis on sharing and passing on what is already known rather than confronting novel situations of developing new knowledge, and hence has more congruence with the cultural perspective. The active construction of new knowledge through social relations is central to activity theory, social constructivism (Morley and Hosking, Chapter 3) and is reflected in recent writing on communities of practice (Wenger, McDermott and Snyder, 2002). Rather than simply a pre-existing consensus, 'shared values' should be seen as being 'worked out' and negotiated in continuing conditions of uncertainty (Little, 1990) within arenas such as department meetings.

Departments are likely to intersect and overlap to varying degrees with communities of practice in different contexts, but they may not be the same. Communities of practice are more loosely knit, and defined by the opportunity to learn and share developing over time and reflected in day-to-day interactions. They share many qualities with the collaborative cultures identified by Nias, Southworth and Yeomans (1989) and Hargreaves (1994) as voluntary, development-orientated and unpredictable. Like the department team, they are bound by a sense of identity but with more partial and marginal members, possibly crossing team boundaries. Rather than being imposed by organizational structures they develop more 'organically' and it is less clear where they begin and end, either in membership or duration. The heart of a community of practice is, then, the knowledge that the members develop and share rather than, (as in the organizational team) a set of outcome-orientated tasks (McDermott, 1999). It can be argued that when a department is also functioning as a community of practice there is a powerful synergy in relation to learning and innovation. This will reflect leadership exhibited by individuals and within groups.

## BOUNDARIES

In Wenger's conception of communities of practice, learning and innovation potential lies in the configuration of strong core practices and active boundary processes, where he formulates modes of belonging in terms of engagement, alignment (with wider processes) and imagination or self-image (Wenger, 1998). An important element of boundary construction in communities of practice is co-ordinating opportunities for engagement in joint activities such as problem-solving, recognizing multiple perspectives and resolving difference. This is particularly likely to occur in a situation where professional identity, social interaction, school organization and pedagogic interests intersect – as in the subject department. Talbert and Siskin found that subject departments as 'core teaching contexts' varied enormously in their professional cultures (Siskin and Little, 1995; Talbert, 1995). The strength and character of what they term professional community heavily mediated effects of institutional conditions and wider education changes on teachers' work lives, which Wenger terms alignment. Talbert importantly points out that strong professional community need not mean strong boundaries; established department cultures can function as more of an open system.

It is, however, at the boundary between subcultures or communities of practice that particular objects , such as the 'reified' curriculum, research findings or aims of the school can become the focus for new understandings and practices, particularly when accompanied by a 'broker'. Such a person, whose influence is often informal, transacts knowledge and practice from other communities, therefore exerting leadership influence. Wenger (1998) suggests that through 'legitimate peripheral participation', much of the work of an organization will be accomplished (or not) through the interaction and overlap of distinct communities of practice. These generative tensions particularly require an intersection of interests, something to interact about, to evaluate innovation against, within an open engagement with differences as well as commonalities. Those communities with a wider repertoire or range of understanding of practice will then have more opportunities for making links between groupings.

## THE STUDY

This small-scale study of three comprehensive schools was designed to explore patterns of association and interaction between teachers in the workplace. Earlescombe is an 11–18 school with a small sixth form, located in a suburban area in the West Country with a fairly homogenous white working-class population. Students achieve around the national average for GCSE passes A*–C. This represents a significant value added to their lower than average Key Stage 3 scores.

Brythnoth is an 11–18 community college serving a rural catchment with islands of socio-economic advantage, but also deprivation. The college was established in 1986 from the amalgamation of two existing schools, with the students and staff of the secondary modern moving to the present site. Like Earlescombe, there is a low percentage of adults in the catchment with higher education experience, while the number of students with some statement of special educational needs is above average. Teachers in both these schools commented on the low aspirations and self-esteem of their intake. OFSTED inspections noted that all the schools studied serve their individual communities well. The teachers at Brythnoth, while enjoying the company of individuals, generally cast the staff as fragmented, isolated and discontent. The lack of social cohesion was symbolized by the main staffroom which was frequently empty at break times.

Kingbourn is a large14–18 upper school and community college drawing students from prosperous villages in a shire county. The proportion of students taking free school meals is low in comparison with the other schools and the range of ability, while broad, has a greater proportion above average than below it. In contrast to Brythnoth and Earlescombe, whose contracting budgets have meant staff losses, the school is expanding. It was designated a 'Beacon School' and is now a Media-Arts College, with 68 per cent of the year group achieving grades A*–C at GCSE in 1998. In contrast to Brythnoth, the teachers characterized the staff as working well together in a rapidly changing, challenging but satisfying environment.

The teachers in this study identified the concept of collaboration as working together for a common purpose or goal in a manner characterized by sharing of values, knowledge and ideas and more concretely, facilities and materials. A 'community of practice' was a term also used, in addition to 'working collectively'. While joint work was viewed positively and there was general consensus in articulating the *theory*, actual descriptions of the *practice* varied widely from what could be described as social staffroom interchange to joint action research. The diversity of responses suggested a lack of understanding of the different forms or strengths of joint work possible.

The project explored the types of associations that occurred between adults in the school as a workplace, through observation, the perceptions of the teachers themselves, and the completion of a grid to indicate where, when and with whom they most commonly interacted. There were 20 possible forms of interaction, from *social talk* to *designing Inset*. Semi-structured interviews explored 'what it is like to work in this school'. Observation and document analysis were also used as part of a micro-ethnographic approach.

The interactions that people were asked to consider were derived from Little's research which found that;

> In successful schools more than in unsuccessful ones, teachers valued and participated in norms of collegiality and continuous improvement (experimentation); they pursued a greater range of professional interactions with fellow teachers including talk about instruction, structured observation, and shared planning or preparation. They did so with greater frequency, with a greater number and diversity of persons and locations, and with a more concrete and precise shared language.
>
> (Little, 1982, p. 325)

Little identified a number of 'critical practices of success and adaptability' most likely to lead to workplace learning and the development of productive joint working relationships, which *might* then be indicative of a community of practice. Those explored in this study were:

- Design and prepare materials together.
- Prepare lesson plans together.
- Observe other teachers (with feedback).
- Persuade others to try an idea or approach.
- Make collective agreements to test an idea.
- Talk 'in public' about what one is learning.
- Design Inset.
- Joint research/evaluation

## PATTERNS OF INTERACTION

The patterns of interaction reported were broadly similar between teachers and schools, as shown on the radial graph (Figure 8.1) (McGregor, 2000b). Engagement was demonstrated particularly through the amount and type of talk reported which varied between and within the schools. Kingbourn teachers reported a far higher number of interactions and almost double the amount of 'critical practices' of strong joint work (Table 8.1).

Table 8.1

| | Average no. interactions per person | % Critical Practices | % within department | % cross curricular |
|---|---|---|---|---|
| Earlscombe | 59 | 22.4 | 46.3 | 4.4 |
| Kingbourn | 91 | 31.7 | 37.8 | 11.3 |
| Brythnoth | 49 | 16.5 | 36.2 | 3.9 |

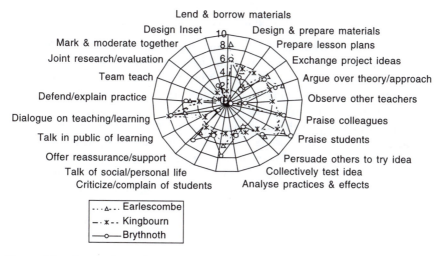

**Figure 8.1** Comparison of percentage

Teachers indicated that *engaging in dialogue around teaching and learning* was particularly important and further included, *arguing over theory, defending* or *explaining classroom practices*, also *exchanging project ideas*, all strongly associated with individuals within departments. Supporting colleagues and social talk were also important.

In workplace practice, designing and producing artefacts such as work schemes together is both a mode of engagement and an indication of the strength of interaction. It is in such exchanges that teachers are most likely to confront and discuss their differences, share experience and develop new knowledge through synergy. This strong form of joint work was less common than simply lending and borrowing materials, which does not require the same level of co-construction. Such 'critical practices of adaptability' were reported least frequently overall. These are precisely the forms of association that Wenger presents as most likely to build and develop communities of practice. On this reading, Kingbourn showed more of the features of a community of practice, although there were differences between departments. Different forms of collaboration were clearly seen to be located in certain places, spaces and times (McGregor, 2000a) with an average of 39 per cent of interactions reported specifically 'within the department'. Informal situations, places and times were most commonly cited as locations of collaboration. Department meetings were mentioned most frequently as times when productive joint work occurred, particularly at Kingbourn where some were structured into the school day.

## DIFFERING CONCEPTIONS OF LEADERSHIP ARISING IN THE STUDY

The importance of leadership in encouraging and sustaining collaborative work and developing collegiality was emphasized in all the study schools but here the focus is on Kingbourn and Brythnoth which had the most widely differing profiles in terms of joint work. Rather than 'from the top', leadership was agreed to operate most effectively throughout the staff, However, at Brythnoth, leadership in the school was commonly conceptualized as hierarchical and related to the status and role of an individual. This seemed to date from the difficult amalgamation 15 years previously, where two post-holders often had to apply for one 'position of responsibility'. A perceived lack of leadership operating at different levels throughout the school was then identified as a barrier to joint work.

In contrast, at Kingbourn, staff valued the opportunities for involvement and participation presented (to some?) by the heads' promotion of 'distributed and multi-level leadership' and 'flattened hierarchies'. However, while concurring with those values, some staff were clear that it was the influence of the head as a transformational leader that created the conditions for this, often through micro-political activity as well as overt strategies (McGregor, 2000a). Kingbourn showed more of the features *characterizing* communities of practice in the level and quality of reported and observable interactions and the emphasis placed on professional learning and enquiry. The school as a whole could not be described as a community of practice; it was too large, formal and heterogeneous. To explore the concept further it will later be necessary to focus on (in this case) the department level.

Commmunities of practice in the workplace are based particularly on engagement or doing things together. At Kingbourn, interaction between subject departments was deliberately encouraged through the creation of 'curriculum areas' and a framework of school improvement groups of self-selected individuals. These groups were based around collaborative enquiry as a means of actively encouraging cross-curricular dialogue and were facilitated and legitimated through resourcing. The allocation of time and other resources is a major way in which subject and school leaders can support collaboration as joint work, but symbolic endorsement is also influential (Little, 1990). This operated most obviously at Kingbourn. 'A community with shared aspirations.

Working with one another outside the "comfort zone" is synergistically powerful. To share, engage, actively seek to give others the opportunity to collaborate' (Head, Kingbourn).

Leadership plays an important role in encouraging reflection on a school's circumstances (or spatiality) and constructing an image of the community, a self-representation of common interests and values, initially through the communication of stories, symbols and statements. Enquiry then provides a means of testing ideas against what is known. It is *through* such shared activities that the existence of common values are explored, negotiated and agreed. At Kingbourn the stated values of the school were regularly revisited on in-service days and discussed in small groups, perhaps modified and then published as a means of their reaffirmation. In this way, a sense of joint enterprise was fostered while at least notionally agreeing core common values, then 'reifying' these as an artefact or document, which also facilitated the development of a common language. At this level it is questionable whether the majority of staff felt they had the opportunity to disagree with the Head, who had more modalities of power within which to operate, although in the discussion groups dissent and debate was present.

Alignment is the dimension in Wenger's (2000) model through which local activities are made congruent with wider organizational and political processes and policies. Those in formal leadership roles such as 'Heads' (of school, department or year, etc.) were seen to have particular opportunity and responsibility to mediate between local activities and wider processes. It is particularly through the dimensions of alignment and imagination that leadership is expressed in the communities of practice model, although it is not explicitly addressed by Wenger.

The third dimension of engagement, or doing things together, was particularly represented in this study by the interactions within the subject department or curriculum area. This is the level at which we might expect communities of practice to arise, where people are more likely to have a common understanding of the enterprise in hand and the ability to identify gaps in knowledge through joint reflection enquiry. Interpersonal relationships of mutuality, trust and respect are crucial in the development of collaborative cultures (Hargreaves, 1994; Nias, Southworth and Yeomans, 1989) and in communities of practice are identified as major components of 'social capital'. The importance of trust, respect and praise was emphasized by teachers in this study time and again, linked to their confidence to share experiences, confront differences and debate them constructively.

## LEADERSHIP IN A COMMUNITY OF PRACTICE

Subject departments are powerful 'practice-relevant configurations' (Nespor, 1994) of people, technologies and ideas, a particular nexus of relationships (McGregor, in press). If practice is particularly a combination of participation, negotiation and reification (Bennett, 2001), these were strongly represented in the collaboration and the social interactions that constructed the science department at Kingbourn. A rich mixture of social, personal and professional talk interwove almost seamlessly when colleagues were in each others' company, strongly suggesting elements of a community of practice overlapping with the pre-existing organizational boundaries of the department (McGregor, in press), which was, as perceived by the rest of the school, cohesive, innovative and successful.

Ogawa (Chapter 2) describes the importance of finding the social spaces, times and places where the contingencies and uncertainties of teaching can be explored in conjunction with ordered elements, creating the opportunity for situated organizational learning. In terms of spatiality, the *places* were made by the interactions The offices of the science departments in both schools were similarly cramped *physical* spaces, but at Kingbourn used to a very different effect, where proximity was actively encouraged as a major factor in developing positive relationships. People were also brought into the office by the desire to consult the up-to-date lists, information and records that were displayed there, and to negotiate over equipment for lessons. In their packed department office at break, where teachers, technicians and trainees gathered, could be seen the reciprocity between material space and the web of past and present social relations that is the spatiality, of the (work)place (McGregor, forthcoming).

In the 'federal' science curriculum area (Busher, 2001) subject leaders deliberately created opportunities to work together on the creation of joint work schemes and curricula. Innovations such as CASE were particularly valued for sharing ideas at a similar level of competence, and were generally welcomed at Kingbourn as providing an opportunity to collaborate, while they were more usually perceived as a burden at Brythnoth. The modelling behaviour of the head of science was important in supporting risk-taking in and the selective adoption of change:

> There is a shared language [in the department], we all understand what we are talking about. With coaching we have to get into each other's classrooms, see it, experience it, talk about it. I try and act as a role model. If I have a lesson that goes wrong or well, I articulate it. I don't use my office, this was a conscious decision. It would decrease open dialogue dramatically.

> (Gregg Parfitt, Head of department, Kingbourn)

But leadership was not confined to his particular role. He was influential in creating processes through which leadership could be expressed by any members of the department, including technicians – perhaps best described as leadership capacity or density (Jackson, 2000). 'Collaboration means having leadership across a wide range of staff, you don't have to be an old hand in the department to have a leadership role' (Gregg Parfitt, Head of department, Kingbourn). This was facilitated and developed through encouraging collaboration and negotiation, formally in meetings and informally at break times, thus exemplifying the notion of leadership as a group function exercised by individuals with different formal status and levels of experience at different times. In contrast, in the Brythnoth science department there was a leadership vacuum, where individuals failed to find leadership either in the head of department or themselves. While being highly internally collaborative, the Kingbourn science department, also had strong links throughout and beyond the school, for example with higher education institutions, the Science Association and the school improvement groups. It was actually functioning as a more open system than was perceived.

They key practices through which power seemed to be operating in the Kingbourn science curriculum area, could be characterized as more *lateral* (and substantially positive) modalities, such as persuasion (rather than coercion) research and collective testing of ideas (rather than imposition) although these were arguably influences in terms of the central imposition of National Curriculum testing. The negotiation of mutual observation and feedback may be seen as quite different in form and content to the monitoring of official government surveillance, such as OFSTED. These collaborative processes mediate and effect learning, which then represents a different conception of power from the notion of a 'top-down' hierarchy.

## BEYOND COMMUNITIES OF PRACTICE

Wenger suggests that individuals participate in local, small-scale communities of practice which help to construct their identities. It is worth introducing here, however, another perspective which develops Lave and Wenger's original concept. Jan Nespor, in a theorized account of the spatiality of the curriculum, argues that the local nature of the situated learning that Lave and Wenger propose fails to take account of how such communities are structured, maintained and connected to one another in space-time. He proposes that the social and psychological are integrated only though a narrow conception of the social, limited to a focus on face-to face interactions taking place in circumscribed settings. Social organization (for most of the population) now links distant times, places and individuals that may never be physically co-present. Wenger (2002) now takes account of this, for example with communities linked by e-mail rather than co-presence. Nespor makes a more fundamental point that the interaction of people, things and ideas actually create the particular community in an ongoing way: 'Communities aren't just situated in time and space, they are ways of producing and organising time and space and setting up patterns of movement across space-time: they are networks of power' (Nespor, 1994, p. 9).

Hence a 'community' is composed of heterogeneous and dispersed elements linked together as a particular space-time. Hosking (1999) suggests the importance of knowing as an ongoing process of making social realities which are 'standpoint dependent', relating to the local social or local historical. A more sophisticated understanding of the relationship between time-space and place is expressed through the new theorizing on spatiality, 'What gives a place (a community?) its specificity is not some long internalized history but the fact that it is constructed out of a particular constellation of relations, articulated together at a particular locus' (Massey, 1993, p. 66).

Certainly in Wenger's earlier work, the community is seen as a container for the learning process rather than necessarily constitutive of it. Learning may be situated, but cognition is not distributed. Spatializing communities of practice would therefore seem to offer a further dimension of understanding to existing organizational and cultural conceptions in addition to a further development of this practice-based theory. Seeing power as emerging from action, through modal effects such as persuasion and collaboration highlights the importance of thinking spatially.

Further, although Wenger (2000) usefully describes the 'reification' of processes, for example through the writing of a textbook, he does not extend the discussion to the interaction between the material and the social that is further developed through a consideration of Actor-Network Theory. This is a body of theoretical and empirical writing, developed by a group of sociologists, which employs a social view of technology, treating social relations, including power and organization as network effects. Networks are seen as materially heterogeneous, a complex set of artefacts actors and structures and a set of socially constructed principles and processes, devised to realise a purpose (Law, 1992; Lawn and Grosvenor, 1999). It treats technologies as active members of networks rather than passive objects, determining solutions, circulating ideas and circumscribing actions (Latour, 1997). 'The classroom' becomes a system of relations between people, ideas, objects and technologies (from the blackboard, to ICT). Communities of practice can then be interpreted as particular configurations of actor networks.

## CONCLUSION

In later formulations of the theory, Wenger (2002) develops the idea that new knowledge as well as learning is produced through interactions, and that through diversity there are creative tensions. While the cultural perspective, and much school improvement literature, assumes that pre-existing beliefs and values are unproblematically congruent and commonly held in 'collaborative cultures', Hosking (1999) suggests (from a social constructivist viewpoint) that American social psychology paradigms have tended to ignore differences in beliefs and values within groups and the generative tensions of conflicts of value inherent in the ongoing construction of social settings. Instead, she proposes that it is testing and negotiating common values through joint practice and learning which strengthens communities of practice. (In spatial terms these are then constantly made and remade through performance). The role of leadership is then in facilitating engagement, imagination and alignment. Formal units such as departments are major sites for teacher learning, but particularly when they intersect with communities of practice where colleagues can share and make meaning together. Collective enquiry and reflection in 'shared influence settings' then gives the possibilities of creating new knowledge (Jackson, 2000). A challenge for leaders in schools is to recognize and nurture communities of practice in their core activities, but particularly facilitate active boundary processes to extend collaboration to collegiality, where leadership can then be demonstrated or exercised by a variety of actors in different situations.

The concept of communities of practice and of situated learning has some considerable utility in explaining patterns of association amongst teachers (and other staff) in secondary schools and challenging monolithic views of culture and community. With other relational and practice-based theorizing, it provides additional tools for interrogating workplace groupings, and moving away from binary formulations such as dichotomizing structure and culture. It provides a framework for exploring situated workplace learning which takes place through formal and informal interactions. In that people belong to various communities of practice which overlap, but may not be contiguous with organizational units or subcultures, the model provides an explanation for the differential capacity for change and improvement, for example in different subject departments in the same school.

The theory of communities of practice suggests further dimensions to the notion of collegiality as powerful joint work, rather than a more instrumental collaboration. What it does not do in this respect, however, is to unpick the important power relationships crucial in decision-making and negotiation. It thereby fails to address, for example, some of the issues around the interaction of micro-politics and 'headship' in schools or the notion that rather than a role or a person, leadership may at times be better understood as a dynamic and fluid process, expressed through different modalities of power and association within groups in the workplace.

Power and leadership are not quite the same and reconceptualizations of leadership in education suggest that leadership can be more usefully seen much more in terms of influence (Hosking, 1999). Current notions of dispersed or distributed leadership, 'multi-level leadership based around values', where values are created together synergistically through strong forms of joint work such as collaborative enquiry (Jackson, 2000) begin to move away from modernist assumptions about leadership being the possession of certain individuals to a focus on leadership processes in context, including adults learning collaboratively.

## REFERENCES

Ball, S.J. and Lacey, C. (1995) Revisiting subject disciplines as the opportunity for group action, in L.S. Siskin and J.W. Little (eds), *The Subjects in Question: Departmental Organisation and the High School*. New York: Teachers College Press.

Bennett, N. (2001) Power, structure and culture: an organizational view of school effectiveness and school improvement, in A. Harris and N. Bennett (eds), *School Effectiveness and School Improvement: Alternative Perspectives*. London: Continuum.

Blackmore, J. (1999) *Troubling Women: Feminism, Leadership and Educational Change*. Buckingham: Open University Press.

Brundrett, M. (1998) What lies behind collegiality, legitimation or control? *Educational Management and Administration*, 26(3), 305–16.

Busher, H. (2001) The micro-politics of change, improvement and effectiveness in schools, in A. Harris and N. Bennett (eds), *School Effectiveness and School Improvement: Alternative Perspectives*. London: Continuum.

Darling-Hammond, L. (1998) Teacher learning that supports student learning, *Educational Leadership*, 55(5), 6–11.

Engestrom, Y., Miettinen, R. and Punamaki, R.-L. (eds) (1998) *Perspectives on Activity Theory*. Cambridge: Cambridge University Press.

Fielding, M. (1999) Radical collegiality: affirming teaching as an inclusive professional practice, Australian Conference on Educational Research, Adelaide.

Foucault, M. (1982) Space, knowledge and power (interview in Skyline, March), in P. Rabinow (ed.), *The Foucault Reader*. London: Penguin.

Fullan, M. (1999) *Change Forces: The Sequel*. London: Falmer.

Gherardi, S. (2000) Practice-based theorizing on learning and knowing in organizations, *Organization*, 7(2), 211–23.

Gitlin, A. (1999) Collaboration and progressive school reform, *Educational Policy*, 13(5), 630–58.

Gronn, P. (2000) Distributed properties: a new architecture for leadership, *Educational Management and Administration*, 28(3), 317–38.

Hannay, L. and Lum, T. (2000) Internalising change capacity in secondary schools through organisational change, BEMAS Research Conference, Robinson College, Cambridge, March.

Hargreaves, A. (1993) Individualism and individuality, reinterpreting the teacher culture, in J.W. Little and M. McLaughlin (eds), *Teachers' Work: Individuals, Colleagues and Contexts*. New York: Teachers College Press.

Hargreaves, A. (1994) *Changing Teachers Changing Times: Teachers' Work and Culture in the Post-modern Age*. London: Cassell.

Hargreaves, A. (1995a) Renewal in the age of paradox, *Educational Leadership*, 52(7), 14–19.

Hargreaves, D. (1995b) School culture, school effectiveness and school improvement, *School Effectiveness and School Improvement*, 6(1), 23–46.

Harris, A. and Bennett, N. (eds) (2001) *School Effectiveness and School Improvement: Alternative Perspectives*. London: Continuum.

Hopkins, D. (2001) *School Improvement for Real*. London: Falmer.

Hopkins, D., Ainscow, M. and West, M. (1994) *School Improvement in an Era of Change*. London: Cassell.

Hosking, D.M. (1999) Social construction as process: some new possibilities for research and development, *Concepts and Transformations*, 4(2), 117–32.

Jackson, D. (2000) The School Improvement Journey: perspectives on leadership, *School Leadership and Management*, 20, 61–78.

Jackson, D. (2000) School Improvement and the Planned Growth of Leadership Capacity, BERA Annual Conference, Cardiff.

Latour, B. (1997) On actor-network theory: a few clarifications, Centre for Social Theory and Technology, Keele University, July.

Lave, J. and Wenger, E. (1991) *Situated Learning: Legitimate Peripheral Participation*. Cambridge: Cambridge University Press.

Law, J. (1992) Notes on the theory of the actor network: ordering, strategy and heterogeneity, *Systems Practice*, 5(4), 379–93.

Lawn, M. and Grosvenor, I. (1999) Imagining a Project: Networks, Discourses and Spaces – Towards a New Archaeology of Urban Education, *Paedagogica Historica*, 35(2), 381–93.

Leithwood, K. and Jantzi, D. (1990) Transformational Leadership: how prinicipals can help reform school cultures, *School Effectiveness and School Improvement*, 1(4), 249–80.

Little, J.W. (1982) Norms of collegiality and experimentation: workplace conditions of school success, *American Educational Research Journal*, 19(3), 325–40.

Little, J.W. (1990) The persistence of privacy: autonomy and initiative in teachers' professional relations, *Teachers College Record*, 91(4), 509–36.

Little, J.W. (1995) Subject affiliation in high schools that restructure, in L.S. Siskin and J.W. Little (eds), *The Subjects in Question: Departmental Organisation and the High School*. New York: Teachers College Press.

Little, J.W. (1999) Colleagues of choice, colleagues of circumstance: response to M. Fielding, *Australian Educational Researcher*, 26(2), 35–43.

Louis, K.S. and Kruse, S. (1995) *Professionalism and Community: Perspectives on Reforming Urban High Schools*. Thousand Oaks, CA: Corwin Press.

Lukes, S. (1974) *Power: A Radical View*. London: Macmillan.

Massey, D. (1993) Power-geometry and a progressive sense of place, in J. Bird, B. Curtis, T. Putnam, G. Robertson and L. Tucker (eds), *Mapping the Futures; Local Cultures, Global Change*. London: Routledge.

Massey, D. (1999) *Power Geometries and the Politics of Space-Time. Hettner Lecture 1998*. Heidelberg: University of Heidelberg.

McDermott, R. (1999) Learning across teams: the role of communities of practice in team organisations, *Knowledge Management Review*, May/June, 32–6.

McGregor (2000a) The challenge of collaboration: what encourages joint work between teachers? BEMAS Research Conference, Robinson College, Cambridge, March.

McGregor, J. (2000b) Travelling together: teachers meeting the challenge of collaboration, *Forum*, 42(1), 15–23.

McGregor, J. (in press) Spatiality and teacher workplace cultures: the department as nexus, in R. Edwards and R. Usher (eds), *Spatiality, Learning and Curriculum*. Greenwood Publishing.

McLaughlin, M. (1993) What matters most in teachers' workplace context? in J. Little and M. McLaughlin (eds), *Teachers' Work: Individuals, Colleagues and Contexts*. New York: Teachers College Press.

McLaughlin, M. and Talbert, J. (2001) *Professional Communities and the Work of High School Teaching*. London: University of Chicago Press.

Nespor, J. (1994) *Knowledge in Motion: Space, Time and Curriculum in Undergraduate Physics and Management*. London: Falmer.

Nias, J., Southworth, G. and Yeomans, R. (1989) *Staff Relationships in the Primary School: A Study of Organisational Cultures*. London: Cassell.

Paechter, C. (2000) *Changing School Subjects*. Buckingham: Open University Press.

Reay, D. and Ball, S.J. (2000) Essentials of female management, *Educational Management and Administration*, 28(2), 145–59.

Retallick, J. (1999) Teachers' workplace learning: towards legitimation and accreditation, *Teachers and Teaching: Theory and Practice*, 5(1), 33–49.

Rose, G. (1999) Performing space, in D. Massey, J. Allen and P. Sarre (eds), *Human Geography Today*. Cambridge: Polity Press.

Sammons, P., Thomas, S. and Mortimore, P. (1997) *Forging Links: Effective Schools and Effective Departments*. London: Paul Chapman Publishing.

Sharp, J., Routledge, P., Philo, C. and Paddison, R. (eds) (2000) *Entanglements of Power: Geographies of Domination and Resistance*. London: Routledge.

Siskin, L. (1994) *Realms of Knowledge: Academic Departments in Secondary Schools*. London: Falmer.

Siskin, L.S. and Little, J.W. (eds) (1995) *The Subjects in Question: Departmental Organisation and the High School*. New York: Teachers College Press.

Talbert, J. (1995) Boundaries of teachers' professional communities in U.S. high schools: power and precariousness of the subject department, in L.S. Siskin and J.W. Little (eds), *The Subjects in Question: Departmental Organisation and the High School*. New York: Teachers College Press.

Wallace, M. and Hall, V. (1997) Towards a cultural and political perspective, in A. Harris, N. Bennett and M. Preedy (eds), *Organisational Effectiveness and Improvement in Education*. Buckingham: Open University Press.

Wenger, E. (1998) *Communities of Practice: Learning, Meaning and Identity*. Cambridge: Cambridge University Press.

Wenger, E. (2000) Communities of practice and social learning systems, *Organization*, 7(2), 225–46.

Wenger, E., McDermott, R. and Snyder, W. (2002) *Cultivating Communities of Practice*. Boston, MA: Harvard Business School Publishing.

# 9

---

# Leaders of Subject Communities

### CHRISTINE WISE

Within English schools there is commonly a role undertaken by a subject specialist known as 'subject leader' or 'middle manager'. These individuals are responsible for an aspect of the academic curriculum and include department heads, faculty heads, curriculum team leaders and cross-curriculum subject co-ordinators. They oversee and lead the teaching and learning, the use of resources and the development of the staff who work within the area. They usually have a tier of management above them and the staff working within the area are considered to be below them in the structure whilst they are working in that role.

A department in an English secondary school is a formal unit of accountability, which is usually organized around a specific subject. However, as Siskin (1994) has argued, and the title of this chapter suggests, a subject can also provide an additional source of identity for teachers over and above that of teacher. This indicates that it might also be helpful to examine the dynamics of departmental leadership from the point of view of the subject unit as a community of practice, and to consider the implications this might have for the role of the subject leader.

Research into leadership within effective schools has shown that it extends beyond the senior management team (Harris, 1999) in what is now becoming referred to as dispersed or distributed leadership. Because of this, it has been increasingly recognized that those at the middle level of leadership or management have a powerful influence over classroom practices (Harris, Busher and Wise, 2001) and are expected to: 'provide professional leadership and management for a subject to secure high quality teaching, effective use of resources and improved standards of learning and achievement for all pupils' (DfES, 2001).

Clearly in most secondary schools the middle manager cannot do this alone so they need to 'secure' high-quality teaching through working with others particularly other teachers. The Department for Education and Skills (DfES) nicely summarizes this with an expectation that the subject leader will: 'Establish clear expectations and constructive working relationships among staff, including

131

team working and mutual support; devolving responsibilities and delegating tasks, appropriately evaluating practice and developing an acceptance of accountability' (DfES, 2001). They do not state to whom the team should feel accountable and this is an important point that we will return to later.

Throughout this chapter the term 'middle manager' will be used to denote individuals acting as academic middle managers, subject leaders and subject managers. It draws on data collected as part of a much wider research project on 'The role of academic middle managers in secondary schools' (Wise, 1999). Some parts of the research were reported in an article specifically on the monitoring role (Wise, 2001) and it is these aspects that will be discussed in some detail here.

Originally the data were analysed assuming a predominately rational bureaucratic model of practice. They will be re-examined here using Wenger's (2000) concept of a 'community of practice' and the potential usefulness of this model will be discussed.

## ROLE SET, ROLE CONFLICT AND THE SUBJECT DEPARTMENT

Central to the original analysis of the data was the concept of role set and the associated concept of role conflict. However, this also provides a potential link to the reconceptualization of the department as a community of practice, so it needs to be outlined briefly here.

An individual's role set is made up of the people whom the role incumbent considers have a legitimate right to influence their decisions and actions whilst acting within that role. This means that an individual may have several different role sets operating concurrently as most people enact more than one role at a time, e.g., teacher, middle manager, parent and partner. The influence may be direct or indirect but it is important that it is viewed as legitimate by the role incumbent otherwise it might be ignored or not acted upon (Howard, 1988, p. 87). Legitimacy might arise from positional authority, subject knowledge, ethical stance or many other sources.

An individual head of department in England might consider some or all of the following to be members of their role set: their subject area colleagues, their senior managers, teachers in other subject areas, pastoral team members, parents, governors, local education authority advisers and inspectors, examination boards, subject associations, local community members and so on. Within this range, however, some will be seen as key members, whose influence is considerable, whilst others are peripheral and of little relevance except, perhaps, in relation to specific tasks or issues.

Wise (1999) found that middle managers considered their subject area team to be the most influential in all areas of decision-making. This was also reflected by their team members who believed themselves to be the most influential group in the middle managers' role set. One middle manager commented: 'It is really, really important to listen to your team's ideas so they have a sense of purpose and being part of it … a shared responsibility' (Wise, 2001, p. 337).

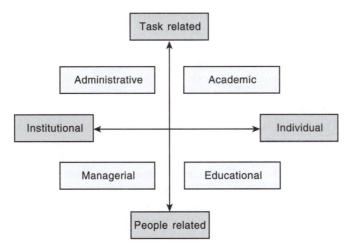

**Figure 9.1** ⸳ A classification of the tasks of the academic middle manager

Wise (1999) also found that middle managers in schools have to contend with conflicting views of their role from their senior managers and their team members. This situation causes role conflict (Handy, 1993, p. 65; Hargreaves, 1975, p. 54) where the different roles the individual is being asked to fulfil are not compatible. With respect to monitoring, for example, the team members are viewed by the middle managers as having the greater legitimate influence over their decisions but the team members are resistant to the idea of monitoring of performance. On the other hand, the senior managers expect monitoring to be taking place and have greater positional authority within the hierarchical structure. In the research (Wise, 1999) the middle managers used the lack of time, expertise and experience as a way of avoiding the conflict and did not, in general, engage in direct monitoring of their team members' performance.

## NORMATIVE ROLE OF THE MIDDLE MANAGER

The exact tasks undertaken by a middle manager vary from school to school, subject to subject, individual to individual but it is possible to draw up a normative list of tasks that are usually undertaken by the majority of middle managers in secondary schools.

In Wise (1999) a classification for these tasks was derived from the work of other writers (e.g., Bailey, 1973; Bennett, 1995; Brydson, 1983; Hughes, 1985; Lambert, 1972; Morris and Dennison, 1982). The model is based on there 'being a continuum between people and things as one dimension and a continuum between institutional and individual aspects as the other dimension' (Wise, 1999, p. 63) which gives four quadrants as shown in Figure 9.1.

These quadrants were called Administrative, Academic, Educational and Managerial for ease of reference and also in part because of the type of tasks that would fall within them. The Academic tasks would be those associated with the organizational paperwork directly supporting the learning of the pupils, such as schemes of work and homework policies, whilst the Administrative tasks would involve the paperwork and administration associated with the whole-school role, such as managing finance and the stock of resources. The Educational quadrant would contain tasks like teaching, liaising with parents and other more people-related aspects of the role, whilst the Managerial quadrant would be those aspects of the role directly associated with the staff within the middle manager's area. Tasks likely to fall within this area are monitoring the progress of students on teaching practice and newly qualified teachers (NQTs) in their induction year, promoting and planning the professional development of staff within the area, deployment of staff to take advantage of strengths, leading and motivating the subject team, co-ordinating the work of the department and monitoring progress through the curriculum.

Each of these quadrants requires a different range of skills on the part of the middle manager. Those in the upper two quadrants require organizational ability, commitment of plans and policies to paper, financial aptitude and other predominately non-person centred skills.

The tasks within the Educational quadrant require the person-centred skills usually expected of a teacher, relating to students and their parents. This is an area where a middle manager might be expected to be exemplary if they are to gain the respect of their subject area colleagues. Descriptions of the subject leader's duties as 'leading from the front', 'leading by example' and being the 'leading professional' all expect the middle manager to be able to demonstrate ability in the 'art' of teaching usually across a range of abilities and ages of students. Their classroom management and use of resources might be expected to provide a model for others to follow. Except where they have a classroom assistant attached to the class, they are working alone with the students, their interpersonal relationships are with individuals who are there to learn. The role is one which they are trained to adopt, are assessed competent in before they are given qualified teacher status and makes up the majority of their working week.

In contrast, their 'Management' role requires interpersonal skills with colleagues who for most of the working week would be considered to be their equals. Some individuals may have been teaching longer, may be senior in the hierarchy or may be more qualified. The middle managers are expected to negotiate access to lessons to monitor what is being taught and how, manage the individuals' professional development in line with perceived weaknesses or with departmental needs and lead curriculum development through persuading colleagues of the benefits.

These are a very different set of interpersonal skills and they are ones in which the new middle manager may have received very little training or guidance. In practice many approach colleagues as they would like to be approached and others simply avoid this area of their responsibility (Wise, 1999). This has been seen as a major problem for a number of years (Ribbins, 1985; Stokes, 1981) and was certainly frowned upon by the Chief Inspector of Schools (1997, p. 14). It may be that an alternative viewpoint that is less hierarchical than the one assumed in the normative model just outlined could help address this issue.

## MONITORING AND THE SUBJECT LEADER

The resistance to change of subject areas and departments has long been a problem to those wanting to implement change in secondary schools (Leask and Terrell, 1997). Monitoring could be viewed as having an hierarchical accountability function where practice is 'checked' by those further up the structure. It is a process where the middle manager, in a bureaucratic structure, checks on the work of the rest of the subject area team to ensure they are carrying out their role as agreed or, often, as instructed. This might involve checking that books are being marked according to an agreed policy, homework is being set, teaching is being carried out according to the norms of the department and the syllabus is being followed. Some of these tasks the middle managers found easier than others (Wise, 1999).

Within each of the three case study schools involved in the study by Wise (1999) there were comments in the staff handbooks or generic job descriptions which made clear the expectation that the middle managers were responsible for monitoring the teaching within their area of responsibility.

It was left to the departments to define quality within their subject area although in one school there were guidelines as to what might be expected of all teachers in the classroom. In practice very few team members were required to show any records or plans to their middle managers and virtually none had experienced any direct observation of their teaching. Indeed, one teacher commented that they had entered a profession and expected to be trusted to work unsupervised. One middle manager commented that '[Monitoring] definitely would be a priority if it wasn't seen as a threat' (Wise, 2001, p. 338). Within the current career structure in England, for example, with classroom observation such an important part of the performance management process, this attitude is unlikely to change unless the purposes and outcomes of monitoring are discussed and agreed.

It is perhaps significant that in many of the departments involved in the research (Wise, 1999) there was no system in place for the middle manager to be observed.

## COMMUNITY OF PRACTICE

A 'community of practice' is a social learning system. According to Wenger (2000, p. 226) competence is both historically and socially defined and is in interplay with our personal experience. When this interplay is in tension, learning takes place (Wenger, 2000, p. 227) and thus our personal development is entwined with the social structures we belong to.

There are three modes of 'belonging' to social learning systems which Wenger (2000, p. 227) posits can be used to define a community. All three coexist but in varying proportions. The first mode is that of 'engagement' which is where working together, producing artefacts, or helping a colleague, shapes our experience of who we are, what we can do and how the world responds to us. The second mode is that of 'imagination'. This is an awareness of a wider community which it is possible only to imagine but within which we might wish to orientate ourselves, such as a nation or the community of science teachers. We cannot know every individual so it requires an act of imagination to place ourselves within it. The third mode of belonging Wenger calls 'alignment', which is the process of aligning our practice with those outside our immediate engagement. This is not a one-way process but one of mutual co-ordination.

Wenger (2000, p. 229) relates our need to participate in communities of practice as 'essential to our learning' and 'at the very core of what makes us human beings'. This is because they are the building blocks of social learning and are the means by which we define competence 'through an experience of direct participation'. They do this, first, by having a collective sense of what the community is about, secondly by interaction, establishing norms and, thirdly, by having a 'shared repertoire' of language, artefacts, history and practices.

In a sense then, a community of practice is about establishing norms that the members conform to, the learning converges, but taken to the limits this would lead to stagnation and would not be about social learning. However, this scenario assumes a fixed boundary with no input from outside the community, which in practice does not happen. At the boundaries, the community is challenged and its learning enhanced, it diverges into new experiences, competencies and practices (Wenger, 2000, p. 233).

By reflecting on the strength of feeling of most middle managers in the research (Wise, 1999) that their colleagues within their own subject area team were their biggest influence it can be seen that there is evidence of a community of practice within most departments or subject areas. This has important implications for schools whose senior managers would normally consider the hierarchical, positional authority of the senior management team to be the strongest influence (Wise, 1999).

The fact that the senior managers were the next most influential group is possibly a sign that the belonging through imagination is weaker and as such might leave the subject area isolated from the wider community. This is evident in schools when some departments are referred to by others as 'mavericks' or as one middle manager described the departments in her school, as 'satellite stations' (Wise, 1999).

However it might also be considered as an internal alignment relationship. The process of alignment is very important in secondary schools with the external accountability of examinations, but there is also the concept of internal alignment with agreed policies and other colleagues or subject areas within the school. The department or subject area effectively has a boundary with the whole-school community which will have its own rules of engagement and judgements of competence. However, alignment is not a matter of just accepting the opinions of others; it is more a process of negotiation to come to somewhere near common agreement. This practice can be observed at many heads of department or middle management meetings where ideas are often loudly and energetically discussed! There are often 'trade-offs' at the whole-school level that allow subject areas to gain some benefit in return for 'falling into line' on another issue.

Within the bureaucratic hierarchical model of management the middle manager is expected to use their positional authority to effect change but behind the closed doors of the classroom they can only rely on occasional monitoring visits to check if their instructions are being carried out. How might this be different if the department or subject area is analysed as a community of practice? From Wenger's (2000) point of view, the community of practice is unlikely to have a single leader who would suffer all the role conflict. Whilst he accepts the need for a 'community co-ordinator' who takes care of the day-to-day work, he also puts forward the idea that the community needs several other forms of leadership which may be enacted by one or two members or widely distributed.

By 'dispersing' the responsibility for 'policing' the performance of the subject area team the extent of the conflict for any one member could be reduced. In the early days of the community it might be necessary for this to be formalized, but gradually this would become a natural action for certain members over particular issues. One member of the community might be responsible for a particular development and would monitor its progress through implementation. Another member of the community might be responsible for leading enactment of whole-school policies within the area and would monitor their functioning. In this way, the designated leader of the area, that is the person labelled by the structure, might be only responsible for monitoring a small part of the work of the subject or area. On other occasions they would be a colleague being observed or monitored.

The leader for each aspect would be likely to be the one judged by the community to have the greatest competence in that area and would therefore have the authority of expertise, which professionals have greater respect for than positional authority. The community members would be the ones judging the competence and, therefore, would charge the leader of that aspect with pursuing the decision of the community; they would be the leading professional on that aspect rather than the professional leader (Wise, 1999).

How does this model of a department working as a community take account of the expectations of external agencies that might have legitimate authority as well as membership of overlapping communities with possibly conflicting norms.

## BOUNDARIES

It is at the boundaries of their subject area that the legitimacy of the role senders diminishes for the middle managers (Wise, 1999). They view the influence of those outside the immediate team to be less valid. However, they do regularly have to interact across the boundaries in their role as a middle manager and in other roles. They are usually part of another team (or possible community) when they meet with other heads of department or subject leaders, yet another team when they are acting as a pastoral tutor, and another again outside the parameters of their school when they meet with other subject specialists at training sessions or examination meetings. In all these circumstances the middle manager's understanding of their role is questioned and their competence challenged.

If the subject area is thought of as a community of practice then these boundary engagements are important and the challenge they pose must be addressed. It might be necessary for the designated leader to set up meetings or opportunities for engagement that allowed the community members, or a subset of them, to discuss the challenge and consider how it might 'fit in' with existing community norms, how the norms might need to adjust to accommodate the challenge or, indeed, how they might challenge the expectation. If, for example, a whole-school change was found to be at odds with the norms within the department which were heavily influenced by the norms of a larger community, such as a subject association, and the process of negotiation did not lead to an acceptable situation for the community, then the change would risk being ignored (Figure 9.2). Minimal compliance or even undermining might follow this, placing the community at odds with the wider community within the organization but strengthening their sense of identity with each other.

Of course, a sort of boundary might appear within the subject area where one or more subject specialists is not prepared to accept all the norms of the remainder of the community. They might be marginalized as individuals, or where their practice was at variance it would be open to greater scrutiny. The situation would be much the same for a new member who was going through the process of being socialized into the ways and norms of the community and considered to have legitimate peripheral participation. In both cases the individuals concerned would offer learning opportunities to the community because there might be questioning of accepted practices or introduction of new ideas for consideration. What might have initially been a clash of ideals might lead to new norms for the community.

Research has suggested (McGregor, Chapter 8, this volume) that there is often more commonality between the same subject departments across a range of schools than there is between different subject departments within the one school. This is evidence of the strong community that can exist within subject specialists. This may derive from their original study of the subject (Siskin, 1994) and affect the way they think and view the world, which will have an impact on their approach to the teaching of their subject.

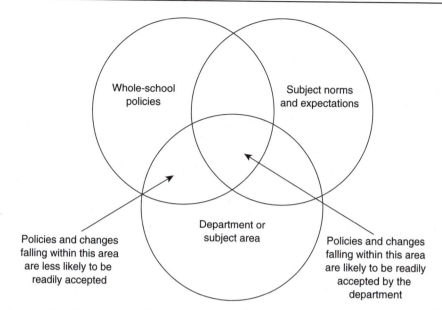

**Figure 9.2**   The norms of the overlapping communities of practice affecting a department or subject area

An example of this would be science teaching, which is frequently carried out in mixed-ability classes in an integrated way. Here there might be a number of subject specialists teaching a subject they are less familiar with for a large amount of the time. For this reason, the normal classroom autonomy of the teacher is often forsaken in return for assistance with teaching the non-specialist area. The acceptance of a variety of leaders is a natural consequence of the integrated nature of the subject. There has to be, however, a fundamental understanding of what the core task is, arrived at through a process of negotiation. The teachers cannot change their approach with each change in subject, so there has to be a sense in which they work together to achieve the outcomes they have agreed upon.

## MONITORING IN A COMMUNITY OF PRACTICE

How might viewing the department as a community of practice help with carrying out this important task?

> People must know each other well enough to know how to interact productively and who to call for help or advice. They must trust each other, not just personally, but also in their ability to contribute to the enterprise of the community, so they feel comfortable addressing real problems together and speaking truthfully.

(Wenger, 2000, p. 230)

The expectation that the department or subject area might work together is not new (Tyldesley, 1984). Donnelly (1990, p. 11) noted that 'the main task of the head of department in the 1990's is to lead staff towards the realisation of a common vision'. Whose common vision is a question that might be raised, and how common, because even within a community of practice the result of the negotiations is unlikely to be completely consensual agreement. The DfES (2001) similarly assumes consensual agreement at some level. It sees the middle manager's role as ensuring all the members of the team behave according to expected and agreed standards, so that a student receives more or less the same experience of a subject regardless of who teaches them. How these standards are communicated will vary according to the expectations of the organization, the team and the middle manager him or herself but usually they are, after a process of discussion, written down as departmental, subject area or similar policy document. It is then, in a bureaucratic structure, the middle manager's responsibility to ensure that they are carried out. The members are held accountable to the policy and their practice is compared to it. How effective this monitoring can be is questionable when only a small proportion of the teaching year can be observed.

In a community of practice this would be seen as a more shared responsibility. Monitoring would be carried out by perhaps every member of the community to help members better reach the ideals negotiated. Where there was disagreement about whether practice seen was in line with agreed norms there would be the opportunity for discussion and development, rather than a punitive measure as might be envisaged in the bureaucratic structure. The monitoring is seen as a developmental learning experience, a chance to share practice rather than be checked on. In this way, the impact might last beyond the immediate observation and, indeed, observation might be sought when new ideas were being tried.

There is a sense in which all monitoring could be said to be about accountability but it is significant who they are accountable to, what they are accountable for and what the outcome will be. If accountability is to their community for agreed norms and values for development purposes, then possibly the process would become less threatening. A good example of this being attempted was in a department in one of the case study schools (Wise, 1999) where the head of department was a young, inexperienced teacher who had a large number of senior staff in his department. They had a system which was more about mutual learning. To avoid conflict he had instituted an arrangement whereby every member of the department observed the teaching of every other member of the department during the course of the year. This led to very stimulating discussions at the departmental meetings when ideas and observations were fed back into the group. This sort of arrangement, a change in purpose for monitoring, could reduce the conflict for the middle manager.

## THE WAY FORWARD

The expectation that middle managers will monitor the teaching of their subject area team on a regular basis has long been established. It has not been accepted by the middle managers as a legitimate expectation for all that time but there is evidence that, even though it is now accepted, it is still not being done (Wise, 1999). Of course 'performance management' in England has made them observe their team members at least once a year, but there is a vast difference between this snapshot and the sort of monitoring of performance that is required to ensure consistent quality and uniformity of experience. This latter type of monitoring could be viewed as part of the engagement process of a community of practice where they develop shared language, repertoires and so on.

When the pressures on the middle manager not to monitor are considered it is not surprising that they avoid the issue. The group within their role set they consider to have the most legitimate power, their team members, is perceived as not expecting to be monitored and, indeed, some are actually hostile to the notion (Wise, 1999). This does, however, cause great role conflict as they know they are expected to monitor by their senior managers who have positional authority within the school structure.

Many training courses currently on offer to middle managers do no more than raise their awareness of what they should be doing. Others, undertaken over a longer period of time, develop the knowledge and understanding of what is required but few impact on the behaviour of the middle manager in their school environment (Harris, Busher and Wise, 2001).

How can the concept of communities of practice help? First, middle managers would need to be made aware of the concept of communities of practice and then given the opportunity to develop their knowledge and understanding. This is necessary so that problems such as the stagnation of the community through isolation from learning at its boundaries are actively avoided.

If the development of a community was seen as being beneficial, there would need to be time for the dialogue to be undertaken that develops shared understandings and resources. Within the current climate in English schools this could not be expected to happen in the margins of participants' time. There are some doubts as to whether a community of practice can be formalized in this way, part of a planned process, but without the time they can never happen at all. There could perhaps, in the first instance, be a policy developed to establish guidelines for monitoring to take place and a division of labour across the community, perhaps each person monitoring a different aspect of the agreed working practices of the community.

Another reason for not participating in monitoring is lack of time (Wise and Bush, 1999). By relieving the middle manager of the sole responsibility for monitoring, some of the problem might be removed. However, the development of shared understanding, trust and sense of commitment will take time to develop and nurture. The concept of the subject area or departmental team as a community of practice may remove some of the unwelcome bureaucratic imposition of traditional monitoring practices but it does not reduce the level of responsibility for the nominated leader or community co-ordinator. Instead of doing the tasks themselves, they are responsible for leading the community of professionals into a realm of common understanding, respect and practice. They would need to lead the negotiation process in the first instance particularly at the boundaries. This could require a whole new range of skills for many.

## REFERENCES

Bailey, P. (1973) The functions of heads of departments in comprehensive schools, *Journal of Educational Administration and History*, 5(1), 52–8.

Bennett, N. (1995) *Managing Professional Teachers: Middle Management in Primary and Secondary Schools*. London: Paul Chapman Publishing.

Brydson, P. (1983) *Head of Departments and Self-evaluation*. Hull: University of Hull, Institute of Education.

Chief Inspector of Schools (1997) *Subject Management in Secondary Schools: Aspects of Good Practice*. London: OFSTED.

Department for Education and Skills (DfES) (2001) *Teaching Standards Framework*. London: DfEs.

Donnelly, J. (1990) *Middle Managers in Schools and Colleges*. London: Kogan Page.

Handy, C.B. (1993) *Understanding Organisations*. London: Penguin Books.

Hargreaves, D.H. (1975) *Interpersonal Relations and Education*. London: Routledge and Kegan Paul.

Harris, A. (1999) *Effective Subject Leadership in Secondary Schools*. London: David Fulton.

Harris, A., Busher, H. and Wise, C. (2001) Effective training for subject leaders, *Journal of In-service Education*, 27(1), 83–94.

Howard, T. (1988) Theoretical and professional perspectives of management in secondary schools with special reference to teachers' perceptions of middle management, unpublished MA thesis, University of Durham.

Hughes, M. (1985) Leadership in professionally staffed organisations, in M. Hughes, P. Ribbins and H. Thomas, *Managing Education: The System and The Institution*. London: Holt Rinehart and Winston.

Lambert, K. (1972) The role of the head of department in schools, unpublished MA(Ed) thesis, University of Southampton.

Leask, M. and Terrell, I. (1997) *Development Planning for Middle Managers*. London: Kogan Page.

Morris, T. and Dennison, W.F. (1982) The role of the comprehensive school head of department analysed, in *Research in Education*, 28, 37–48.

Ribbins, P. (1985) The role of the middle manager in the secondary school, in M. Hughes, P. Ribbins and H. Thomas, *Managing Education: The System and the Institution*. London: Holt Rinehard and Winston.

Siskin, L.E. (1994) *Realms of Knowledge: Academic Departments in Secondary Schools*. London: Falmer.

Stokes, P. (1981) Monitoring the work of teachers, in M. Marland and S. Hill (eds), *Departmental Management*. London: Heinnemann Educational.

Tyldesley, N. (1984) New directions in departmental leadership, in P. Harling (ed.), *New Directions in Educational Leadership*. Lewes: Falmer.

Wenger, E. (2000) Communities of practice and social learning systems, *Organization*, 7(2), 225–46.

Wise, C. (2001) The monitoring role of the academic middle manager in secondary schools, *Educational Management and Administration*, 29(3), 333–41.

Wise, C.S. (1999) The role of academic middle managers in secondary schools, unpublished PhD thesis, University of Leicester.

Wise, C. and Bush, T. (1999) From teacher to manager: the role of the academic middle manager in secondary schools, *Educational Research*, 41(2), 183–95.

# 10

---

# Understanding Curriculum Leadership in the Secondary School

JOHN O'NEILL

## INTRODUCTION

Seventy years ago, Willard Waller argued the need to portray the complex social world of the school in concrete fashion. In his terms, 'to be concrete is to present materials in such a way that characters do not lose the qualities of persons, nor situations their intrinsic human quality' (Waller, 1932, Preface). For Waller, the analysis of typical practices drawn from the routine work of the school could provide greater insights for teachers and school executives. In turn, knowledge about the complexities of schools might encourage 'real' or 'natural' manifestations of personal leadership based on an understanding of how schools actually function as social 'organisms' as opposed to the 'formal' leadership 'of the person who must be a leader because of the position he (*sic*) holds' (*ibid.*, p. 446).

Much of what has been written about educational leadership since then has failed to provide any further understanding of the 'tangled web of interrelationships' such as those which Waller explored in his study of American high schools in the 1930s. This collection of essays is one indication of the pressing need to challenge theoretical and methodological orthodoxies in the study of educational leadership. These orthodoxies have been dominated by what Ogawa and Bossert (1995) call a technical-rational perspective. According to Grace (1993, p. 354) such analyses of educational leadership suffer from 'reductionist tendencies'. They focus on identifying and proselytizing any behaviours and dispositions that appear to offer the potential to more efficiently lubricate the implementation at school level of centrally mandated policies. In doing so, they ignore the historical, cultural, moral and political economies of schooling within which individuals and groups of educators seek possibilities for exerting greater control and self-determination of their work (Foster, 1986).

143

The failure of orthodox conceptions of educational leadership is evident in the emergence of a supposedly 'new' educational leadership research orientation that acknowledges the socially constructed, fluid nature of educational practice. Morley and Hosking (Chapter 3 in this volume) refer to their version of this new orientation as 'a social psychology of organizing'. The related concept of 'communities of practice' has recently come to symbolize the tenor of the new leadership research wherein the phenomenon of 'leadership' is no longer regarded as something abstract and reified but may only be articulated and enacted in social settings through the talk and relationships (i.e., the practice) of people who engage in common purposeful activities (i.e., the community). In this chapter, I consider specifically the work of Etienne Wenger, arguably the most influential contemporary authority on communities of practice (Wenger, 1998; Wenger, McDermott and Snyder, 2002).

However, a social psychology of organizing or community of practice metaphor can pay insufficient attention to the cultural, political, historical and occupational contexts in which social practice unfolds. In the case of curriculum leadership, talk and social practice occur within workgroup and school settings that are shaped in quite specific ways by both contemporary and historical *education* policy texts: curriculum, pedagogy, assessment and their management to name but a few. Work such as that of Morley and Hosking and Wenger can therefore generate only partial insights on educational practice precisely because the educational context is incidental rather than integral to the analysis. In contrast, the broader policy scholarship approaches discussed in this chapter demand that the analysis of the social practices of teaching and curriculum leadership be undertaken in the relational settings of specifically educational talk and work. Decontextualized analyses also fail to articulate fully and explicitly the relationship between knowledge, power and educational practice. In terms of this chapter's focus, there is a pressing need to consider important questions such as whose definitions of 'curriculum leadership' dominate talk and work in real educational settings, how have these become embedded in day-to-day workgroup practices and why have they become common-sense or taken-for-granted assumptions about the way that teachers ought to interact with each other?

This chapter is based on a study of teacher and curriculum development that sought a deeper understanding of how teachers develop their practice (O'Neill, 2001). I did not begin the study with any fixed assumptions about what 'curriculum leadership' in secondary schools would or should be but, instead, wanted to understand, from their positions and experiences (Bourdieu, 1996; Habermas, 1990), how the practitioners in the four secondary schools in the study conceptualized and went about their day-to-day work, and how those in formal positions of authority contributed to its development. In this sense, my approach was consistent with the social constructionist positions of both Morley and Hosking (Chapter 3 in this volume) and Wenger (1998) according to which concepts such as 'curriculum leadership' are not objective practices but, rather, they are produced and sustained intersubjectively by the collective talk and work of people who come together to engage with purpose in common social activities. However, the really crucial point to be argued in this chapter is that this talk and work does not take place in some antiseptic social 'bubble'. There is a complex of official policies and regulations at work as well as institutional, workgroup and classroom norms. Teachers negotiate these on a daily basis and it is only as they do so that the concepts of 'teaching' and 'curriculum leadership' come to have any substantive meaning for those involved.

The chapter continues below with a brief overview of the study itself, followed by a discussion of the theoretical approach taken. I then reconsider the theoretical framework with specific regard to Wenger's work on 'communities of practice' and critique any impact the latter might have on the study of educational leadership in practice.

## CURRICULUM LEADERSHIP IN SECONDARY SCHOOLS

My study examined teacher and curriculum development in New Zealand in the period of intense curriculum policy reform of the mid-1990s.

The study attempted to understand the constraints within which secondary school teachers conduct their work and how they seek to exercise their individual and collective agency in order to gain more control and knowledge of their occupational circumstances. The study linked contemporary dilemmas of practice to longer standing, embedded tensions of curriculum content, pedagogy and assessment. It identified continuities and discontinuities of secondary schooling practice in the decades since the 1940s and showed how contemporary policy options and proposed solutions were simply the latest staging post in a protracted sequence of political efforts to solve 'problems' of curriculum and credentialling.

In some respects, the official policy texts introduced in the 1990s spoke directly to teachers' own pragmatic concerns and aspirations. Thus, teachers and curriculum leaders engaged creatively and energetically with the challenges posed by official trials of internally assessed qualifications in the senior secondary school because these appeared to offer the opportunity to end secondary teachers' long search for meaningful alternatives to examination-dominated schemes of work, assessments and credentials. However, curriculum innovation always took place alongside other day-to-day routines and seasonal patterns of work. For curriculum leaders in my study, these multiple demands meant that any potential benefits of voluntary curriculum innovation had constantly to be weighed against its costs in terms of other workgroup priorities, the energies and dispositions of fellow workgroup members and their personal health and well-being.

My approach echoed the aims and methods of Waller in the 1930s and is consistent with that of a considerable body of scholarship in education. However, the methods and findings of such scholarship are rarely mentioned in the contemporary 'educational management studies' (Grace, 1993) literature that continues to be dominated by the technical-rational approach. This omission is puzzling not least because the broader policy analysis approaches described below appear to afford teachers and researchers the opportunity to gain the sort of deeper and keener understandings of the 'richness of interactions, exchanges of meaningful information, and shared learning' that Wenger (1998, p. 261) argues are the features of true 'communities of practice'.

## ANALYSING CURRICULUM LEADERSHIP IN CONTEXT

In this part of the chapter, I argue that the range of 'education policy scholarship' approaches I drew on for my study offers insights on aspects of educational practice such as teaching and curriculum leadership that go beyond those provided by analyses using 'communities of practice' or a 'social psychology of organizing' metaphor. In doing this, it is important to explain the specific usage here of key terms such as 'policy', 'text' and 'discourse'.

A number of educational researchers have attempted the analysis of contemporary practice within its lived political, cultural and historical contexts. Common to almost all the examples discussed below is a consideration of the relationship between knowledge and power: how historical practices and power relations constitute contemporary social arenas within which certain forms of language, knowledge and practice are conceptualized, articulated, allowed, preferred and regulated, while others are marginalized, silenced or excluded (Foucault, 1980). The essential point to be made is that these approaches are, like teaching and learning, 'supremely contextual' (Kliebard, 2002, p. 137) in that they require the researcher to examine the effects of particular education policy texts at specific configurations of time and place. Consequently, the meaning and purpose of educational or curriculum leadership also come under critical scrutiny and cannot simply be taken as given. It is not possible, therefore, to use such research – as much of the orthodox and 'new' educational leadership literatures both attempt – to abstract readily generalizable principles of leadership action or 'recipes for what to do in particular circumstances' (*ibid.*), in other quite different policy contexts and institutional settings.

## POLICY SCHOLARSHIP

In his study of school leadership, Grace makes a sharp distinction between what he calls the 'policy science' and the 'policy scholarship' approach (Grace, 1995; 1998). The former is concerned with the identification of specific leadership behaviours through supposedly value-free and objective research. The latter, in direct contrast, seeks actively to understand the practice of leadership in its historical context on the basis that 'many contemporary historical problems or crises in education are, in themselves, the surface manifestations of deeper historical, structural and ideological contradictions in education policy' (Grace, 1995, p. 3). Grace argues that what is 'relevant here is a commitment to locate the matter under investigation in its historical, theoretical, cultural and socio-political setting and a commitment to integrate these wider relational features with contemporary fieldwork data. In this sense policy scholarship is used as an essay in wider and deeper understanding' (*ibid.*). Grace eschews a reductionist, predictive science of individual leadership behaviour in favour of a complex, historically grounded critical analysis of how, in his case, English headteachers engage with enduring moral, ethical and practical dilemmas amidst a shifting, interventionist policy terrain.

Grace's critical scholarship approach is based on the social theory framework of Fay (1975, in Grace, 1998). Fay suggests that a critical social science must (a) uncover the historically embedded nature of flaws in the social order; (b) develop theories which demonstrate the structural contradictions that underpin these flaws; (c) produce theories that speak to and in the language and experiences of the social actors involved; and (d) be illuminative and educative for the social actors involved rather than manipulative of them.

Thus in terms of understanding curriculum leadership, we might want to ask questions such as: which dilemmas is the official model of curriculum leadership intended to address? And, how have these dilemmas come to be as they are?

## POLICY ETHNOGRAPHY

Using a complementary approach to Grace, Smyth and Shacklock analysed the regulative effects for teachers of the accreditation processes they must go through to secure 'Advanced Skills Teacher' (AST) status in Australia. The authors identified four competing discourses of teaching 'on and about' the AST initiative, which they called 'official', 'preferred', 'resistant' and 'indigenous' (Smyth and Shacklock 1998, p. 10), and examined 'the clash' between these. Moreover, the authors 'consider it important that teachers have the opportunity to access discourses about their work which counter the constraints by drawing upon language and conceptual apparatuses different to those that see teaching primarily as economic work' (*ibid.*, p. 197). To facilitate this, they set out to 'develop a conversation between the macro-forces shaping teachers' work and the specific micro-forces as lived and experienced by teachers in their everyday lives as workers' (*ibid.*, p. 6). Indeed, the axiology of the study was explicitly political in that the authors 'believe there is a pressing need for accounts of what is happening to teaching that enable teachers to reclaim the voices/discourses/practices of schools' (*ibid.*, p. 27). In attempting to meld together topical, localized teachers' accounts with a critical analysis of the macro forces of structural adjustment as these shaped the development of the AST initiative, the authors described their work as an exercise in 'policy ethnography'. On the basis that policy development is always 'a contested struggle over "representation" and "exclusion" of particular viewpoints and sets of interests culminating in temporary truces or uneasy settlements' (*ibid.*, p. 29), they wanted to explore:

what happened when authorities sought to impose a (well-meaning) policy on teachers from which they had been excluded during formulation. We were also interested in the response of teachers as they came to understand what this policy meant for them in the context of their work, and how much they were prepared to tolerate a redefinition of their teaching.

(*Ibid.*)

Consequently, as researchers we might want to ask questions such as: whose definition of curriculum leadership is being used in schools? Or, how do teachers talk about curriculum leadership in their day-to-day work?

## POLICY SOCIOLOGY

Smyth and Shacklock draw on Ball's studies of 'policy sociology' in which he construes educational reform as a complex discursive struggle for ascendancy. For Ball (1990; 1994), this complexity demands that we conceptualize more clearly what 'policy' is if we are to study its constituent processes, contexts and effects. He makes a distinction between policy as text and policy as discourse. Policy texts, he argues, are 'interventions in practice'. Although they encourage certain readings and reactions, texts vary in the degree to which they intentionally allow for local interpretation and adaptation. Those who produce policy documents cannot directly control how policy as text is read, interpreted and responded to locally because: 'a response must still be put together, constructed in context, offset against other expectations. All of this involves creative social action, not robotic activity. Thus, the enactment of texts relies on things like commitment, understanding, capability, resources, practical limitations, cooperation and (importantly) intertextual compatibility' (Ball, 1990, pp. 18–19).

The mediation of policy texts is a social process that hinges on language and communication. To reflect this Ball articulates a conception of policy as discourse wherein policy texts circulate in social (or educational) spaces as one 'voice' in a cacophony of competing claims for power and influence in the shaping of practice. Drawing on the work of Michel Foucault, Ball notes that discourses are 'about what can be said, and thought, but also about who can speak, when, where and with what authority. Discourses embody meaning and social relationships, they constitute both subjectivity and power relationships' (Ball, 1990, p. 17). Discourses, then, articulate, shape and constrain what may be thought, said and done. Educational policies as textual interventions are attempts to change the ways in which teachers, or curriculum leaders, or students, as 'subjects' think, act and interact. Thus, argues Ball, ideally, we also need to study 'policy trajectories', i.e., their discursive effects over time in what he calls the contexts of 'influence', 'policy text production', 'practice', 'outcomes' and 'political strategy' (Ball, 1994, pp. 26–7).

Here, we might want to consider, for example, how officially promulgated models of curriculum leadership are intended to change teachers' behaviour and thinking and the extent to which, in reality, practitioners actually comply with official expectations of 'good practice'.

## POLICY ARCHAEOLOGY

Also drawing liberally on a Foucaultian framework, Scheurich (1997) takes this policy 'trajectory' notion a stage further in his 'policy archaeology'. Scheurich criticizes existing approaches to policy studies which, he argues, take for granted the construction of social problems (real or symbolic) as if they were 'medical diseases' for which solutions, in the form of policy, are proposed. Yet for Scheurich, existing approaches fail 'to question or critique the "natural" emergence of social problems' (*ibid.*, p. 26). Scheurich asks us to consider why and how certain aspects of social or educational practice become identified and named as problems in the first place, and others not. This becomes the first of his four 'arenas of study or focus', namely 'the study of the social construction of specific education and social problems' (*ibid.*, p. 27). The second, and most abstract, he calls the 'social regularities arena' in which he seeks to identify the tacit networks of 'regularities' and 'rules of formation' that constitute the historically specific conditions which allow a range of education problems and policy options to be identified. Third, is the policy solution arena that similarly 'involves the study of how the range of possible policy choices is shaped by the grid of social regularities' (*ibid.*, p. 101). Fourth, is a critical examination of the social regularities that constitute policy studies itself as a field of practice. Scheurich then applies each of the stages to some real educational 'problems', for example, the development of integrated health, welfare and social services as a policy solution to the perceived problem of underachievement among 'target groups' of poor, ethnic minority and single-parent children.

In the context of this chapter, we might usefully consider both the emergence of 'leadership' as a solution to the 'problem' of 'ineffective' schools and the continuing reluctance in many contemporary educational leadership discourses to engage with the literature on critical policy scholarship (Smyth, 1993).

## CRITICAL DISCOURSE ANALYSIS

Drawing on discourse theory, Luke claims that 'many educational analyses have difficulty showing how large-scale social discourses are systematically (or for that matter unsystematically) manifest in everyday talk and writing in local sites' (Luke, 1995, p. 11). Luke argues that 'every waking moment is caught up in engagement with text of some kind' (*ibid.*, p. 13). Texts are forms of 'language in use'. Language (meanings, statements, words and concepts) infuses social institutions such as schools, the media and government. Language constitutes discourse. The language of discourse makes possible different ways of being, thinking and acting for individuals because 'texts position and construct individuals, making available various meanings, ideas, and versions of the world' (*ibid.*). Language texts, therefore, both liberate and constrain the range of possible identities and behaviours.

A key point is that individuals' freedom to take up or contest positions within such discourses is constrained on the basis of 'their prior experiences with language and texts, their available stock of discourse resources' (*ibid.*, p. 15). Thus, in examining 'curriculum leadership' discourses, both in official texts and everyday workgroup practice, we might want to analyse how teachers respond to specific forms of language use in policy texts and from where, historically, their own forms of analysis and response appear to derive.

## INTERACTIONIST ETHNOGRAPHY

Luke's discussion helpfully focuses on the exercise of individual and collective human agency. This, clearly, is fundamental to any consideration of how teachers collectively define and develop their practice in particular workgroup and school contexts. That said, some of the approaches discussed above may appear to shift our orientation too far from schooling and the exercise of leadership within the 'context of practice' that is a central concern of this chapter. In contrast, in Hammersley's definition of 'interactionist ethnography', the emphasis

> is on researching the experience, perspectives and actions of those involved; teachers, children, students and others. This is to be done not in abstract fashion but by treating perspectives and actions as socially grounded, both in the immediate contexts in which people live and work, and within the wider framework of global society.

> (Hammersley, 1999, p. 2)

For Hammersley, the value of the interactionist perspective in studies of educational practice is that it focuses on the ways in which teachers in schools, workgroups and classrooms respond to the demands of externally imposed educational policy texts: 'In particular, the stress has been on the ways in which teachers have not only managed to sustain their emotional survival, but have also kept open some space to make available crucial opportunities for learning by children and young people' (*ibid.*).

In one sense, the difference articulated here is merely one of perspective, focus or balance. In Hammersley's definition, teachers and their practice 'figure' against a 'background' of policy. In other approaches discussed above, historical, cultural and political contexts are in sharper focus than the more immediate and localized context of practice. Clearly, all these discursive strands of social experience exist and interact. The issue is clarifying the criteria against which decisions may be made about which elements of the phenomena being studied to focus on, which to include, which to exclude, which to choose to give voice to, which to silence; or in Grace's (1998) terms, how do we endeavour to promote the integrity of our research? Moreover, how can we approach our research in such a way as to elicit meaningful data on the discursive articulation and enactment of curriculum leadership in specific educational settings?

## CRITERIA OF INQUIRY

Carspecken (1996, p. 26) argues that all researchers of social practice are interested in 'the same basic things', namely; 'social action (and its patterns)'; 'subjective experiences' and 'conditions influencing action and experience'. However, our 'social ontology', the way we view existence, and the consequent assumptions we make about the social world, suggest particular ways of approaching our research. Indeed, this is as true for Morley and Hosking, and Wenger, and the other contributors to this volume, as it was for me in my study. According to Carspecken, qualitative researchers have a greater need to make these social ontologies explicit because of the range and diversity of options for studying social experience. Below, I set out the criteria of inquiry drawn from the discussion in the previous section that over the course of several years' fieldwork, reading and thinking became clarified and adopted for my study. In doing so, I hope to show that the various policy scholarship approaches just discussed lend themselves to specific and unique ways of examining the phenomenon of curriculum leadership and, to borrow Waller's words from the introduction to this chapter, do so 'in such a way that characters do not lose the qualities of persons, nor situations their intrinsic human quality'.

First, my early contacts with secondary teachers and curriculum leaders whose experiences, beliefs, actions and understandings were occupationally similar but culturally different from mine encouraged me to seek a 'wider and deeper understanding' (Grace, 1995, p. 3) of their practice. To achieve this the study of contemporary teaching practice and its localized challenges in specific work sites needed to be contextualized in the history, politics and culture of teaching in New Zealand.

Second, if the research was to be 'humane' these teachers' voices and experiences needed to form an 'integral part of the analysis' (Grace, 1998, p. 219). I was concerned to ensure also that their own accounts of practice, and of what was important in that practice, rather than my a priori theories, shaped the study.

Third, I wanted to document teachers' 'creative social action' (Ball, 1994, p. 18) in response to central reforms and to assess the extent to which they 'were prepared to tolerate a redefinition of their teaching' (Smyth and Shacklock, 1998, p. 29). In this regard, it was important to identify the various overlapping discourses of teaching, curriculum and management that were in circulation, the 'clashes' between them and teachers' reading of them.

Fourth, the study as a whole would need to examine the origins of selected contemporary educational policy texts, why these were deemed to be important, the discourses they variously interrupted and engendered and their effects, over time, on practice (Scheurich, 1997).

Finally, through the articulation and examination of 'language in use' (Luke, 1995, p. 11) in local sites, it would be possible to explore with these teachers their individual and collective identities and positioning; and how these were 'crafted in the dynamics of everyday life' (*ibid.*, p. 14). A related area of interest here was how teachers 'managed to sustain their emotional survival' (Hammersley, 1999, p. 2) in order to be able both to maintain existing practices and respond to (read, reinterpret, adapt) the demands of new curriculum (content, pedagogy, assessment) and management texts in circulation.

We turn now to consider the application of Wenger's 'community of practice' metaphor to the domain of educational leadership. What, if anything, might a 'new' leadership approach based on a social constructionist conception of teachers' work within schools as 'communities of practice' add to our understanding of the phenomenon of curriculum leadership?

## CURRICULUM LEADERSHIP WITHIN A 'COMMUNITY OF PRACTICE'

It might be helpful to begin by imagining Wenger's work as a textual intervention in a field of practice – to use Ball's term (above) – in this case, the field of educational leadership research. What effect might such a textual intervention have on the study of leadership in educational settings? Will the ideas, metaphors and language it contains materially alter the ways in which the study of curriculum leadership is conceptualized and analysed?

On first inspection, Wenger's widely read 1998 book, *Communities of Practice: Learning, Meaning and Identity*, would appear to offer little of relevance to schooling (it is based on a study of claims processors in the medical insurance industry) and even less to the study of educational or curriculum leadership (leadership merits only two entries in the index of the book). Wenger's work is based on a social theory of learning that comprises four basic premises; first, 'we are social beings', second, 'knowledge is a matter of competence with respect to valued enterprises', third, 'knowing is a matter of participating in the pursuit of such competences' and, fourth, 'meaning is ultimately what learning is to produce' (*ibid.*, 1998, p. 4). In his book, these four premises are numbered, indented within the text and presented as a list. Each numbered point is elaborated briefly with a sentence of comment or example. On the next page in the book there appears a Venn-type diagram of the components of Wenger's social theory of learning. Each of the four parts is then briefly defined in another numbered list that appears below the diagram.

Throughout each chapter the presentation of text is carefully structured to combine diagram, bullet points and lists with constant reiteration and summation of the key points. The book divides into two almost equal parts (the first on 'practice', the second on 'identity'). In each chapter, a lexicon of key terms is defined, elaborated and constantly referred back to in subsequent chapters. Most of the key terminology is Wenger's own and, although the empirical basis of the book is a study of claims processing practice, the discussion is mostly context free.

If one reads the text chapter by chapter from the beginning, the exposition of the argument is precise, clear and logical, leading the reader through; if, however, one jumps in at the middle it can be very difficult to grasp the concepts and terminology he employs.

Wenger's is a curious book, then. His abstract analyses of learning, social practice and individual and communal identity are meticulous, exhaustive, insightful and challenging. It was easy enough to apply Wenger's conceptual frameworks of 'meaning', 'practice', 'community' and 'identity' and the more detailed terminology that accompanied these, to the explanations of their work given by the teachers and curriculum leaders in my study. On revisiting the discussion of curriculum leadership above, it was not difficult to apply specific, clearly defined labels to aspects of individual and collective practice within each of the teacher workgroups. After a while, though, this became an empty exercise inasmuch as it served more to demonstrate that the labels and terminology of his community of practice metaphor could be applied accurately to these teachers' experiences than it did to explain further what was going on within the specific field of teachers' social learning. Wenger's framework confirmed for me that my own analysis appeared sound, but it did not add greatly to my understanding of teaching or curriculum leadership practice.

In a sense, this is not at all surprising. Wenger draws deeply and widely on the disciplines and literatures of the social sciences. However, none of this is evident in the main body of his text. The text itself gives the appearance of being a completely novel framework for organizational analysis that deploys a distinctive set of terms, concepts and schema. It is only in the 20 pages of endnotes and the six pages of bibliography where the text may be firmly and visibly located within a range of social science scholarly traditions.

Ironically, it is this very body of theory and research that is often studiously avoided by those working in the area of educational management and leadership. In education, there already exist significant literatures on the complexities of 'practice' and 'identity' in schooling and on the history, politics and culture of educational administration and leadership. Why should Wenger succeed where others have failed to have their analyses recognized and appropriated by those working in the field of educational leadership?

Arguably, the key lies in the construction of Wenger's text itself. The various terms, concepts, diagrams and schema provide a veneer of ready applicability to complex social situations – including the social processes of schooling within which leadership practices are produced. These frameworks are accessible in a non-threatening way, helping the observer of social practice to unpack and label social interaction in educational settings without being forced to understand its political, historical and cultural provenance. In this regard, the community of practice metaphor may encourage a more sensitive and empathetic analysis of schooling processes and this in itself would be valuable.

However, until and unless those who study educational leadership for a living are prepared to engage more actively with the intellectual traditions that underpin work such as Wenger's (including the established field of educational studies), it is debatable whether our understanding of educational leadership as a form of social practice will progress much further. To put it crudely, the superficial and acritical content of much of the educational management studies literature suggests that the researchers involved may in effect be acting as no more than intellectual camp-followers in each new education policy skirmish. Critical policy scholarship, in contrast, demands a painstaking, reflexive approach to the understanding of educational practice. Anyone who turns to Wenger for a quick fix on educational leadership and its improvement may well find the same.

## CONCLUSION

The different possibilities outlined above have already begun to play themselves out, albeit not yet in education. With two corporate management consultant colleagues, Wenger has recently written a new book, *Cultivating Communities of Practice* (Wenger, McDermott and Snyder, 2002) published by Harvard Business School Press (the title and choice of publisher are not accidental, I think). Ironically, where his 1998 book argued carefully against the reification of management and leadership, and against the possibilities of instrumentally managing a 'community' of human beings, the 2002 book appears to offer advice on precisely how to 'cultivate' organizations and their members as communities. Whereas the 1998 book studiously avoided prescriptions, the 2002 book openly offers 'seven principles for cultivating communities of practice' (Wenger, McDermott and Snyder, 2002, p. 49). 'Management' and 'managers' (including 'champions' and 'sponsors') now merit 16 entries in the index (seven in 1998) and 'leadership' (including 'coordinators' and 'thought leaders') a further 29 (two in 1998). What the authors call 'the conceptual foundations' (*ibid.*, p. xi) are limited to the opening two chapters and the remainder of the book is devoted to the 'cultivation' process. The bibliography for the 1998 book drew widely from the applied and critical social sciences; that for the 2002 book almost exclusively from the management science and organizational theory literature. Ironically, in place of Wenger's idiosyncratic lexicon and decontextualized analysis in 1998, in 2002, the text is organized around standard management concerns such as 'measuring and managing value creation' (Wenger, McDermott and Snyder, 2002, p. 161) and the examples given are all from the corporate and commercial services sectors. In many senses, the 2002 text reads like any other mainstream management and leadership textbook, and the careful and disinterested social science scholarship that underpinned the 1998 text has been excised.

How and why should this happen? Happily, Michael Apple's (1990, pp. 105–22) analysis of the use of management theory in education, specifically in the area of curriculum, is particularly illuminating in this regard.

Apple shows how twentieth-century North American curriculum theorists borrowed *selectively* from systems management theory in order to justify the use of explicit objectives and outcomes in curriculum design. Although done in the interests of 'efficiency', it also firmly established and maintained control of the curriculum in the hands of administrators, not teachers. Significantly, what these 'curriculists' borrowed was not systems theory *in totum*, complete with its disciplinary traditions of intellectual enquiry and conflict, but rather 'educators have borrowed only the language, often only the surface language (what I have called the reconstructed logic) and have, hence, pulled the terminology out of its self-correcting context ... we have yet to learn the dangers of appropriating models from disparate fields and applying them to education' (*ibid.*, p. 113).

Apple's remarks, and the parallel example of the appropriation of Wenger's scholarship for more instrumental purposes should alert us to the dangers of divorcing the study of social practice from specific policy contexts and intellectual traditions. In the case of educational and curriculum leadership, the potential dangers, and solutions, are only too apparent. The study of educational leadership needs to be undertaken within forms of scholarship that require us to locate contemporary social practice within a broader historical, cultural and occupational analysis. Indeed, such approaches would appear essential if we are to approach a more informed and complete understanding of the practice of leadership in educational settings.

## REFERENCES

Apple, M. (1990) *Ideology and Curriculum* (2nd edn). New York: Routledge.

Ball, S. (1990) *Politics and Policy Making in Education: Explorations in Policy Sociology.* London: Routledge.

Ball, S. (1994) *Education Reform: A Critical and Post-structural Approach.* Buckingham: Open University Press.

Bourdieu, P. (1996) Understanding. *Theory, Culture and Society,* **13**(2), 17–37.

Carspecken, P. (1996) *Critical Ethnography in Educational Research.* London: Routledge.

Fay, B. (1975) *Social Theory and Political Practice.* London: George Allen and Unwin.

Foster, W. (1986) *Paradigms and Promises: New Approaches to Educational Administration.* Buffalo, NY: Prometheus.

Foucault, M. (1980) *Power and Knowledge: Selected Interviews and Other Writings.* New York: Pantheon.

Grace, G. (1993) On the study of school leadership: beyond education management, *British Journal of Educational Studies,* **41**(4), 353–65.

Grace, G. (1995) *School Leadership. Beyond Education Management. An Essay in Policy Scholarship.* London: Falmer.

Grace, G. (1998) Critical policy scholarship: reflections on the integrity of knowledge and research, in G. Shacklock and J. Smyth (eds), *Being Reflexive in Critical Educational and Social Research* (pp. 202–17). London: Falmer.

Habermas, J. (1990) *Moral Consciousness and Communicative Action,* trans C. Lenhardt and S. Weber Nicholsen. Cambridge, MA: MIT Press.

Hammersley, M. (1999) Introduction, in M. Hammersley (ed.), *Researching School Experience: Ethnographic Studies of Teaching and Learning* (pp. 1–13). London: Falmer.

Kliebard, H. (2002) *Changing Course: American Curriculum Reform in the 20th Century*. New York: Teachers College Press.

Luke, A. (1995) Text and discourse in education: an introduction to critical discourse analysis, *Review of Research in Education*, **21**, 3–48.

Ogawa, R. and Bossert, S. (1995) Leadership as an organizational quality, *Educational Administration Quarterly*, **31**(2), 224–43.

O'Neill, J. (2001) Shards of teacher and curriculum development in four New Zealand secondary schools, unpublished PhD thesis, Massey University.

Scheurich, J. (1997) *Research Method in the Postmodern*. London: Falmer.

Smyth, J. (ed.) (1993) *A Socially Critical View of the Self-managing School*. London: Falmer.

Smyth, J. and Shacklock, G. (1998) *Remaking Teaching: Ideology, Policy and Practice*. London: Routledge.

Waller, W. (1932) *The Sociology of Teaching*. New York: Wiley.

Wenger, E. (1998) *Communities of Practice: Learning, Meaning and Identity*. Cambridge: Cambridge University Press.

Wenger, E., McDermott, R. and Snyder, W. (2002) *Cultivating Communities of Practice: A Guide to Managing Knowledge*. Boston, MA: Harvard Business School Press.

# SECTION 3

# THE PERSPECTIVES AND PROFESSIONAL DEVELOPMENT

# 11

## Assessing the Impact on Practice of Professional Development Activities

NIGEL BENNETT

### INTRODUCTION

This chapter reviews some data from a pilot study that examined the impact of programmes of leadership and management development on practice in schools (the 'IMPPEL' project). The project sought to disconnect judgements about the impact of development programmes from the programme objectives, and to measure impact from the point of view of participants and their work colleagues. The interviews and data analysis focused on the knowledge, skills and abilities that were expected of leaders and managers by participants in the programmes and their colleagues. In this chapter I shall reanalyse some of the data to examine the potential of institutional theory, as presented by Rodney Ogawa in Chapter 2, when examining the impact on individuals and schools of a particular programme of professional development.

### INSTITUTIONAL THEORY AND THE IMPPEL PROJECT

An analysis of the impact of professional development on professional practice depends on our understanding of practice and the influences that affect it. Ogawa argues that schools and teachers are surrounded by uncertain and contradictory expectations and face uncertainty as to what teaching – education's 'core technology' – involves and requires. Schools as organizations have to resolve these contradictions and help individual teachers cope with the daily uncertainty of their contacts with their students – and one another. Leadership is a key activity in this process, and we have to have a clear picture of where it is located and what it involves. Even this, however, is itself uncertain.

### UNCERTAINTY

Uncertainty exists at both organizational and individual level. Although there is broad agreement about the role of education, this soon breaks down when we start to analyse what this means in practice. This can give rise to arguments about, for example, the relative importance of raising academic achievement compared to generating social cohesion, and governments can introduce policies that favour certain articulations of the role, such as the publication of league tables of academic performance and giving parents the right, in theory, to choose their children's schools. Schools have to respond to the tensions created by these complex pressures, whilst taking account of how other neighbouring schools respond.

Uncertainty also exists as to what are the most effective teaching strategies. 'Best practice' can be argued to be defined in terms of a particular dominant perception of education, or even a dominant academic group, as Bucher and Strauss (1961) demonstrated in relation to medical practice. Such domination can change over time: It could be argued that 'progressive' teaching became 'best practice' in the 1970s through the domination of initial teacher training by specialists in primary education, but that 'traditional' models came back into favour as their secondary colleagues reasserted control.

## KNOWLEDGEABILITY AND CAPABILITY

Discussions of 'best practice', create uncertainty in our minds, questioning existing practice, and making us consider how it might be improved. This uncertainty is, of course, an opportunity for learning about alternatives.

But even when teachers can acquire a 'best practice toolkit' of teaching strategies, they still need to know and when and how to apply the techniques or skills it contains. In Ogawa's terms, this is the combination of knowledgeability and capability that defines the boundaries of practice. 'Knowledgeability' is what enables teachers (or others) to act in ways that they know or believe will produce a similar outcome. It includes personal convictions and understandings as well as 'facts'. Knowledgeability thus combines facts and values as a basis for action. 'Capability' is what ensures that teachers can and do select from among alternative possible acts. Without it, knowledge is useless; equally, it has to rest upon sound knowledge in order to be demonstrable. Capability invests a degree of control of a situation in the individual exercising it. This analysis holds for leadership and management activity as much as for teaching, as Goleman, Boyatzis and McKee (2002), for example, demonstrate. However, it is important to note that both knowledgeability and capability exist and are generated in social as well as individual settings. Individual teachers' prior professional training and development is blended with their experience in classroom and staffroom to define both what is known and what is acceptable activity in using that knowledge. Such social interaction creates a sense of certainty by defining the boundaries of legitimate action and may also limit the extent to which changes in such practice are deemed acceptable. Individual teachers may have the capability to apply newly obtained knowledge, but if their actions step outside the boundaries of what is acceptable then they will have to think carefully before doing it. Knowledgeability and capability are defined by a social community of practice as well as by individual capacity.

## LEADERSHIP AND CERTAINTY

To create sufficient order or certainty to enable individuals to do their job, members of an organization have to interpret the environmental signals, relate them to the resources available and plan ways of matching resources to expectations (Goldring, 1997; Weindling, 1997). Teachers require sufficient freedom to deploy their knowledgeability and capability, and the certainty of knowing the boundaries within which these actions are acceptable. Every organization embodies a culture – a set of norms that defines 'proper' action and limits individual uncertainty.

Leadership is a key activity in the creation of such certainty, as Goddard, Morley and Hosking and Gronn all demonstrate in this volume. Some sort of direction and co-ordination is necessary to develop and sustain sufficient certainty to enable individuals to act and to retain some collective coherence. Leadership thus becomes defined as reducing the level of uncertainty surrounding individual and collective activity by creating an orderly environment in which it can take place.

From this perspective, leadership is only to be found in situations of uncertainty, and exists in the relationships between individuals and groups when one party in the relationship is less uncertain than the other(s). Because this allows for leadership to be exercised by any individual at any time, it removes it from formal position and allows it to be seen as an organizational quality, widely dispersed throughout the organization and mobile within it.

Organizations can only cope with changing and competing external demands if they are themselves able to change, and as Rosenholtz (1989) and Stoll and Fink (1996) point out, this requires that people in organizations are willing to learn new skills and ideas. Learning is, therefore, a key element in coping with uncertainty, and is likely to have meaning only when it occurs in situations of uncertainty. Effective leadership therefore, like effective teaching, is to be found when the means of reducing uncertainty is concerned with sustaining sufficient uncertainty that learning can continue. As Ogawa puts it, good leadership creates organization which simultaneously embraces order and disorder, or certainty and uncertainty. Consequently, we can search for the impact of leadership and management development programmes in terms of the ways in which they create a sufficient balance between certainty and uncertainty to allow participants to exercise and extend their knowledge and capability on behalf of others to create a similarly constructive balance.

## TWO KINDS OF UNCERTAINTY

We can differentiate between two kinds of uncertainty. The first relates to the nature and purpose of the job being done. At the organizational level this relates to the balance between the values of its members (or key members) and perceived wider social expectations. At the individual level, it relates to the job that they do. In relation to this study, it asks, what is my job as a subject leader or head of department? What am I supposed to do? We may call this *job-related uncertainty*.

The second form of uncertainty is more tightly focused. Ogawa suggests that teachers and professionals seek to deal with it by drawing on their knowledgeability and capability. But embedded in these is a sense of certainty that their knowledgeability and capability is sufficient. If they find themselves faced with new tasks or obligations, this may create uncertainty about the strength and adequacy of both knowledgeability and capability. When this occurs, we may talk of *technical uncertainty*.

In the analysis that follows, therefore, I shall seek and analyse data relating to the following questions:

- To what extent do the teachers experiencing leadership and management development programmes do so from positions of uncertainty about their work? Is this uncertainty job-related, technical, or both?
- To what extent do the programmes appear to enhance both the teachers' knowledgeability and their capability in relation to leadership and management activities? How far do they and their colleagues agree about the nature and degree of enhanced knowledgeability and capability as changed practice?
- To what extent is their ability to exploit their knowledgeability and capability aided or hindered by structural or cultural elements within the school, and to what extent are these the result of formal policies created within the school?

Before undertaking this reanalysis, however, it is appropriate to outline very briefly the nature of the project from which the data are being drawn.

## THE IMPPEL PROJECT

The Impact on Practice of Programmes of Leadership and Management Development (IMPPEL) project set out to create a means by which schools and individuals could assess the nature and extent of impact of professional development on their work without reference to the programme objectives. Its pilot phase, with which this chapter is concerned, is described more fully in Bennett and Smith (2000). The data that will be reanalysed here are drawn from a set of interviews with secondary school heads of department who were taking part in a competency-based management development programme officially focused on developing skills in target-setting. None of them had received more than a couple of days' training in leadership or management before joining the course.

The data were gathered by interviewing the course participants (our 'focal interviewees') and asking them to identify up to six colleagues with whom they worked most closely in their school work (their role set). These teachers were also interviewed, giving us a more rounded perception of changes in our focal interviewees' practice (if any) occurring during or soon after their participation in the course. The conceptual framework within which our questioning and initial analysis was conducted was a very traditional, instrumental view of leadership and professional development, strongly influenced by the competency movement of the 1980s and 1990s (Boyatzis, 1982; Jirasinghe and Lyons, 1996), with its one-way relationship between leader and led. However, we found the data suggested both a mutuality between focal interviewees and their role set and a significant role for the school's culture in influencing the impact of the course on their colleagues and the school.

## REANALYSING THE IMPPEL DATA

1. *To what extent do the teachers experiencing leadership and management development programmes do so from positions of uncertainty about their work?*

There was in fact considerable certainty about the nature of the management and leadership duties of headteachers and their heads of department (HODs). Headteachers were expected to set the direction of the school, create a vision for staff to follow, and create a culture for the school, Heads of department were expected to put this vision into effect, planning and monitoring schemes of work, securing resources and allocating staff to classes. They were expected to provide advice and support to departmental colleagues when wanted, and to ensure staff development took place. Managers and leaders, then, were expected to create an orderly environment.

The HODs interviewed shared these views, emphasising their planning, monitoring and support responsibilities. Esther and Ruth[1] were working with newly qualified teachers (NQTs) and so emphasized their support and training functions, and Esther's NQT in particular agreed that this took place. But although each of them expressed certainty about how they should do their job, they went about it quite differently. Esther assisted her NQT to grow as a teacher by increasing her chances to take a lead herself through preparing schemes of work and, eventually, taking responsibility for the department's lower school curriculum. In this she was helped by her NQT being a subject specialist, which her other department colleague was not, and being out of school sometimes attending the management development course. Ruth encouraged and promoted discussion – her departmental meetings were described as in-service sessions because of the number of new ideas they discussed – but Mary was far more formal and directive in her approach, and reluctant to promote such discussion. So we may suggest that technical uncertainty about doing their job led each HOD to create their own understanding of it, developing individual knowledgeability and capability.

In terms of its avowed focus, the course addressed a major issue of technical uncertainty: how to meet a government requirement to set justifiable and measurable targets against which to assess pupil progress. It provided both a statistically based approach to the process and, through its assessment, a reason to put it into practice that might persuade reluctant colleagues to co-operate. However, other forms of learning also occurred. The course was based on a generic competency-based management course, and covering that ground led all the participants interviewed to become more aware of issues in their management and leadership practice that they had not considered. Thus the course generated uncertainty about practice even as it generated technical certainty about target setting.

The four HODs responded differently to this challenge. Peter's situation meant that he could make little of this learning, as will be indicated below. Ruth and Mary, moving into more senior roles in their schools, were aware of some aspects of their work, such as communication skills, but preferred to look to more experienced colleagues for help rather than exploring insights from the course. They sought to create certainty out of their work situation and to draw on others' professional knowledge and capability.

Esther, however, spoke of a dramatic reappraisal of both her responsibilities and her approach to carrying them out. As she put it, she started 'managing people rather than running systems', and ceased to be 'Miss Efficient', handing down instructions for people to follow. Instead she became a facilitator, using departmental meetings as opportunities for discussion rather than transmitting information, learning to listen to colleagues' opinions and encouraging them to be critical. Two important things seem to be happening here. First, the course created both job-related and technical uncertainty. Previously, she felt she knew what her job was and how to do it. Now, she was not sure. Second, she acquired through the course considerable new knowledge: both a new understanding of the nature of the work and awareness of the particular actions that might be appropriate to achieve it in practice. Third, she obtained through her work on the programme opportunities to practise what she was learning, so creating a capability to apply the knowledge that she was acquiring, and develop it into enhanced knowledgeability.

These teachers, then, approached the course from a position of technical uncertainty about a new task they faced – target-setting – but certain overall of their approach to their work and secure in the knowledgeability and capability that produced it. Ruth and Mary achieved technical certainty to complement their existing job-related certainty. Esther, however, had to re-create her job-related certainty as a result of having her knowledgeability, and therefore her capability, undermined by her learning. She had been able to create new knowledge and had the opportunity and freedom at school to extend her knowledgeability and generate a sense of capability in its use.

2. *To what extent do they appear to enhance both their knowledgeability and capability in relation to leadership and management activities? How far do they and their colleagues agree about the nature and degree of enhanced knowledgeability and capability as changed practice?*

It is, perhaps, worth reminding ourselves that 'knowledgeability' is not the same as 'knowledge': It contains both a sense of what might be done and a valuation of what should be done. A key question for a study of impact is therefore the extent to which new knowledge that might be acquired from the course becomes an aspect of what the individual *values* as knowledge and is capable of using.

Three of the four course participants interviewed spoke of greatly enhanced knowledgeability and, perhaps through the competency-based assessment involved, enhanced capability in its use. Even fellow departmental heads who were hostile to the initiatives they were trying to put in place acknowledged the additional sophistication they brought to them. Their knowledgeability and capability was further enhanced by the nature of the projects they undertook for course assessment, which were taking place on a whole-school basis rather than just within their department. Even though they felt more certain about the target-setting process, and more certain it was the right way to do it, they were working on a wider stage with a large number of colleagues with whom they had not previously worked. This generated both job-related and technical uncertainty, and a search for new knowledge and capability to cope with it.

Ruth and Mary looked to their senior colleagues for this rather than to the course, apparently seeking certainty from social support and from the collective knowledgeability and capability that informed existing practice within their school. Esther, likewise, sought social support, but as we suggested above, her enhanced knowledgeability and capability had been developed in relation to her formal departmental role rather than in a whole-school role – although she was developing a similar role to Ruth and Mary in promoting target setting more widely. Her sense of enhanced knowledgeability and capability in her leadership and management practice was corroborated by the interviews with both her departmental colleague and her headteacher, whose descriptions of how she was doing her work substantially confirmed her own perception of her new-found approach to her work.

Peter, on the other hand, achieved much less in this field than the other three. Only his immediate line manager saw him as having enhanced his knowledgeability and capability to any great extent, either in relation to target-setting or more generally. It may be significant that he was in a relatively junior position in his school relative to the other HODs studied, and his target-setting project was very limited in scope. He was allowed to repeat it a year later, but on an even more reduced scale. In the absence of any room to develop his role significantly, all Peter achieved was more knowledge of an approach to target-setting, with only very limited opportunities to develop capability within it.

We may propose, therefore, that all our respondents indicated enhanced knowledgeability and capability in relation to the specific focus of the course studied, in that they had acquired new knowledge and internalized its underpinning values, and this judgement was corroborated by their colleagues whom we interviewed. These colleagues were the teachers whom our HODs identified as the key members of their role set – the staff with whom they worked most closely. This enhanced knowledgeability and capability helped create order out of uncertainty, even when, in Esther's case, that uncertainty had been created by her early learning on the course. The course's target-setting projects further served to create levels of organizational uncertainty which the course participants' knowledgeability and capability could serve to reduce, and created a whole-school leadership role for middle-ranking staff. However, there was a considerable difference between the degree of uncertainty created for Peter and that created for our other HODs, and the extent to which new knowledge was embedded in their knowledgeability and turned into practice by the development of capability. It is to the reasons for this that we turn in considering the last of our three questions.

3. *To what extent is their ability to exploit their knowledgeability and capability aided or hindered by structural or cultural elements within the school, and to what extent are these the result of formal policies created within the school?*

As the previous discussion suggests, both school structure and culture influenced how the additional knowledge and capability generated by the course were exploited by the participants. Indeed, school culture and an individual's seniority within the structure may limit the degree to which capability in the deployment of new knowledge can be achieved. Our data suggest four aspects of the individual's organizational environment in particular: the degree of uncertainty at senior levels within the organization concerning its practice in relation to environmental pressures; the extent to which middle-ranking staff are given opportunities to develop their work on a wider stage than their formal position might permit; colleagues' attitudes towards those who would exploit their enhanced knowledgeability and capability; and the extent to which there was already a readiness to adopt or encourage the activities involved in exploiting enhanced knowledgeability and capability.

First, there was the extent to which the school itself could be characterized as existing in a state of uncertainty. At two of the schools the senior staff interviewed felt under great pressure to implement important central government initiatives, and wanted help to do it. One school's local authority had put in place a statistical system for setting and monitoring student achievement targets, but the headteacher and her senior staff all felt unable to make it work. Consequently, they took advantage of every opportunity that came along. When the course was first put forward, schools were only allocated one place each on it. Apart from Peter's headteacher, who only took up the one place, all of the schools studied negotiated themselves extra places – one of them managed eight instead of the one they were allocated.

This was essentially technical uncertainty. More profound job-related uncertainty at the whole-school level resulted from the extent to which senior staff saw the development of their colleagues as a key aspect of their work, even if it resulted in their gaining promotion and moving on. It was the job-related certainty of the schools' senior staff that created circumstances in which individual and organizational uncertainty could flourish more widely in the school. In Ogawa's analysis, this is good leadership practice. Mary, Ruth and Esther all worked in schools whose headteachers expressed this position, whereas Peter did not. Esther's headteacher argued that when a young teacher with outstanding ability joined the school, they should be given every opportunity to develop and extend their experience from the very beginning. The teacher almost always moved on to a new post within three or four years, but the advantage to the school in terms of the contribution they made to its activities while they were there was well worth the sacrifice. This philosophy generated a culture in which teachers' individual knowledgeability and capability could be developed whilst contributing to an uncertainty that would promote school learning and development. Mary's headteacher emphasized the value of excellent teachers with questioning minds in promoting changes in practice without which the school would ossify. A constant supply of 'new blood' was essential to keep new ideas coming into the school. These schools had established very robust systems for identifying individual staff's professional development needs, although they showed different degrees of balance between defined organizational development needs as articulated in a school development plan and the individual professional development needs of the teaching staff. The same kinds of policies were to be found in Peter's school, but there was a far less robustly expressed philosophy of 'giving able teachers their heads' than at the other three.

Second, there was the extent to which middle-ranking staff received opportunities to deploy their knowledge and develop knowledgeability and capability on a wider stage than their formal responsibilities might normally permit. Peter's headteacher appeared reluctant to do this. Although Peter was described as 'outstandingly able', he was given no opportunity to develop his target-setting knowledge more widely: indeed, he was not even given sufficient resources to develop the work in his own responsibility area. When an advanced version of the programme was introduced, the deputy head was given the school's place.

The other three headteachers actively promoted a wider role for their course participants. Middle-ranking rather than senior staff were given places on the programme, as the school capitalized on interest shown in the past and identified 'high fliers' who would benefit. Having committed resources to their teachers' participation in the course, the headteachers sought to promote them, although only in one case – Mary – were sufficient resources available to achieve this. Esther had to continue as departmental and year head, but her project involved developing school-wide systems for target-setting and providing appropriate in-service training for her school colleagues. There was no surprise when she gained a promotion elsewhere. Mary and Ruth discussed the focus of their projects for the advanced course with their headteachers, so that the school could benefit directly in policy terms at the same time as the teachers benefited personally.

A third factor was colleagues' attitudes towards the course participants. By and large, the course participants' role sets whom we interviewed, especially their departmental colleagues, were supportive of the work, and this made it easier for them to exploit their new knowledge and develop capability in its use. But our HODs also stated that the target-setting initiative received only 'patchy' acceptance, and one head of department colleague clearly saw it as an affront to his professional competence – a demonstration, perhaps, of uncertainty about the boundaries of his role. Mary implicitly demonstrated the degree of resistance that she experienced when she stated that because the course carried a qualification she could always ask colleagues to do something 'to help me with my NVQ', rather than having to persuade them to participate by justifying it to them. Only Esther's colleagues did not appear to be showing much resistance to the work, and this may have been because the school had already been working on target-setting for some time. She was simply providing a more rigorous, consistent and efficient approach to the task.

Finally, in the three schools where the course participants received considerable freedom to develop their knowledgeability and capability on a school-wide stage, senior staff were already interested in target-setting. Indeed, it appeared that the local vocational training agency set up the course precisely because this was an issue that heads were concerned about, and the head-teachers sent teachers on it because it chimed with immediate needs. The stronger the concern, the more staff the heads sought to place on the course. Crucially, therefore, it appears that the relationship between the school and its environmental expectations created a demand for legitimate practice that could be facilitated by the course.

In summary, then, we can suggest that cultural and structural factors played an important part in creating opportunities for the individual teachers to develop an extended knowledge base that provided the stimulus for enhancing their knowledgeability and capability in practice. This cultural orientation towards professional development as a means of exploiting high levels of ability whilst preparing high-flying staff for a successful career was given additional impetus in this case by external pressure from central government policy. The course provided an opportunity to respond effectively and to a high standard to external requirements to introduce a target-setting scheme for monitoring pupil progress. Developing and exploiting knowledgeability and capability was a means of generating renewed legitimacy for the school in relation to central government requirements.

## CONCLUSION: CONTINUING PROFESSIONAL DEVELOPMENT AS 'EMBRACING UNCERTAINTY'?

This reanalysis of IMPPEL data suggests at least six ways in which the concepts of knowledgeability and capability in responding to situations of uncertainty or disorder might be helpful when looking at the impact of professional development.

1) Uncertainty as opposed to order gives us a means of examining how knowledgeability and capability provide order-creating responses to individuals' conceptualization of their responsibilities. Conversely, when that conceptualization is challenged, the search for knowledgeability and capability becomes more demanding. Esther's move from departmental leadership as running systems to departmental leadership as managing

people was a major reconceptualization that created that need for significantly new knowledge and, through the opportunity to develop capability in its use, significantly enhanced knowledgeability.

2) Uncertainty as a basis for learning is helpful when thinking about what professional development should involve. In particular, it helps us distinguish between the kinds of order and uncertainty that professional development activities can create. Esther's experience of the course was more profound than that of the others interviewed because it went beyond the technicalities of target-setting to a new understanding of her role and responsibilities. Instrumental professional development that secures greater order without challenging the order it creates itself is likely to have less impact on personal development in the long run than more reflective professional development that sustains a cyclical relationship between the creation of knowledgeability and the creation of more uncertainty.

3) Conversely, creating too much uncertainty can separate individuals from their sense of knowledgeability, so that their capability becomes unimportant in the new context. With this comes a lack of confidence and, possibly, alienation and a loss of self-worth. A balance between order and certainty is needed for learning to be effective. In three of the schools, moves were already afoot to undertake target-setting, so the initiatives were more likely to succeed than at the fourth.

4) Schools faced with changing external demands may seek legitimacy through sponsoring individual members of staff to develop greater knowledgeability and capability that can then be used to assist others. Senior managers and leaders have to bear in mind the danger of moving too far from the knowledgeability and capability that underpins current practice, whilst recognizing that too much order can create a lack of responsiveness to new knowledge and demands and, ultimately, ossification. Only when a school reaches a crisis such as being declared to be 'failing' by its inspectorate might such wholesale change be considered: then, school staff must respond to an authoritative statement that their knowledgeability and capability are inadequate and that capability in new forms of knowledge is required.

5) The social nature of learning has been demonstrated in two ways: through the responses colleagues made to new knowledge in action, and through individuals looking to other colleagues for assistance as they take up new responsibilities. The first serves to delimit the range of new knowledge that is acceptable in that particular setting – knowledgeability – and the second acknowledges sources of professional learning that can derive from the knowledgeability and capability of others. In addition, a wider cultural perception within the organization, that is sponsored by the headteacher and other senior staff, will help to generate or limit the extent to which learning is a social rather than an individual activity.

6) The way in which middle ranking staff were both creators of uncertainty and sources of knowledgeability and capability is a clear demonstration of

the potential disconnection of 'leadership' from 'position'. What counted in the cases examined here was the knowledgeability and capability of individuals in a particular situation and set of relationships, not whether they held formal leadership positions.

It appears, then, that a view of organizations as sources of order in situations wherein knowledgeability and capability provide the means of dealing with endemic uncertainty has utility when considering ways of exploring the impact of professional development on both individuals and the organizational context of their work. It will certainly provide a framework for analysing the data from the second phase of the project to set alongside more traditional approaches, one that plays down the degree of rationality that underpins such learning and renders the relationship between individuals, the organization and their professional development more tentative than traditional models of training appear to do.

## NOTE

1. All names are pseudonyms.

## REFERENCES

Bennett, N. and Smith, R.E. (2000) The impact of CPD on educational management, *Professional Development Today*, 3(2), 71–82.

Boyatzis, R. (1982) *The Competent Manager: A Model for Effective Performance*. New York: Wiley.

Bucher, R. and Strauss, A. (1961) Professions as process, *American Journal of Sociology*, 66, 325–34.

Goldring, E. (1997) Educational leadership: schools, environments and boundary spanning, in M. Preedy, R. Glatter and R. Levačić (eds), *Educational Management: Strategy, Quality and Resources* (pp. 290–9). Buckingham: Open University Press.

Goleman D., Boyatzis, R. and McKee, A. (2002) *The New Leaders: Transforming the Art of Leadership into the Science of Results*. London: Little, Brown.

Jirasinghe, D. and Lyons, G. (1996) *The Competent Head: A Job Analysis of Heads' Tasks and Personality Factors*. London: Falmer.

Rosenholtz, S.J. (1989) *Teacher's Workplace: The Social Organization of Schools*. New York: Longman.

Stoll, L. and Fink, D. (1996) *Changing Our Schools*. Buckingham: Open University Press.

Weindling, D. (1997) Strategic planning in schools: some practical techniques, in M. Preedy, R. Glatter and R. Levačić (eds), *Educational Management: Strategy, Quality and Resources* (pp. 218–33). Buckingham: Open University Press.

# 12

## Preparing for Leadership in Education: In Search of Wisdom[1]

### PETER RIBBINS

### 1  PROLOGUE

In this chapter I will consider wisdom in leadership and in doing so will say something about what this might mean for leader preparation in education. This will require a meditation on philosophy and its place in the theory and practice of leadership. In attempting this I will consider the relevance of values by drawing on aspects of my own and other research into leadership. This reflects my long-standing belief that the generation of wisdom ('sophia') requires two things: the grounding of 'action on better theory, on the best theory available' (Hodgkinson, 1991, p. 111); and, the grounding of theory on better accounts of action, on the best accounts of action available (Ribbins, 1999a). My discussion will seek to make *sense* of sophia. In doing so it will call for *sensibility* and conclude with a search for *synthesis*. These are contested matters. If I tread cautiously, this reflects a commitment to the wisdom of an old African proverb that 'Only a fool tests the depth of the water with both feet'.

### 2  SENSE

'Sense' is complex. Collins Cobuild (1987) identifies 14 meanings. The three relevant to my discussion stress understanding, values, judgement, reason and behaving and the links between each of these:

1)  'if you have a sense of something, such as duty or justice, you believe that it is valuable' (*ibid.*, p. 1315);
2)  'sense is the ability to make good judgements and to behave in a practical and reasonable way' (*ibid.*, p. 1316); and,
3)  'when you make sense of something, you succeed in understanding it' (*ibid.*, p. 1316).

Following Aristotle, Hodgkinson (1991, p. 112) reminds us that:

> man has three distinct ways of knowing; three approaches to the world, three
> modes of action. They are *theoria*, *techne* and *praxis*. *Theoria*, or theory, repre-
> sents our knowing function in its purest form as it seeks to abstract, generalize,
> induce and deduce from a world of sense data that is given and that needs to be
> explained ... In its higher reaches, it offers the prospect of *sophia*, that transcen-
> dent wisdom of which *philosophy* is supposed to be the lover.

In modern times the distinction between *theoria* and *techne* (technology or the
applied sciences) has become entrenched in an unhelpful dichotomy between
theory and practice. For Begley (1999) the missing link is *praxis*. As such
'achieving praxis in educational administration is a function of three leadership qualities: the pursuit of administrative sophistication by individual
administrators, the development of sensitivity to the value orientations and
needs of self and others, and the synergy which results when the first two
qualities are consciously cultivated' (*ibid.*, p. 1). What might this mean for
leadership in education?

From the end of the Roman World, Boethius, as philosopher and administrator, has much to tell us. He wrote *The Consolation of Philosophy* in prison
facing imminent execution. As Greenfield movingly describes it:

> as he awaits his death he thinks back on his career and writes, thus bringing a new
> insight to the administrative task. Few of us will face the horror that Boethius did,
> but I am convinced that potentially there is that same dimension in all adminis-
> trative rule, a kind of horror. The wielding of power is terrible, and the more
> power, the more terrible. If there is to be some kind of humanizing of that power
> a contemplative, philosophical dimension must and should be brought to it.
> Perhaps to do the thing at all requires ... a meditation on values.
>
> (Greenfield and Ribbins, 1993, p. 262)

Boethius (1969, p. 41) shared Plato's view that:

> commonwealths would be blessed if they should be ruled by philosophers or if
> their rulers should happen to have studied philosophy ... the reason why it (is)
> necessary for philosophers to take part in government was to prevent the reins of
> government falling into the hands of wicked and unprincipled men to the destruc-
> tion of the good ... the only consideration to impel me to any office was a general
> desire for good. This was the reason I had no alternative but grimly to resist evil ...
> (and) to struggle to defend justice ...

But how common amongst leaders are these compulsions?

For Hodgkinson (1996, p. 8) 'other things being equal, (organizations) will
wish to appoint the "wisest" men or women to its administrative offices'. However,
'this desire is likely to be couched in terms neither of philosophy nor wisdom
but rather of such qualities as sophistication, credibility, know-how, cleverness,
integrity, common sense and vision'. In contrast he argues 'Administrators
ought to be wisdom seekers. Socrates declared that the unexamined life was

not worth living. We shall extend this dictum ... to "The unexamined value is not worth holding", and more immediately, "Unexamined administration is not worth doing"'.

How might leaders attain wisdom? Some have claimed that the holding of high office enables leaders to become wiser. But as Boethius (1969, pp. 70, 71) warns: 'honour is not accorded to virtue because of the office held, but to the office because of the virtue of the holder ... when high office is bestowed on unworthy men, so far from making them worthy, it only betrays them and reveals their unworthiness'. If we want wise leaders we should not rely on office to make them so. Rather we must elect or appoint those who are already wise or those who can become so by training or by other means to high office. But is this realistic?

Greenfield, like Plato, believed it possible to enable leaders to become wiser. If this is to be achieved then the

> ultimate training of a leader would be a kind of philosophical withdrawal to look at the larger issues in fresh perspective ... A deeply clinical approach to the training of administrators is needed ... Our training is disjointed, reflection is separated from action, thinking from doing, praxis from the practical. Why do we throw people at these jobs, expecting them to do well with almost no experience ... offering them no analysis of their experience?
>
> (Greenfield and Ribbins, 1993, p. 260)

In a recent paper (Ribbins, 1999b, p. 77) I listed three sets of questions[2] that I believe those involved in the training of educational leaders ought to address:

1) What is good leadership? What is a good leader? How can those with good potential be identified and encouraged to prepare for leadership? How can those with significant leadership responsibilities be encouraged to improve? How good is the evidence?
2) What should a curriculum for developing and sustaining good leaders and leadership look like? How should it be taught? What standards should it entail? How should it be assessed? How good is the evidence?
3) What is the evidence that if such a curriculum were to be developed and taught, it would have a significant beneficial effect on how those graduating actually lead?

In their original form, these questions were put to Anthea Millet, then Chief Executive of the Teacher Training Agency (TTA) at the end of a lecture in which she had outlined the agency's proposals for a comprehensive programme of headship training in the UK. She struggled to meet their challenge. Even so, it seemed clear that 'the TTA, with their new headship qualifications and their initiatives in middle management, have set out a hugely ambitious programme – nothing of its scale or complexity have been attempted elsewhere' (Glatter, 1997, p. 190). Since then responsibility for such leadership development has passed to the National College for School Leadership (NCSL).

Whilst it is as yet too early to be sure what this will mean, there are indications that some things are changing whilst others are not.

It would be helpful if review evidence on these programmes could be made more freely available than was sometimes the case with the TTA. Thus, for example, the findings of a major review of the National Professional Qualification for Headteachers (NPQH) undertaken by the National Foundation for Educational Research (NFER) has never been published. This despite the fact that, if rumour is correct, it was largely positive. I regret this, not least because my limited feedback from course members and tutors (Ribbins, 1999b) has been less so and therefore I continue to share the concerns about the NPQH expressed by a number of distinguished headteachers. As Sir David Winkley has pointed out, what is under offer is

> the kind of training programme that covers every conceivable possibility ... The problem I have with this is that it's possible to go through this kind of process and still not be terribly good as a head ... The danger is of creating a conception of school leadership as a managerial enterprise, as a tick list – you do all these things and then you're going to be a very competent head – that does not follow.
>
> (Pascal and Ribbins, 1998, p. 22)

Given this, he believes that what is needed is training that includes a substantial philosophical and psychological dimension. This is so because 'it doesn't matter how many courses you've been on, and how much you know intellectually about the process of being a head if you don't develop an appreciation of yourself as a person ... you will never make a good head' (*ibid.*, p. 22).

Such a view, and it is not uncommon, suggests that my anxieties are not just the angst of an academic. Reflecting on the limitations of functional competency-based methods of training for management development, Glatter (1997, p. 190) warns of the need to avoid an approach that is narrow, atomistic and bureaucratic. What is surely crucial is how such programmes understand what meaning is to be given to such concepts as 'good leader' and 'good leadership'. In this regard, even those who favour a competency-based approach stress the importance of what Cave and Wilkinson (1992) 'have called the "higher order capacities" to do with judgement, intuition, political acumen and the like. Personal qualities like integrity, stamina and commitment as well as value systems were seen as fundamental' (Glatter, 1997, p. 190). It is by no means always obvious how the TTA packages, or those from the NCSL, will enable candidates for headship to develop, let alone demonstrate, such higher-order capabilities. It could be that government thinking has shifted in recent years. For example, the Green Paper on *Teachers: Meeting the Challenge of Change* (DfEE, 1998) makes only two references to 'competency'. In its place, however, there are many references to 'standards' and 'skills'. This offers little consolation to those who advocate a less mechanistic and managerialist view of leadership for education. This, along with the highly prescriptive nature of much that is proposed, could indicate a government seeking to improve school effectiveness and pupil achievement 'by make teaching as teacher proof and school leadership as headteacher proof as possible' (Ribbins, 1999b, p. 78). Teachers and headteachers, it seems, are no longer to be regarded as knowledgeable and capable about what they do and trusted to do it (see Ogawa, Chapter 2, this volume).

On these matters, ideas developed by Sergiovanni (2001) are illuminating. Reflecting upon the recent history of the USA, he outlines two 'discredited theories' for running schools. They bear an uncanny resemblance to government policy in England and Wales since 1988. Pyramid Theory came first. This 'assumed that the way to accomplish school goals was to control what people in schools did (by having) one person assume responsibility'. But 'as the number ... to be supervised increased, management burdens needed to be delegated to official managers and an hierarchical system of management emerged'. Soon 'rules and regulations were developed to assure that all of the managers thought and acted in the same way, and to provide guidelines for teachers and others who were being managed ... so that they too thought and acted in the same way' (*ibid.*, p. 1).

But

> schools and school systems became too complex and it was impossible to control things directly anymore. So we switched to the Railroad Theory (which) assumed you could control the way people thought and acted indirectly by *standardizing the work* they did (by) anticipating all the teaching, learning, curriculum, assessment and management problems likely to come up. The answers and solutions were developed by higher authorities that represented tracks for all teachers and for all schools to follow ... Once the track was laid out, teachers, and schools needed to be trained to follow the tracks properly and monitoring systems needed to be set up to be sure the tracks were followed.
>
> (*Ibid.*, p. 1)

Sadly, 'in many places the Railroad Theory didn't work either. Teachers and schools did not like being put into straight-jackets [*sic*], teachers complained of being "deskilled", and everyone agreed we needed a new approach' (*ibid.*). A key problem with these and similar approaches is that attempts to separate ends and means disempower and demoralize headteachers and teachers, and diminish dramatically the scope for parents, pupils and other members of the local community of a school to be involved in democratic decision-making. Furthermore, as Sergiovanni maintains, there is little reason to believe that such an approach will actually result in much worthwhile school improvement.

It is not just influential members of recent governments in the USA and UK who have advocated splitting responsibility for ends and means in the determination of educational policy and practice. Such a view has also been taken by a number of distinguished administrative theorists. As Simon (1957) once put it, the organization is a bus and the administrator its driver – who does not, nor should, determine matters to do with destination, route, timetable and the like. Greenfield dismisses (Greenfield and Ribbins, 1993, p. 139) this approach arguing that: 'It is an enormous error to conceive of administration as a science rather than a moral art ... Simon led the science of administration down a narrow road which in its own impotence is inward-looking, self-deluding, self-defeating, and unnecessarily boring.'

If, then, values, with morals and ethics, are, as Hodgkinson (1991, p. 11) claims, 'the very stuff of leadership and administrative life', this should be sufficient reason for administrators to consider them and for such a study to be at the heart of their development. Specifically there are at least three excellent reasons for this:

> Firstly, by doing so he/she may gain self-knowledge and self-understanding. Secondly, it should lead to a better understanding of one's fellows thus enhancing the possibility of a greater empathy, sympathy and compassion but also gaining a sophisticated acceptance and recognition of the negative side of human character. Thirdly, a knowledge of value theory is necessary if we are to make progress with the problems of division, antagonism and conflict which beset organizations and societies. The leader is one who can best perceive and best resolve value conflicts. If there are no value conflicts there is no need for leadership.
>
> *(Ibid.)*

Leaders may need such an understanding of themselves. As Erasmus has claimed, 'Fruitless is the wisdom of him who has no knowledge of himself'. They may also require a sophisticated understanding of values. But is there any evidence that they want this?

Three influential modernist propositions have colluded to discourage serious thinking about values in general and their place in administration in particular (Ribbins, 1999c):

1) That values are not fit subjects for meaningful discussion;
2) That values are not respectable topics for sophisticated modern discourse; and
3) That in any case science will tell us all there is to know about values.

The first and third of these are related in so far as they rest on similar claims about the primacy and possibilities of science more or less narrowly defined, what of the second?

Wilson (1997, p. viii) describes our time as one in which

> science has challenged common sense; one theory of science holds that we can never have knowledge, as opposed to mere opinion, about morality. Anthropologists have shown how various are the customs of mankind ... the dominant tradition in modern philosophy asserts that no rational foundation can be given for any (moral) judgement.

Does the 'mirror that modern scepticism has held up to mankind's face reflect what we wish to see?' *(ibid.,* p. x). Wilson believes not. On the contrary:

Most ordinary men and women ... wish to make moral judgements but their culture does not help them to do it. They often feel like refugees living in a land captured by hostile forces. When they speak of virtue, they must do so privately, in whispers, lest they be charged with ... being 'unsophisticated', or if they press the matter, 'fanatics' ... our reluctance to speak of morality and our suspicion, nurtured by the best minds, that we cannot 'prove' our moral principles has amputated moral discourse at the knees.

(*Ibid.*, pp. x, xi)

This has serious consequences. It means that although 'most of us have a moral sense, (we) have tried to talk ourselves out of it' (*ibid.*, p. ix). Given the closed character of an epoch which purports to value openness so highly, and the intolerance of our new age of tolerance, people tend to 'flinch ... at least in public' from addressing fundamental value issues (*ibid.*, p. xi). As customarily used today, the 'word "values" finesses all the tough questions. It implies a taste or preference and recalls to mind the adage that there is no disputing taste' (*ibid.*, p. xi). This is a bleak conclusion but as Wilson points out most of us 'don't really mean our beliefs are no more than tastes ... Arguments about values often turn into fights about values ... That is not the way we discuss our taste for vanilla ice cream' (*ibid.*, p. xi). Is such passion relevant to administrators? This question takes us from sense to sensibility.

## 3 SENSIBILITY

Sensibility seems simpler than 'sense'. Collins Cobuild (1987) has two definitions – 'someone's sensibility is 1. their ability to experience deep feelings ... 2. a tendency they have to be easily influenced or offended by things that other people say and do' (*ibid.*, p. 1316).

From the perspective of the first of these definitions, Greenfield, is sceptical but suggests how improvements might be made:

I have sensed in speaking to leaders in education ... how very impoverished their real world is. They don't see beyond a narrow horizon. They don't see the problems of education except in rather technological terms, or if they do see it, if they talk about it in larger terms, they are sentimental and platitudinous. We need leaders in education who can think about the larger issues ... But it will be an uphill struggle ... The headlong pressure to act, to do, to be the leader militates against a reflective attitude – a stance which is needed for the growth of worthwhile values, and of character. That is what I see as the ultimate in the nurture of leaders through training. It would be aimed at persons in power, fostering awareness of values and of the value choices that face them, and thereby perhaps assisting character growth.

(Greenfield and Ribbins, 1993, pp. 258, 259)

Greenfield's claim that leaders in education are reluctant to reflect on value issues does not square with the findings of my studies of headteachers or with Hodgkinson's experience:

> Real life administrators are often thought to have a minimal attention span, a contempt for all things intellectual and a pride in their tough images, but I have found that when you start talking about values you can establish an instant rapport with them. Values are the key to their interest. They know what you are talking about. You are onto something which is important to them.
>
> (Quoted in Ribbins, 1993a, p. 15)

Certainly, the 34 educational leaders whose views are reported in some depth in *Headship Matters* (Ribbins and Marland, 1994), *Understanding Primary Headteachers* (Pascal and Ribbins, 1998), *Headteachers and Leadership in Special Education* (Rayner and Ribbins, 1999) and *Leaders and Leadership in the School, College and University* (Ribbins, 1997) talk a great deal of their efforts to achieve a shared vision and of their struggle to clarify and apply their educational and other values in practice.

Brian Sherratt, of Great Barr, the largest school in the UK identifies 'building the ethos of the school ... and working at it daily' as 'absolutely crucial'. Given this, he emphasizes, the importance of stressing again and again that: 'we have these *values,* this is the way we do these things' (Ribbins and Marland, 1994, p. 170). And if 'On the whole teachers tend to say "That's philosophy, it's nothing to do with ... the realities of the job"'. (But) 'it can be, and if they can see the principles which drive the way the institution wants to do things, and if this can be broken down into the things they do in the classroom and the yard ... they will accept that this stress on values can be helpful' (*ibid.*, p. 170).

In developing this view, Sherratt, like most of the 34, stressed that despite the difficulties he still saw his 'role as leading professional and chief executive' (*ibid.*, p. 186). However, as Mike Gasper, an experienced primary school headteacher stresses, this is becoming harder:

> the nature of the job has become more difficult ... if you start looking at all that you are supposed to do it is impossible ... You get the feeling the world is conspiring to undermine everything you believe in or think you should be doing. The day-to-day, week-to-week activity is very much reactive rather than proactive, unfortunately. Again we are trying desperately to lift ourselves out of this.
>
> (Pascal and Ribbins, 1998, pp. 126, 127)

Coping with such a situation requires various strategies including the need 'to decide your own priorities ... to decide what we are going to do and why ... a clear philosophy' (*ibid.*, p. 127) and the need to work ever harder.

These interviews reveal again and again the commitment that so many of these headteachers expect of themselves sometimes at great personal cost. As Peter Downes, head of a large community comprehensive school, confesses 'I work too hard. I probably work about 75–80 hours a week' (Ribbins and Marland, 1994, p. 99). Primary headteachers also work too hard or at least too long. Sue Beeson reveals 'I get to work at 7.45 am and rarely leave before 6.00 p.m.

and take home two or three hours' work most nights ... I don't know what all this works out on average but it is a long week ... I am rarely conscious of being without a thought of school for any length of time' (Pascal and Ribbins, 1998, p. 81).

Such commitment has a price. Peter Downes acknowledged 'the difficulty in working such long hours is that I find myself having to make certain decisions without having given the matter enough thought or without having read widely enough' (Ribbins and Marland, 1994, p. 99). Sue Beeson remarked: 'I'm in my fourth year as head of this school (her second primary school headship). In another couple of years I would like to retire. Whether I will I don't know. The more you know the harder it gets. I would be 52. I think I'll be burnt out by then' (Pascal and Ribbins, 1998, p. 81). John Evans, an experienced head of a large community school in Cornwall concluded:

> Some of my best headteacher friends have retired because of illness or stress. I am talking of people I rate highly who are not just looking for a way out. To survive you've got to be much tougher than in the past. I'm diabetic with serious stomach problems and think this is stress related. It's part of the job.
>
> (Rayner and Ribbins, 1999, p. 184)

Gronn (Chapter 4, this volume) examines this phenomenon in the context of an illuminating discussion of the notion of 'work intensification'. This, he argues, refers to 'new work practices which entail significantly increased levels of output, with expectations of output enshrined in employment contract-based performance indicators and productivity targets' (p. 65). Interestingly, he links this development with the kind of 'proletarianization of the work of school personnel' (p. 65) discussed above (see also Ogawa, Chapter 2, this volume).

For my part, whilst some of the headteachers I have studied accept that their work is less professionally satisfying than it used to be, and that this is a direct result of educational reforms implemented over the last decade or so, the majority would not. Many stressed their continuing responsibility for the nature and quality of the curriculum and pedagogy within their own schools and argued that this had not disappeared with the introduction of a national curriculum and national systems of assessment. As Michael Marland puts it: 'I very much see myself as a curriculum manager. I do not see the legislation as having greatly affected this' (Marland and Ribbins, 1994, p. 149). For Brian Sherratt, 'some heads are more comfortable retreating into their administrative duties as a defence against the hard intellectual and personal effort required to make sense of the curriculum ... Some heads seem to enjoy becoming a kind of financial clerk ... one illusion is to believe that this is something new' (ibid., p. 191). Those who have chosen this route have been willing collaborators in, rather than victims of, the proletarianization of their work.

In contrast John Evans speaks for many when he says: 'I cannot think of anything that I would rather do than be the headteacher of a big comprehensive school' (ibid.). How is such dedication to be accounted for? Three explanations come to mind. First, perhaps Boethius was too pessimistic; might it be that there is something about the office of headship that attracts many unusually dedicated men and women? Second, our sample may be untypical of the mass of headteachers (but see Passmore, 1995). Third, it could be that the office attracts workaholics. In passing, it should be stressed that this is a kind of pathology and pathologies, especially in superordinate leaders, can be dangerous to the individual and to the organisation. As Kets de Vries (1995, p. 208) puts it:

> parallels can be drawn between individual pathology ... and organizational pathology, the latter resulting in poorly functioning, or 'neurotic', organizations in which the 'irrational personality characteristics' of principal decision-makers can seriously affect the overall management process ... At the head of a 'neurotic' organization ... one is likely to find a top executive whose rigid, neurotic style is strongly mirrored in the nature of inappropriate strategies, structures and organizational cultures of his or her firm. If this situation continues for long, the organization may self-destruct.[3]

So much for sensibility, what can be said of synthesis?

## 4  SYNTHESIS

Collins Cobuild (1987) notes three meanings for 'synthesis', only one of which is relevant to my discussion. In this 'A synthesis of different ideas ... is (described as) a mixture or combination of these ideas ... in which they blend together' (*ibid.*, p. 1484). In exploring leadership and leadership development in education, I believe that the pursuit of understanding, even of wisdom, requires both empirical rigour and conceptual clarity. In thinking about the place of synthesis in enabling this I will say something about the need for an appropriate research model *and* for a comprehensive conceptual map.

In exploring what an appropriate *model for research* into leadership might look like, I have argued for an approach with a concern for *agency* and *structure* viewed within contexts shaped by the interaction of macro (societal), meso (institutional) and micro (individual) relationships (Gronn and Ribbins, 1996). Such a view emphasizes the significance of context in describing and accounting for social phenomena. As Morley and Hosking (Chapter 3, this volume) put it: 'the relationship between people and contexts is one of mutual creation: so, people create contexts and contexts create people' (p. 43). My own interest in this area has been mainly in the development and extensive use of a three level model of research (Ribbins, 1993b; 1999a). In what follows I will restrict myself to a brief sketch of its main features.

*Level 1: A situated portrait approach* – presents sets of portraits of the views of individual school leaders across a range of themes, each of which is reported in some depth (Pascal and Ribbins, 1998; Rayner and Ribbins, 1999; Pashiardis and Ribbins, 2003).

*Level 2: A multi-perspective approach* – offers an access to the views of the particular school leader being portrayed along with those of significant others (teaching and other staff, pupils, parents, governors, members of the local area, etc.) in the school community.

*Level 3: A multi-perspective in action approach* – relatively few studies explore what school leaders say (and what significant others say about them) in the context of what they all then actually do. To undertake this the researcher must engage in observational investigation. The following examples of studies of headteachers are classified into three categories according to the extent to which the headteacher is the focus of the study and his or her status in undertaking the research. *Category 1* studies treat the headteacher as one amongst a number of actors at the school to be studied. He or she is regarded by the researcher as a subject of study rather than as an active partner in the research process (e.g. Ribbins, 1999a). *Category 2* studies focus upon a particular headteacher but regard her or, more usually, him as a subject to be studied not as an active partner in the research. *Category 3* studies identify the headteacher as the main subject of the research and as a full co-researcher. Since 1989 I have been involved in such third-level research with Brian Sherratt at Great Barr.

Recent developments in leadership in education as theory and practice in the UK have stimulated the search for a *comprehensive map of the field* (see Gunter and Ribbins, 2002a; Ribbins and Gunter, 2002). The NCSL has given its support to this venture, not least by sponsoring the involvement of Geoff Southworth[4] in leading a key seminar held at the University of Reading in October 2001. Such an acknowledgement of the need for a map of the field of leadership by a body carrying a national responsibility for leadership development in schools is very welcome, if somewhat belated. It is hard to see how it would be possible to give a persuasive answer to the three questions listed earlier without such a map. In addition, a map would enable greater clarity in determining what needs to be known, what is known, and how any shortfall between the two might be tackled.

The DfEE and TTA have sought to identify standards for headteachers and other school leaders that set 'out the professional knowledge, understanding, skills and attributes necessary to carry out effectively the key tasks of that role' (DfEE, 2000, p. 1). This attempt has some of the characteristics of an exercise in mapping. Much the same might be said of the NCSL's attempt to develop a leadership development framework for schools (NCSL, 2001). But whatever their merits as presently constituted these attempts at mapping are partial and may overemphasize substantive aspects of school leadership as against those that focus on the nature of research and knowledge in the field. I would argue that a comprehensive map requires attention be given to both these dimensions and to their interaction.

With regard to the latter Helen Gunter and I have argued in a keynote paper given at the opening session of an ESRC Seminar Series on the theme of

Challenging the Orthodoxy of School Leadership that much more attention needs to be given to the nature of knowledge production in the field of educational leadership. In attempting to progress this we advocate an approach involving the study of mappers (who), mapping (how, why and where) and maps (what). We outline our thinking on this through the medium of six related typologies: Producers, Positions, Provinces, Practices, Processes and Perspectives. It is our belief that these typologies can be used to describe and explain knowledge production in the field and that they have the potential to support professional practice by field members. More specifically 'they can enable questions and activity surrounding research, theory, policy and practice to be scoped and, the choices that are made along with orientations towards them to be opened to scrutiny' (Gunter and Ribbins, 2002b, p. 1).

## 5   EPILOGUE

Strenuous and sometimes expensive attempts have been made in the UK and in many other countries in recent times to produce programmes of leadership development opportunities in a variety of educational contexts. This represents an improvement on past practice but there is reason to doubt if these programmes as presently constituted offer satisfactory answers to the three sets of key questions identified earlier in the chapter. For this to be possible, it is necessary to make a case in terms of sense, sensibility and synthesis in our understanding of the praxis of leadership and the preparation of leaders. It is hard to see how this can be achieved without a map of the field. Achieving this will not be easy. The maps presented at Reading and developed subsequently (Gunter and Ribbins, 2002a; Gunter and Ribbins, 2002b; Ribbins and Gunter, 2002; Southworth, 2002) represent points of departure on what is likely to be a demanding journey.

## NOTES

1. The origins of this chapter lie in three linked keynote presentations given by Christopher Hodgkinson, Paul Begley and Peter Ribbins at the BEMAS National Conference that was held in Manchester in 1999.

2. These questions are substantially modified versions of those that were voiced initially by Benjamin Levin at the 1997 Annual National Conference of BEMAS.

3. Had space permitted, these ideas could have led to a much fuller discussion of the notion of pathology and the ways in which different kinds of leadership pathology can lead to various types of organizational neurosis. On this Hodgkinson (1996, pp. 187–212) has identified 15 kinds of leader pathology and Kets de Vries (1995, p. 209) five types of 'neurotic' organization, each reflecting the pathologic characteristics of their chief executive: the dramatic, the suspicious, the detached, the depressive and the compulsive.

4. As of May 2002, Southworth has been appointed to head up the Research Division of the NCSL.

# REFERENCES

Begley, P. (1999) The praxis of educational administration: sophistication, sensitivity and synergy. Paper presented to the Conference of the British Educational Management and Administration Society on Values, Equity and Leadership, UMIST, September.

Boethius (1969) *The Consolation of Philosophy*, Trans. V.E. Watts. London: Penguin.

Cave, E. and Wilkinson, C. (1992) Developing managerial capabilities in education, in N. Bennett, M. Crawford and C. Riches (eds), *Managing Change in Education: Individual and Organisational Perspectives*. London: Paul Chapman Publishing.

Collins Cobuild (1987) *English Language Dictionary*. London: Collins.

Department for Education and Employment (DfEE) (1998) *Teachers: Meeting the Challenge of Change* (Green Paper). London: DfEE.

Department for Education and Employment (DfEE) (2000) *National Standards for Headteachers*. London: DfEE.

Glatter, R. (1997) Context and capability in educational management, *Educational Management and Administration*, 27(3), 253–67.

Greenfield, T. and Ribbins, P. (1993) *Greenfield on Educational Administration: Towards a Humane Science*. London: Routledge.

Gronn, P. and Ribbins, P. (1996) Leadership in context: Postpositivist approaches to understanding educational leadership, *Educational Administration Quarterly*, 32(3), 452–73.

Gunter, H. and Ribbins, P. (2002a) Leadership studies in education: towards a map of the field, *Educational Management and Administration*, 31(1), 387–416.

Gunter, H. and Ribbins, P. (2002b) Challenging orthodoxy in school leadership studies: old maps for new directions? Keynote speech from a seminar held at the University of Warwick in November.

Hodgkinson, C. (1991) *Educational Leadership: The Moral Art*. New York: SUNY.

Hodgkinson, C. (1996) *Administrative Philosophy. Values and Motivations in Administrative Life*. London: Pergamon.

Hodgkinson, C. (1999) Theoria: sex, sin and seduction. Paper presented to the Conference of the British Educational Management and Administration Society on Values, Equity and Leadership, UMIST, September.

Kets de Vries, M. (1995) The leadership mystique, *Leading and Managing*, 1(2), 193–211.

National College for School Leadership (NCSL) (2001) *Leadership Development Framework*. Nottingham: NSCL.

Pascal, C. and Ribbins, P. (1998) *Understanding Primary Headteachers*. London: Cassell.

Pashiardis, P. and Ribbins, P. (eds) (2003) *The Making of Secondary School Principals on Selected Small Islands,* in *International Studies in Educational Administration*, 31(2), Special Edition.

Passmore, B. (1995) Heads call time on long hours. *Times Educational Supplement*, 16 June, 11.

Rayner, S. and Ribbins, P. (1999) *Headteachers and Leadership in Special Education*. London: Cassell.

Ribbins, P. (1993a) Conversations with a *condottiere* of administrative value, *Journal of Educational Administration and Foundations*. 8(1), 13–28.

Ribbins, P. (ed.) (1997) *Leaders and Leadership in the School, College and University*. London: Cassell.

Ribbins, P. (1999a) Context and praxis in the study of school leadership, in P. Begley and P. Leonard (eds), *The Values of Educational Administration* (pp. 125–40). London: Falmer.

Ribbins, P. (1999b) Understanding leadership: developing headteachers, in T. Bush, L. Bell, R. Bolam, R. Glatter and P. Ribbins (eds), *Educational Management: Redefining Theory, Policy and Practice* (77–90). London: Paul Chapman Publishing.

Ribbins, P. (1999c) Foreword, in P. Begley and P. Leonard (eds), *The Values of Educational Administration* (pp. ix–xviii). London: Falmer.

Ribbins, P. and Gunter, H. (2002) Mapping leadership studies in education: towards a typology of knowledge domains, *Educational Management and Administration*, 30(4), 359–86.

Ribbins, P. and Marland, M. (1994) *Headship Matters*. London: Longman.

Sergiovanni, T. (2001) Moral authority, community and diversity: leadership challenges for the 21st Century, in K. Wong and C. Evers (eds), *Leadership Quality for Schooling: International Perspectives* (pp. 1–12). London: Falmer.

Simon, H. (1957) *Administrative Behaviour*. New York: Free Press.

Southworth, G. (2002) Mapping the field of school leadership, draft summary paper from a seminar held at the University of Reading in December 2001.

Wilson, J. (1997) *The Moral Sense*. New York: Free Press.

# SECTION 4

# REVIEW AND OVERVIEW

# 13

## Comparing and Contrasting the Perspectives: Mapping the Field of Educational Leadership

### HELEN GUNTER

This book is a map of the field of educational leadership and as such it is first, topographical as it seeks to chart underlying knowledge claims; second, it is geographical, as the authors have taken up positions and seek to position others in how they have engaged with knowledge claims; third, it is political, in which boundaries have been drawn that control access and exit; and fourth, it is practical as it enables the map reader to have route ways and sign posts through a complex and dynamic field (Gunter and Ribbins, 2002). I intend in this final chapter to be both a map reader and user, and as such contribute to the dynamism of mapping. Consequently I need to reflexively explain where I am beginning my journey and how I have interpreted and understood the terrain ahead, and the meaning it has generated for my own intellectual journey within the field. In doing this I intend to use an approach to maps, mapping and mappers developed by Peter Ribbins and myself through our collaborative work on field development (Gunter and Ribbins, 2002; Ribbins and Gunter, 2002).

### READING AND USING MAPS

Picking up and reading a text such as this book requires us to orientate ourselves and ask questions about purpose and scope. The editors tell us that that the book is about 'analysing critically' what they label as 'conventional' or 'orthodox' views of leadership, and as such they divide the book into three sections beginning with theories, moving onto the interplay between theories and empirical work, followed by analysis of the implications of this work for professional development. As such the map is constructed in a particular way with a rationale, and hence we can expect to know the territory we are about to enter and the landscape that we expect to unfold. Therefore the reasons for the production of this edited collection can be encapsulated by Weindling's (2001) description of why we use maps:

- To delimit territories and define boundaries.
- To show the known from the unknown.
- To identify features in the landscape.
- To show the relationship and distance between different places.
- To help the traveller navigate a course.
- To warn the traveller of potential dangers – 'here be dragons'.

While the field itself is dynamic and shifting, this book as a map seeks to chart and so stabilize meaning about theory and practice at one point in time and space, though how and why we engage with the book over time and in varied contextual spaces will have stabilities and flexibilities that affect interpretations and practices. In this way the book cannot and does not seek to be comprehensive, mainly because like Harry Potter stepping onto a staircase in Hogwart's School, where you think you are going might not be where you arrive.

We need to understand who the map readers or travellers are, and ask questions about how useful our maps are to them. In this way, some travellers are on a package tour in which they are given access to knowledge in a controlled way, and as such may or may not be given this book either in whole or part. Other mappers, as distinct from the editors and chapter authors, will decide what is and is not worth knowing, and may or may not reveal this to the traveller. Other travellers will be pioneer trekkers who will either actively seek out this text as a guide or will fortuitously happen across it. However, whether we are tourists or trekkers we do need to note that we not only use the maps as we go, but also create new maps in the process through our own charting or theorizing. Consequently, map readers as users and producers of the knowledge landscape are actively engaged with others in charting and creating new frontiers. We need to acknowledge that those who we might expect to be on the territory can also be joined by others who inhabit the territory but who might not be recognized as legitimate members. For example, Peter Ribbins and I have both argued that we need to work for an inclusive approach:

> Whilst leadership is multi-voiced and multi-sited we know that some voices are louder than others and some sites are more privileged than others. We are also aware that while we may continue to work for the democratisation of knowledge through our professional practise as researchers and teachers, this is a contested position and so the struggle is more than just asking what we know about leaders, leading and leadership, but is also about the structures that seek to determine what is worth knowing and who the knowers are.
>
> (Gunter and Ribbins, 2002, p. 412)

Such a claim needs to be located in the experiences of the mappers so far, and so this commitment to broadening what is known and what is worth knowing, is located in professional practice as a mapper, and it is to this that I now turn.

## A STARTING POINT

I first began to publicly map the territory through an analysis of knowledge claims that I playfully but seriously labelled Jurassic Management (Gunter, 1997). This is a metaphor for providing meaning about education as a theme park, and it is drawn from Michael Crichton's 1991 best seller, *Jurassic Park* (Crichton, 1991), in which he shows, through a combination of drama and scientific argument, that instrumental systemic organizational control dressed up in a benign language of vision and mission can have uncertain consequences and may sometimes even be dangerous. It seems that management strategies such as planning and problem-solving, and cultural integration processes such as teams cannot determine the future, but are being used seductively to train managers into the illusion of control. Visioning seems to be the solution to a rejection of scientific and bureaucratic models, and so while we should no longer operate management by objectives we can have a vision of a future state that we can move towards. Jurassic Park failed because visioning is based on a knowledge claim that cause and effect are close together, and by drawing on chaos theory Crichton (1991) shows that living systems are inherently unpredictable and so the emphasis should not be on determining outputs but on the critical choices that managers have to make at different times in the life of the organization.

Jurassic Management is evident in an education industry focused on the promotion and implementation of theme park strategies and processes. The scanning of bookshelves and training courses demonstrate a dominance of management by ringbinder in which generic management strategies and processes are applied to educational organizations. For example, headteachers/ principals are told by government agencies (Hopkins, 2001; TTA, 1998), private consultancies (Forde, Hobby and Lees, 2000) and academics (Caldwell and Spinks, 1988; 1992; 1998; Leithwood, Jantzi and Steinbach, 1999) that they should be leaders and engage in transformational leadership by the creation and communication of a vision. The drive to create and maintain the integrated and stable organization is strong, and yet it is based on limited knowledge claims with an impoverished approach to personal and organizational histories, theory and theorizing, research and researching. Transformational leadership dominates the language and is the promoted good practice of how schools should be led, and it connects with the modernization of education within England over the last 20 years (Gunter, 2001a). It is consistent with the iterative emergence, over time and often inconsistently, of the performing school and performing teacher where the purpose of schools and the workforce are to deliver according to externally determined targets and curricula. This privileges certain knowledge claims particularly around technicist problem-solving techniques. These are being supported by approaches to knowledge production, storage and retrieval-based systematic reviews that use keywording to select, label and organize knowledge (Ribbins and Gunter, 2003). Furthermore, communication of knowledge through bullet points and electronic presentation systems facilitates clarity and acceptance at the expense of meaning and engagement (Gunter and Willmott, 2002).

Given my emerging position within the field, I am clearly in sympathy with the purpose of this book. There is much within the opening chapter by the co-editors that is consistent with the arguments made above about the hegemony and intellectual impoverishment of transformational leadership. Furthermore, I am happy to be associated with a text that seeks to generate alternative understandings, and put into the public domain work that is central to how we work to democratize knowledge by having access to ideas about *challenging the conventions*. However, this is itself contested because, using Blackmore's (1999) terminology, we can be positioned as 'trouble', but we need to be 'troubled' by such positioning, and we should continue to be 'troubling' through dialogue and practice. The continued dominance of Jurassic Management within what is promoted as good educational leadership and organizational practice makes such critical engagement challenging. The climate is one where intellectual work can be tolerated, but more often than not is ridiculed as exotic and irrelevant to real lives and the urgency of action. Nevertheless, what might be seen as a hegemonic and impenetrable settlement of knowledge truths actually remains fragile and is being contested through theory, research and practice. Hence, this book affords us the opportunity to gaze across the field at other possible ways of knowing, and enables us to reread familiar maps in new and interesting ways.

## JOURNEYING BEYOND JURASSIC MANAGEMENT

Making sense of and understanding debates within or about the field needs to be described and explained, and recent work with Peter Ribbins has generated an approach to maps, mapping and mappers that has a number of dimensions, and is presented in Figure 13.1.

This work is in the process of being reported (Gunter, 2001a; 2001b; 2002a; 2002b; Gunter and Ribbins, 2002; Ribbins and Gunter, 2002; Ribbins and Gunter, 2003). The five typologies developed from these 'P's are concerned not only with knowledge but also with who the knowers are and what knowledge is used for. In this chapter space only allows me to make passing reference to four of the Ps because I intend to interrelate my reading of the book to the five knowledge provinces as the prime focus.

Ribbins and Gunter (2002) identify five knowledge provinces and these are shown in Figure 13.2.

The identification of these five knowledge provinces is based on an analysis of the publication outputs of the field in which reading and analysing texts produced clusters around differentiated approaches to purpose (Bush *et al.*, 1999, Gunter, 2001a). Knowledge provinces mean what is being asserted as constituting the truth underpinning the intention behind any leadership activity. For example, at one end of the continuum, in what Ribbins and Gunter

| Provinces | claims to the truth regarding how power is conceptualized and engaged with |
|---|---|
| Practices | the practice in real time, real life contexts of leaders, leading and leadership |
| Producers | the people, and their roles (e.g. practitioner, researcher), who are knowers through using and producing what is known |
| Positions | the places (e.g. training session; consultancy) where knowers use and produce what is known |
| Processes | the research processes (e.g. observations and interviews) used to generate and legitimate what is known |

**Figure 13.1**  The dimensions of knowledge production in the field of educational leadership

| Knowledge provinces | Knowledge claims are concerned with... |
|---|---|
| Conceptual | Philosophical questions of morality, rights, life and humanity |
| Critical | Issues of power and social justice |
| Humanistic | Lived lives and experiences |
| Evaluative | Measuring effectiveness and identifying the conditions for improvement |
| Instrumental | Providing prescribed action for change |

**Figure 13.2**  Knowledge provinces in the field of educational leadership
*Source:* (based on Ribbins and Gunter 2002)

(2002) call conceptual approaches, claims are made around the value of intellectual work in comparison with instrumental in which direct action is the outcome. For conceptual approaches what matters are fundamental questions about how we want to live and organize our work, while instrumental approaches seek activity compliance.

The co-editors in framing purposes do not locate the book within the evaluative or instrumental domains. They seek to distance this book from the prescriptive purposes underpinning the models of transactional and transformational leadership and the 'conventional literature'. Furthermore, they draw on knowledge claims that are not concerned to statistically measure the effectiveness of role incumbents on organizational effectiveness. Instead they seek to:

> explore the utility and explanatory power of three particular perspectives on leadership, drawing on institutional theory, activity theory as developed in theories of distributed leadership, and the implications of the concept of communities of

practice. We will also examine further the value of a view of leadership that rests on contingency theory.

(Bennett and Anderson)

My reading of the chapters shaped by the typology presented in Figure 13.2 suggests that they can be described and understood primarily through the conceptual and critical knowledge provinces, with a preference for humanistic methodologies. Goddard, Gronn, Morley and Hosking, and Ogawa have a clear conceptual purpose in which issues of values are at the core of what they are interested in. Their unease with how leadership is being defined and promoted has prompted challenges based on other understandings of humans, teachers as humans, organizations as formal and informal associations of humans:

> In this chapter I do not attempt to provide a single conceptualization of what leadership is, nor do I attempt to develop a scale by which leadership ability might be measured and analysed. To do so would be to suggest that leadership is a concept which can be pinned down like a butterfly on a board, or bottled like glacial water, and that a single person can, on their own, provide the consumers with such a product.
>
> (Goddard)

> So strong is the attributed symbiosis between these two analytical constructs [i.e. leaders and followers] that they are like the horse and carriage in the song about marriage: you cannot have one without the other. But why not? Why, are organization members automatically assumed to fit into either of these binary categories? And why has the claim that there can be no leadership without followers become a truism? If we consider the other siblings, it is apparent that, with the possible exception of power, no other family member is portrayed in binary terms. In the case of power, the dualism of the powerful and the powerless is the closest one gets to anything as conceptually hard and fast as leaders and followers, and yet this power dichotomy has never been anywhere near as thoroughly embedded in the public or academic consciousness as the leader–follower binary.
>
> (Gronn)

> What we shall try to do, explicitly, is to draw out some of the themes in a more general critique that we have emphasized and that others have not. That is to say, if we have had a distinctive part in any debate about 'new leadership' it has been because, first, we have a general view about the nature of social psychology of organizing ... and that, second, we have applied this general view to the study of leadership in particular.
>
> (Morley and Hosking)

In this chapter, I consider the institutional and organizational context of teaching, explaining that teachers work as direct agents of the social institution of education. Teachers, thus, stand at the boundary between social order, as defined by institutions and reflected in the structures of school organization, and the potential chaos, or uncertainty, that would result if they failed in their mission. I then explore the complexity and thus uncertainty that teachers encounter in deploying a multidimensional knowledge base.

(Ogawa)

What holds these chapters together is an interest in investigating leadership is a social and socializing process:

A sign on a door does not a leader make ... The role of leadership is not *contained* within a single individual by virtue of their positional authority; however, the function of leadership is *exercised* by individuals acting within a certain organizational position.

(Goddard)

A distributed view of leadership demands that we de-centre 'the' leader, a requirement that contradicts the ruling scholarly illusions of the last two decades or so which have privileged high-profile, vision-driven individuals who, allegedly, engineer transformational turnarounds.

(Gronn)

leaders should participate in relational processes in ways that:

- link their own knowledge and experience intelligently to that of others;
- (help to) organize negotiations within ('internal') and between ('external') groups;
- deal with cognitive and political aspects of the core problems in their (individual and collective) decision-making tasks;
- focus on key dilemmas in their individual and collective tasks.

This line of argument could be said to upgrade the role of 'followers' and to downgrade that of 'leaders'. Leaders do have special responsibilities, but one is not to ignore the contributions of their followers.

(Morley and Hosking)

Leadership is cultural, developing structures on which symbolic activities focus to shape and reinforce norms and values that guide the relations and interactions that occur in professional communities, both within schools and between schools and the profession. Culture produces group solidarity and, consequently, co-ordinated action ... Finally, along with other participants in school organizations – including administrators, students and parents – individual teachers and professional communities provide leadership by developing structures that can affect all levels of school organization.

(Ogawa)

Consequently the authors recognize the struggles 'from' and 'for' within leadership, and the moral issues within professionally social and socializing relationships are endemic in theorizing leaders, leading and leadership. For Gronn, the empirical data shows the dilemma of mediating policy directives while enabling the division of labour to be operable within a local context, and in working issues like this through, Ogawa talks about leaders being 'knowledgeable' and 'capable'. Indeed, communication is enhanced according to Morley and Hosking by how 'participants experience the emerging processes as legible, coherent and open-ended', and as such our styles of interaction might change but underlying values do not (Goddard). What these underlying philosophical discussions generate are questions about agency and structure, or the interplay between the individual (practices, and choices within and about practice) and collective cultures and traditions (what determines and shapes practices and choices). These authors seek to challenge current orthodoxies through the social sciences as the means by which alternative understandings can be generated and developed. In turning to the social sciences they are within the tradition of the field (see Gunter, 2002a), and this is welcome given the intellectual impoverishment of much of what has been promoted as leadership in the last 20 years (Gunter, 2001a).

All the authors are seeking to say something about power. Not about power as a property of a role incumbent's job description, but how it is exercised within complex organizational and social interactions. This enables a division of labour to be identified, and so the dynamics of leadership as a relationship can be thought through. Consequently, tough issues regarding the current promotion of distributed leadership and communities of practice are worked through and are not resolved into neat and tidy prescriptions. This is the strength of such analysis, because the danger of complete resolution could be the design of the randomized controlled trial to see if 'it' works or not, and/or the production of the instrumentalized ringbinder. As Gronn argues, these matters are not new, practitioners as mappers within the field already experience and practise distributed power relationships, and are members of communities of practice, and they need the opportunity to explore this and to work through what it means rather than have 'good practice' distilled as bullet points. In particular, we need to know much more about what it means to do the distributing and to be distributed to, and to ask: what are the actualities and possibilities for leadership to be exercised separately from those who do the distributing? Engaging with the social sciences in this way enables us to be inclusive as it connects with the realities of what it means to practice leadership (e.g., see Winkley, 1998), and the necessary intellectual work facilitates dialogue which is so crucial to how we seek to understand actual and proposed action.

Engaging with issues of power takes the authors on to the critical territory, and as such we can identify how they are interested in the interrelationship between leadership within and external to the organization. Issues of 'distribution' and of 'communities' are not just for the organization but are inevitably inclusive of students, parents and localities. Goddard, and Ogawa, both remind us that the school has not been separate from this but, as all the authors note, the promotion of a preferred model of a school leader has denied the recognition of leadership within wider networks. If we are going to work for inclusive leadership then we need to undertake a 'policy archaeology' (Morley and Rassool, 1999, p. 131) so that we can track particular models of leadership, where their origins lie and how they are being promoted. In this way we can juxtapose particular developments in order to generate new insights in the way Gronn asks questions about the interrelationship between distributed leadership and the intensification of work. This enables the link between the supposedly enhanced agency of the worker and the nature of their work to be critically reviewed within the context of rapid, and often inhuman, restructuring across the private and public sectors.

It is intended that the authors in Section 2 build on the conceptual and critical work through the presentation and analysis of humanistic empirical work. These chapters also show the same concern regarding the current state of leadership theorizing and research, and through their critical reading of Section 1 they then take forward the analysis of values and power through their research. The authors are not constrained by Section 1 but are stimulated by it to review their empirical work and/or to develop the theoretical analysis. The emphasis in these chapters is on the stress data and how best to research leaders, leading and leadership. The stress is on capturing the meaning of those engaging in leadership mainly through interviews, and their words are reproduced to illustrate the analysis. The existence of and possibilities for distributed leadership are examined:

> The high performer's drive for excellence, as shown by the leadership of the three heads in the study, did lead to intensification of work that was not desirable in the long term. However, some of the intensification did seem to be necessary, particularly in stage one, in order to raise morale and move forward. Others then had to develop capability in dimensions of their role performance, not just as teachers, but also as leaders. This aligns with Gronn's characterization of distributed leadership as having to have a finely tuned tolerance for ambiguity. If school leaders are to 'acquire a sense of how events coalesce, fuse and flow' then they need to be able to develop synergies within the whole school, so that work intensification does not become a hindrance to distributed leadership practices, but an impetus for them.
>
> (Crawford)

> The interactive relationships between restructuring, distributive leadership and reculturing provide a glimpse into the difficulties associated with fostering and sustaining significant change in secondary schools. Yet, as the experiences of the school investigated ... suggest, such change is possible if the conditions support an internal challenge to taken-for-granted assumptions and provide a means through distributed leadership to permit participants to become deeply engaged in and to own the process.
>
> (Hannay)

[it] is one that ultimately empowers those within the organization to take leadership responsibility. It requires emotional intelligence, the ability to trust in others to lead and vast amounts of empathy. Here leadership is a shared commodity owned by those who work within the school and by those who work on behalf of the school.

(Harris and Day)

The existence of and possibilities for communities of practice are explored:

Formal units such as departments are major sites for teacher learning, but particularly when they intersect with communities of practice where colleagues can share and make meaning together ... A challenge for leaders in schools is to recognize and nurture communities of practice in their core activities, but particularly facilitate active boundary processes to extend collaboration to collegiality, where leadership can then be demonstrated or exercised by a variety of actors in different situations.

(McGregor)

If the subject area is thought of as a community of practice then these boundary engagements are important and the challenge they pose must be addressed. It might be necessary for the designated leader to set up meetings or opportunities for engagement that allowed the community members, or a subset of them, to discuss the challenge and consider how it might 'fit in' with existing community norms, how the norms might need to adjust to accommodate the challenge or, indeed, how they might challenge the expection. If, for example, a whole-school change was found to be at odds with the norms within the department which were heavily influenced by the norms of a larger community, such as a subject association, and the process of negotiation did not lead to an acceptable situation for the community, then the change would risk being ignored. Minimal compliance or even undermining might follow this, placing the community at odds with the wider community within the organization but strengthening their sense of identity with each other.

(Wise)

What the analysis does is to show the complex nature of these investigations, and how there is a need for more work. For example, O'Neill shows how an education policy scholarship approach enables a critical evaluation of how Wenger's theories are being used within the field:

until and unless those who study educational leadership for a living are prepared to engage more actively with the intellectual traditions that underpin work such as Wenger's (including the established field of educational studies), it is debatable whether our understanding of educational leadership as a form of social practice will progress much further. To put it crudely, the superficial and acritical content of much of the educational management studies literature suggests that the researchers involved may in effect be acting as no more than intellectual camp-followers in each new education policy skirmish. Critical policy scholarship, however, demands a painstaking, reflexive approach to the understanding of educational practice. Anyone who turns to Wenger for a quick fix on educational leadership and its improvement may well find the same.

(O'Neill)

This does alert us to the intellectual work needed to engage with theory if we are to avoid the unreflexive borrowing of language without the underlying conceptual framework. Indeed, O'Neill is right to point out that the field must operate within 'forms of scholarship that require us to locate contemporary social practice within a broader historical, cultural and occupational analysis'. Hence central to the core purpose of the book in 'challenging the conventions' is to problematize field scholarship and practice, and in doing this important connections are made with Section 3 in which how we prepare for and develop leadership is a core theme.

Consistent with O'Neill's analysis is Gronn's worry about the development of 'designer leadership':

> Designs for leaders intrude significantly into the domain of school leaders' work because they operate through highly structured and externally imposed regimes of assessment and accreditation, the intention of which is to license or authorize the initial appointments of education professionals and to guarantee their continuing engagement in professional practice in conformity with sets of desired norms.

As Gronn goes on to point out, this regulation of the formation of leaders is at odds with his own work on distributed leadership, and also with the goals of the chapters in this edited collection. The challenge for the challenging goal of Section 3 is to analyse the implications of the previous chapters for professional development. In doing this the two authors capture for us the problematics of knowledge and knowing, and are consistent with my own arguments in favour of conceptually informed practice (Gunter, 2001a). In other words, instead of putting our energies into how we procedurally read, categorize and weigh the literature as procedurally linear disembodied reviews, we need to focus on how and why the literature is read and used by its users, and how this produces knowledge and knowing (Gunter, 2001a; Ribbins and Gunter, 2003).

Bennett investigates the 'impact' issue regarding professional development, and in so doing shows how the fixation with 'best practice' creates an understanding of impact that is highly instrumental (this is how to do it) and evaluative (this is what we know from measuring it). By challenging the knowledge claims underpinning this, Bennett is able to explore the complexities in control and order, and so is able to show how knowledge and knowing create meaning through which learning and hence professional development take place. This takes the book full circle because it returns to the philosophical underpinnings of much of what we are interested in when we ask questions about the location and exercise of power. Ribbin's approach asks us to think about agency and structure, and means and ends in how we approach the activity of leadership, and so we are able to think about becoming a leader (or not) as educational and educative rather than about training and being trainable. Furthermore, as Ribbins argues, we are unable to take these matters forward without an explicit approach to maps, mapping and mappers, and as such this book is a contribution to scanning the territory that exists beyond the instrumental and evaluative.

## TRAVELLER'S REST

I began reading this book with a predisposition of wanting to go beyond Jurassic Management, and see field members positioning themselves on other parts of the territory. I have not been disappointed. These chapters show that, first, there are other positions in the production and use of knowledge and that we need to acknowledge and understand the validity of intellectual work. Second, there are other knowledge provinces such as conceptual and critical that reveal important understandings of the theory and practice of leadership. Third, the practice of leadership cannot be charted without recognition of what it means to know and to practice knowing because this legitimizes the generation of alternatives to those that are promoted and preferred. Fourth, the procedures used in reviewing published maps needs to be more than procedural because what we weigh as important is not through disinterested abstraction but through our engagement with people.

Beyond Jurassic Management is a vibrant field of knowledge production that reveals productive struggle about ideas. It is a place where the territory remains unsettled and this is a good sign because researchers are exercising their agency at a time when there is a pattern of activity that could lead to the closing down of spaces where new ideas and collaborations develop. There is no place for doubt, disclosure and debate in the world of designer leadership. However, as these chapters (and other research) show, the realities of leadership are such that mappers (including practitioners) need the opportunity to engage critically with what is taking our interest. In doing this we need to challenge 'new', and in this book I tripped over 'new leadership' on more than one occasion but was left asking what was new about it, and why would we want to call it this. As Hartley (1998) has argued, we are in danger of a 'modernist makeover' in which we take on the language and labels but the knowledge claims underpinning 'new' models remain modernist rational control systems. These chapters are asking us to think otherwise about leadership to that which we are being presented with in policy texts and by knowledge entrepreneurs, and we can only do this if we are reflexive about our work. I began the book convinced that binaries such as 'leader' and 'follower' do not help, and I leave the reading confirmed in this, and so we should not be producing new binaries of old and new, but challenging categories and labels in ways that help us interrogate knowledge and knowing.

In this way the book has been successful in legitimizing the right to challenge as mainstream activity. What is of interest is in the differences rather than a synthesis, and through critical review it is hoped that insights will be developed that move the agenda forward. For my own part, in calling for maps to be developed, used and challenged, there are key learning outcomes from this work that the field could take note of in developing its research agenda: first, theory is not there to be applied like a coat of paint, but to generate vibrant understandings; second, such an engagement requires an open approach to reflexivity about who we are and what we are doing so that our position as mediators of knowledge is transparent; third, in critiquing particular models of leadership and producing alternatives we need to debate the emancipatory function of the social sciences and how this links to our conceptualization of the future. The interrelationship between researching leadership and changing leadership needs to be high on our agenda. In completing the reading of this book we could be dissatisfied because we have been given the opportunity to think but we might worry about what we actually do on a Monday morning. The revelation is that thinking and doing are not separate but are interconnected and, as the authors show, are alive and well within the field.

## ACKNOWLEDGEMENTS

I would like to thank Professor Peter Ribbins who I have been collaborating with in developing recent work on knowledge production in the field. This chapter directly links to the other papers where we have been developing our ideas (Gunter and Ribbins, 2002; Ribbins and Gunter, 2002; 2003).

## REFERENCES

Blackmore, J. (1999) *Troubling Women: Feminism, Leadership and Educational Change*. Buckingham: Open University Press.

Bush, T., Bell, L., Bolam, R., Glatter, R. and Ribbins, P. (eds) (1999) *Educational Management: Redefining Theory, Policy and Practice*. London: Paul Chapman Publishing.

Caldwell, B. and Spinks, J. (1988) *The Self Managing School*. Lewes: Falmer.

Caldwell, B. and Spinks, J. (1992) *Leading the Self Managing School*. London: Falmer.

Caldwell, B.J. and Spinks, J.M. (1998) *Beyond the Self Managing School*. London: Falmer.

Crichton, M. (1991) *Jurassic Park*. London: Arrow.

Forde, R., Hobby, R. and Lees, A. (2000) *The Lessons of Leadership*. London: Hay Management Consultants Ltd.

Gunter, H. (1997) *Rethinking Education: The Consequences of Jurassic Management*. London: Cassell.

Gunter, H. (2001a) *Leaders and Leadership in Education*. London: Paul Chapman Publishing.

Gunter, H. (2001b) Critical approaches to leadership in education, *Journal of Educational Enquiry*, 2(1), 94–108.

Gunter, H. (2002a) Purposes and positions in the field of education management: putting Bourdieu to work, *Educational Management and Administration*, 30(1), 3–22.

Gunter, H. (2002b) Rethinking education: beyond Jurassic Management, inaugural lecture, Adjunct Professor of Educational Management, Unitec, Mount Albert, Auckland, New Zealand, 9 July.

Gunter, H. and Ribbins, P. (2002) Leadership studies in education: towards a map of the field, *Educational Management and Administration*, 30(4), 387–416.

Gunter, H. and Willmott, R. (2002) Biting the bullet, *Management in Education*, 15(5), 35–7.

Hartley, D. (1998) In search of structure, theory and practice in the management of education, *Journal of Education Policy*, 12(1), 153–62.

Hopkins, D. (2001) *Think Tank Report to Governing Council*. Nottingham: National College for School Leadership.

Leithwood, K., Jantzi, D. and Steinbach, R. (1999) *Changing Leadership for Changing Times*. Buckingham: Open University Press.

Morley, L. and Rassool, N. (1999) *School Effectiveness: Fracturing the Discourse*. London: Falmer.

Ribbins, P. and Gunter, H. (2002) Mapping leadership studies in education: towards a typology of knowledge domains, *Educational Management and Administration*, 30(4), 359–86.

Ribbins, P. and Gunter, H. (2003) Leadership studies in education: maps for EPPI reviews? in L. Anderson and N. Bennett (eds), *Evidence Informed Policy and Practice in Educational Leadership*. London: Paul Chapman Publishing (forthcoming).

Teacher Training Agency (1998) National Standards for Headteachers. London: TTA.

Weindling, D. (2001) SCRELM Mapping exercise: some notes and preliminary thoughts. Paper presented to the SCRELM Seminar, Reading University, 13 December.

Winkley, D., with Pascal, C. (1998) Developing a radical agenda, in C. Pascal and P. Ribbins (eds), *Understanding Primary Headteachers*. London: Cassell.

# Index